The Internet

ILLUSTRATED, Sixth Edition

Gary P. Schneider
Jessica Evans
Katherine T. Pinard

COURSE TECHNOLOGY
CENGAGE Learning

Australia • Brazil • Japan • Korea • Mexico • Singapore • Spain • United Kingdom • United States

COURSE TECHNOLOGY
CENGAGE Learning

The Internet—Illustrated, Sixth Edition
Gary P. Schneider
Jessica Evans
Katherine T. Pinard

Executive Editor: Marjorie Hunt

Associate Acquistions Editor: Brandi Shailer

Senior Product Manager: Christina Kling Garrett

Associate Product Manager: Michelle Camisa

Editorial Assistant: Kim Klasner

Director of Marketing: Cheryl Costantini

Marketing Manager: Ryan DeGrote

Product Marketing Specialist: Kristen Panciocco

Developmental Editor: Kim T. M. Crowley

Senior Content Project Manager: Jill Braiewa

Art Director: Heather Hopkins

Print Buyer: Fola Orekoya

Text Designer: Joseph Lee, Black Fish Design

Proofreader: Chris Clark

Indexer: Rich Carlson

Permissions Specialist: Janice Jutras

QA Reviewers: Serge Palladino, Jeff Schwartz

Cover Artist: Mark Hunt

Compositor: GEX Publishing Services

For product information and technology assistance, contact us at
Cengage Learning Customer & Sales Support, 1-800-354-9706
For permission to use material from this text or product, submit all requests online at **cengage.com/permissions**
Further permissions questions can be emailed to
permissionrequest@cengage.com

Library of Congress Control Number: 2009936221

ISBN-13: 978-0-538-75098-1

ISBN-10: 0-538-75098-7

Course Technology
20 Channel Center Street
Boston, MA 02210
USA

Cengage Learning is a leading provider of customized learning solutions with office locations around the globe, including Singapore, the United Kingdom, Australia, Mexico, Brazil, and Japan. Locate your local office at: **www.cengage.com/global**

Cengage Learning products are represented in Canada by Nelson Education, Ltd.

To learn more about Course Technology, visit **www.cengage.com/coursetechnology**

To learn more about Cengage Learning, visit **www.cengage.com**

Purchase any of our products at your local college store or at our preferred online store **www.ichapters.com**

Printed in the United States of America
1 2 3 4 5 6 7 15 14 13 12 11 10 09

About This Book

Welcome to *The Internet—Illustrated, Sixth Edition*! Since the first edition of this title published back in 1999, millions of students have used various texts in the Illustrated Series to master software skills and learn essential computer concepts. We are proud to bring you the latest edition of this book that presents the most current and essential topics relating to the Internet that today's students need to know.

This book is designed to teach students of all levels the most essential topics and skills for navigating and harnessing the power of the Internet. The unique design of this book, which presents each skill on two facing pages, makes it easy for novices to absorb and understand new skills and for more experienced users to progress through the lessons quickly, with minimal reading required. This new edition includes updates on the latest Internet developments and tools including Microsoft® Internet Explorer® 8 and Mozilla® Firefox® 3. It includes expanded coverage of managing browser tracks, and information on the SmartScreen Filter in Internet Explorer 8 and Phishing and Malware Protection in Firefox. It also now features coverage of Windows Live™ Mail and includes information on microblogs.

This latest edition also reflects feedback that we gathered over the last year from instructors who have used previous editions of this and other books in the Illustrated Series. As a result of all this feedback, we made improvements that you suggested and preserved the features that you love. And, of course we covered all the key new developments relating to the Internet. We are confident that this book and all its resources will help students of all levels master the basics of using the Internet.

Author Acknowledgments

We want to thank the outstanding team of professionals at Course Technology for making this book possible. The editorial, development, and production staff members have done their usual outstanding job. We are grateful for the continuous support and encouragement of our spouses, Cathy Cosby and Richard Evans. We also thank our children for tolerating our absences while we were busy writing.

Gary P. Schneider and Jessica Evans, New Perspectives Series Authors

As usual, Course Technology put together a fantastic team. Thank you to Christina Kling-Garrett who always sounds so calm when I talk to her. And thank you especially to Kim Crowley who makes tackling the Internet an easy task.

Katherine T. Pinard, Adapting Author

Preface

Welcome to *The Internet—Illustrated, Sixth Edition*. If you are new to computers, this book will provide you with the most relevant and essential information you need to know to become a proficient Internet user. If you already know a little bit about the Internet, you will be able to easily skim through topics that you already know and focus only on information that is unfamiliar to you.

The unique page design of the book makes it a great learning tool for both new and experienced users. Each skill is presented on two facing pages, so that you don't have to turn the page to find a screen shot or finish a paragraph. See the illustration on the right to learn more about the pedagogical and design elements of a typical lesson.

What's New in This Edition

We've made changes and enhancements to this edition to make it the best ever. Here are some highlights of what's new:

- **Content Updates** Updated to include Internet Explorer 8, Firefox version 3.5, and Windows® 7.

  Coverage of the SmartScreen Filter in Internet Explorer and Phishing and Malware Protection in Firefox.

  Coverage of microblogs.

  Increased coverage of managing browser tracks.

- **Coverage of InPrivate Browsing** and InPrivate Filtering in Internet Explorer and Private Browsing in Firefox.

Each two-page spread focuses on a single skill.

Concise text introduces the basic principles in the lesson and integrates a real-world case study.

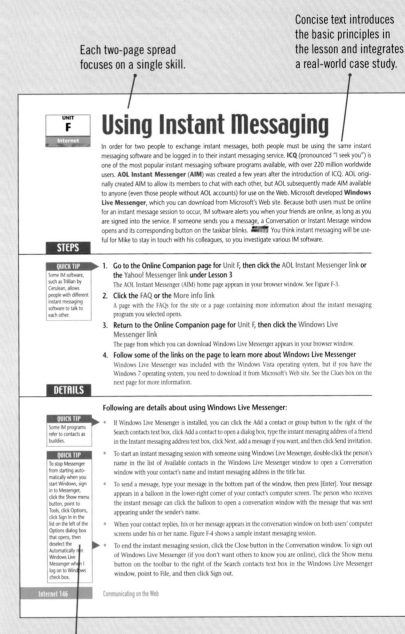

Hints appear, right where you need them—next to the step itself.

Every lesson features large, full-color representations of what the screen should look like as students complete the numbered steps.

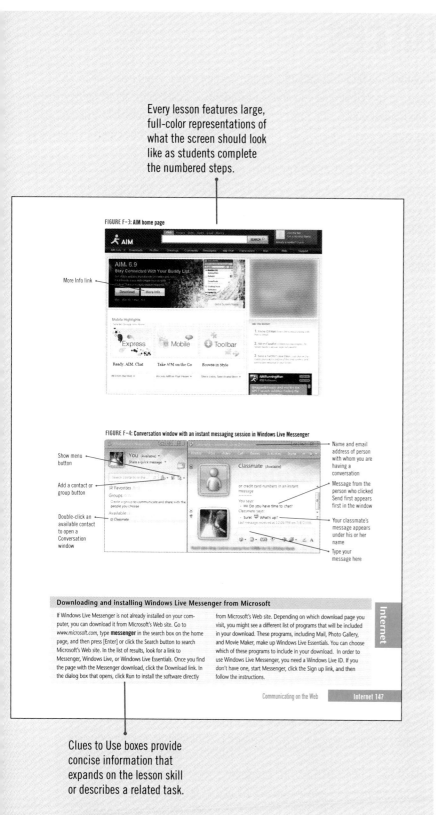

FIGURE F-3: AIM home page

More Info link

FIGURE F-4: Conversation window with an instant messaging session in Windows Live Messenger

Show menu button

Add a contact or group button

Double-click an available contact to open a Conversation window

Name and email address of person with whom you are having a conversation

Message from the person who clicked Send first appears first in the window

Your classmate's message appears under his or her name

Type your message here

Downloading and installing Windows Live Messenger from Microsoft

If Windows Live Messenger is not already installed on your computer, you can download it from Microsoft's Web site. Go to www.microsoft.com, type **messenger** in the search box on the home page, and then press [Enter] or click the Search button to search Microsoft's Web site. In the list of results, look for a link to Messenger, Windows Live, or Windows Live Essentials. Once you find the page with the Messenger download, click the Download link. In the dialog box that opens, click Run to install the software directly

from Microsoft's Web site. Depending on which download page you visit, you might see a different list of programs that will be included in your download. These programs, including Mail, Photo Gallery, and Movie Maker, make up Windows Live Essentials. You can choose which of these programs to include in your download. In order to use Windows Live Messenger, you need a Windows Live ID. If you don't have one, start Messenger, click the Sign up link, and then follow the instructions.

Internet

Communicating on the Web   Internet 147

Clues to Use boxes provide concise information that expands on the lesson skill or describes a related task.

Assignments

The lessons feature a realistic case study. The assignments on the light purple pages at the end of each unit increase in difficulty. Additional case studies provide a variety of interesting and relevant exercises for students to practice skills.

Assignments include:

- **Concepts Reviews** consist of multiple choice, matching, and screen identification questions.
- **Skills Reviews** provide additional hands-on, step-by-step reinforcement.
- **Independent Challenges** are case projects requiring critical thinking and application of the unit skills. The Independent Challenges increase in difficulty, with the first one in each unit being the easiest. Independent Challenges 2 and 3 become increasingly open-ended, requiring more independent problem solving.
- **Real Life Independent Challenges** are practical exercises to help students with their everyday lives.
- **Advanced Challenge Exercises** set within the Independent Challenges provide optional steps for more advanced students.
- **Visual Workshops** are practical, self-graded capstone projects that require independent problem solving.
- **Web Resources Supplement** *The Internet—Illustrated, Sixth Edition* features an Online Companion (OC) Web site. Use the OC to access all the links referenced in the book. Because the Internet changes frequently, the OC will also contain any updates or clarifications to the text after its publication.

v

Instructor Resources

The Instructor Resources CD is Course Technology's way of putting the resources and information needed to teach and learn effectively into your hands. With an integrated array of teaching and learning tools that offer you and your students a broad range of technology-based instructional options, we believe this CD represents the highest quality and most cutting-edge resources available to instructors today. Many of these resources are available at *www.cengage.com/coursetechnology*. The resources available with this book are:

• **Instructor's Manual**—Available as an electronic file, the Instructor's Manual includes detailed lecture topics with teaching tips for each unit.

• **Sample Syllabus**—Prepare and customize your course easily using this sample course outline.

• **PowerPoint Presentations**—Each unit has a corresponding PowerPoint presentation that you can use in lecture, distribute to your students, or customize to suit your course.

• **Figure Files**—The figures in the text are provided on the Instructor Resources CD to help you illustrate key topics or concepts. You can create traditional overhead transparencies by printing the figure files. Or you can create electronic slide shows by using the figures in a presentation program such as PowerPoint.

• **Solutions to Exercises**—Solutions to Exercises contains files students are asked to create or modify in the lessons and end-of-unit material. Note that these solutions do not include software programs students are instructed to download in Unit G. Also provided in this section is a document outlining the solutions for the end-of-unit Concepts Review, Skills Review, and Independent Challenges.

• **Data Files for Students**—To complete Units C and G in this book, your students will need Data Files. You can post the Data Files on a file server for students to copy. The Data Files are available on the Instructor Resources CD, the Review Pack, and can also be downloaded from *www.cengage.com/coursetechnology*. In this edition, we have included a lesson on downloading the Data Files for this book on page xvii.

Instruct students to use the Data Files List included on the Review Pack and the Instructor Resources CD. This list gives instructions on copying and organizing files.

• **ExamView**—ExamView is a powerful testing software package that allows you to create and administer printed, computer (LAN-based), and Internet exams. ExamView includes hundreds of questions that correspond to the topics covered in this text, enabling students to generate detailed study guides that include page references for further review. The computer-based and Internet testing components allow students to take exams at their computers, and also saves you time by grading each exam automatically.

CourseCasts—Learning on the Go. Always Available... Always Relevant.

Our fast-paced world is driven by technology. You know because you're an active participant—always on the go, always keeping up with technological trends, and always learning new ways to embrace technology to power your life.

Let CourseCasts, hosted by Ken Baldauf of the Florida State University, be your guide into weekly updates in this ever-changing space. These timely, relevant podcasts are produced weekly and are available for download at *http://coursecasts.course.com* or directly from iTunes (search by CourseCasts). CourseCasts are a perfect solution to getting students (and even instructors) to learn on the go!

Brief Contents

Contents

Unit C: Using Email   **53**

Unit F: Communicating on the Web   141

Unit G: Downloading Programs and Sharing Files   165

Unit H: Extending Browser Capabilities   193

Unit I: Increasing Web Security   213

Illustration Credits

Unit A

Figure A-2 Courtesy of © 2009 Google

Figure A-3 Courtesy of Lifehacker.com

Figure A-4 Courtesy of © 2009 University of Massachusetts Online

Figure A-5 Courtesy of © Computer History Museum

Figure A-8 Courtesy of Source: National Coordination Office for Networking and Information Technology Research and Development, Arlington, Virginia, USA

Figure A-9 Courtesy of Source: Adapted from Netcraft Web Survey (http://www.netcraft.com)

Figure A-10 Courtesy of the U.S. Geological Survey. Source: (http://www.usgs.gov)

Figure A-11 Courtesy of Copyright © 1994–2009 W3C

Figure A-12 Courtesy of © 2009 Internet Corporation For Assigned Names and Numbers. Source: http://www.icann.org

Figures A-15 and A-16 Courtesy of D-Link Systems, Inc.

Figure A-17 Courtesy of © Ariel Skelley/Getty Images

Unit B

Figures B-2 and B-4 Courtesy of Atlanta Pet Rescue & Adoption

Figure B-5 Courtesy of Scottish Council for Voluntary Organisations

Figures B-6–B-7; B-9, B-12, B-14–16; B-20, B-22, B-24, B-26–27; B-29 Courtesy of © 2009 Microsoft Corporation. All rights reserved. Microsoft product screenshot(s) reprinted with permission from Microsoft Corporation

Figures B-6, B-8, B-10, B-13, B-17–19; B-21, B-23, B-25–26, B-28, B-30 Courtesy of Copyright © 2005–2009 Mozilla. All rights reserved.

Unit C

Figures C-1–C-41 Courtesy of © 2009 Microsoft Corporation. All rights reserved. Microsoft product screenshot(s) reprinted with permission from Microsoft Corporation

Unit D

Figures D-1, D-3, D-10, D-18 Courtesy of Yahoo! Inc. ® 2009 by Yahoo! Inc. YAHOO! and the YAHOO! Logo are trademarks of Yahoo! Inc.

Figure D-2 Courtesy of © 2009 Lycos Inc. All Rights Reserved

Figures D-6, D-16–D-17: D-22–D-23 Courtesy of © 2009 Google

Figures D-7 and D-20 Courtesy of © 2009 Microsoft Corporation. All rights reserved. Microsoft product screenshot(s) reprinted with permission from Microsoft Corporation

Figure D-8 Courtesy of Wolfram Alpha LLC, a Wolfram Research Company (www.wolframalpha.com)

Figure D-9 Courtesy of Copyright © 2000–2009 Gigablast, Inc. All rights reserved.

Figure D-11 Courtesy of © 2009 InfoSpace, Inc. All rights reserved.

Figure D-12 Courtesy of © 1999–2009 KARTOO S.A.

Figure D-13 Courtesy of © awesomelibrary.org

Figure D-14 Courtesy of Copyright © 2008, Librarians' Internet Index, LII. All rights reserved.

Figure D-15 Courtesy of © 1994–2009 INFOMINE, The Regents of the University of California. System developed and supported by the Library of the University of California, Riverside, IMLS and FIPSE.

Figure D-19 Courtesy of Copyright © Vivisimo, Inc. 2000–2009. All rights reserved.

Figure D-21 Courtesy of the National Science Foundation and the University of Utah

Unit E

Figures E-1 and E-2 Courtesy of Yahoo! Inc. ® 2009 by Yahoo! Inc. YAHOO! and the YAHOO! logo are trademarks of Yahoo! Inc

Figure E-3 Courtesy of Imaginova Corp.

Figure E-4 Courtesy weather.com

Figures E-5 and E-19 Courtesy of Accuweather, Inc. 385 Science Park Road, State College, PA 16803 (814) 237-0309 © 2009

Figure E-6 Courtesy of © 2009 Google

Figures E-7, E-18, and E-21 Courtesy of © 2009 Microsoft Corporation. All rights reserved. Microsoft product screenshot(s) reprinted with permission from Microsoft Corporation

Figure E-8 Courtesy of Copyright © 2009 Idearc Media LLC. All rights reserved.

Figure E-9 and Figure E-17 Courtesy of © 1996–2009 WhitePages.com, Inc.

Figures E-11 and E-20 Courtesy of © 2009 SYSTRAN Software, Inc. All rights reserved.

Figure E-12 Courtesy of Annette Nellen, Professor of Accounting & Taxation, San Jose State University

Figures E-13 and E-14 Wikipedia® is a registered trademark of the Wikimedia Foundation, Inc.

Figure E-15 Courtesy of © 2005–2009 The Board of Trustees of the Leland Stanford Junior University

Unit F

Figure F-1 Courtesy of © 2009 Topica Inc.

Read This Before You Begin

Frequently Asked Questions

What are Data Files?

A Data File is a file that you use to complete some of the steps in the units and exercises. If any Data Files are required to complete the steps in a unit, they are listed on the unit opener page.

Where are the Data Files?

Your instructor will provide the Data Files to you or direct you to a location on a network drive from which you can download them. Alternatively, you can follow the instructions on the next page to download the Data Files from this book's Web page.

What software was used to write and test this book?

This book was written and tested using a typical installation of Microsoft Windows 7 with Aero turned off. The browsers used are Microsoft Internet Explorer 8 and Mozilla Firefox 3.5. Windows Live Mail version 2009 and Window Live Hotmail were used in Unit C. Windows Mail version 6, Outlook Express running under Windows XP, Mozilla Thunderbird 2.0, and Gmail are covered in an appendix. Windows Live Messenger Version 2009 was used in Unit F.

Do I need to be connected to the Internet to complete the steps and exercises in this book?

The exercises in this book assume that your computer is connected to the Internet. If you are not connected to the Internet, see your instructor for information on how to complete the exercises.

What do I do if my screen is different from the figures shown in this book?

This book was written and tested on computers with monitors set at a resolution of 1024 $\times$ 768. If your screen shows more or less information than the figures in the book, your monitor is probably set at a higher or lower resolution. If you don't see something on your screen, you might have to scroll down or up to see the object identified in the figures.

Downloading Data Files for This Book

In order to complete the lesson steps and exercises in Units C and G in this book, you will need Data Files. A **Data File** is a file that you use to complete some of the steps in these units. Your instructor will provide the Data Files to you or direct you to a location on a network drive from which you can download them. Alternatively, you can follow the instructions in this lesson to download the Data Files from this book's Web page.

1. Start Internet Explorer, type www.cengage.com/coursetechnology in the address bar, then press [Enter]

2. When the Web site opens, click the Student Downloads link

3. On the Student Downloads page, click in the Search text box, type this book's ISBN: 9780538750981, then click Go

QUICK TIP
You can also click Student Downloads on the right side of the product page.

4. When the page opens for this textbook, in the left navigation bar, click the Download Student Files link, then, on the Student Downloads page, click the Data Files link

5. If the File Download – Security Warning dialog box opens, click Save. (If no dialog box appears, skip this step and go to Step 6)

TROUBLE
If a dialog box opens telling you that the download is complete, click Close.

6. If the Save As dialog box opens, click the Save in list arrow at the top of the dialog box, select a folder on your USB drive or hard disk to download the file to, then click Save

7. Close Internet Explorer and then open My Computer (Windows XP) or Computer (Windows Vista) or Windows Explorer and display the contents of the drive and folder to which you downloaded the file

8. Double-click the file 75098-1d.exe in the drive or folder, then, if the Open File – Security Warning dialog box opens, click Run

QUICK TIP
By default, the files will extract to C:\ CourseTechnology\ 75098-1

9. In the WinZip Self-Extractor window, navigate to the drive and folder where you want to unzip the files to, then click Unzip

10. When the WinZip Self-Extractor displays a dialog box listing the number of files that have unzipped successfully, click OK, click Close in the WinZip Self-Extractor dialog box, then close Windows Explorer, My Computer, or Computer

You are now ready to open the required files.

Understanding Internet Basics

Files You Will Need:

No files needed.

The Internet offers many communication tools and information resources. To use the Internet effectively, you need to know what it is, what tools and information are available on it, and how you can connect to it. Roland Kenney owns Nostalgic Sweets, a small chain of candy stores in Ohio that offers various types of candy from an earlier era—namely the 1950s, 60s, and 70s. He wants to start selling his products via the Internet, and he asked you to come up with a plan for developing a Web site and then marketing and selling Nostalgic Sweets products. As part of your research, you need to investigate the ways people use the Internet and the best way to connect to it.

How do people use the Internet?

How has the Internet impacted society?

Who invented the Internet?

How did the Internet grow into its current form?

How does the World Wide Web work?

Who controls the Internet?

How are networks created?

How do computers connect to the Internet?

What are the types of Internet connections?

How Do People Use the Internet?

The **Internet** is a collection of computers all over the world that are connected to one another. The **World Wide Web** (or, simply, the **Web**) is a subset of the computers on the Internet, and its purpose is to organize the vast resources on the Internet to make them more easily accessible to users. Documents formatted to be viewed on the Web are called **Web pages**, and a **Web site** is a collection of related Web pages stored on a computer connected to the Internet. You start your research for Roland by learning about several of the common uses for the Internet.

DETAILS

The following are common ways people use the Internet:

- **Obtain Information**

  Millions of Web sites offer information on almost any imaginable topic. Some sites provide information organized like an encyclopedia. Other sites offer specialized types of information, for example, digital camera reviews, recipes for Mexican food, or instructions for growing houseplants. Still others provide up-to-date news. Many sites are available for free, some sites make money by selling advertising space, and some companies charge the user to access the information. Figure A-1 shows a Web page from the NASA Web site.

- **Communicate**

  Using tools on the Internet, you can communicate electronically with people all over the world.
  - You can send and receive electronic mail messages (**email**) between two or more computers, you can send messages that are read by the receiver as soon as you send them (**instant messages** or **IMs**), or you can communicate with people using their personal pages on social networking sites such as Facebook or Twitter.
  - You can conduct electronic meetings in which all participants view the same computer desktop over the Internet, or set up a video conference for participants in different locations.
  - You can create an online journal (a **blog**) in which you write and store entries for public viewing. Most online journals include an interface that lets readers comment on the posted entries. Figure A-2 shows the start page for creating your own blog on the Blogger Web site.
  - You can discuss almost any topic you can imagine in electronic discussion groups. You can join a discussion stored in a location on the Internet, or send messages to people who have subscribed to a list.

- **Buy and Sell Goods and Services**

  All kinds of businesses provide information about their products and services on the Internet. Some companies, such as Amazon.com, exist only on the Web, while others, such as American Eagle Outfitters, maintain a Web site to supplement sales in their physical stores.

- **Download Software**

  Many Web sites offer software to download and install. Some software is free; other software must be paid for before you can use it.

- **Access Multimedia**

  You can subscribe to a music downloading service and download songs that you can transfer to an MP3 player. You can also watch movie previews, news clips, television programs, or videos posted by ordinary people.

- **Play Online Multiuser Games**

  Online adventure games, such as World of Warcraft, allow hundreds, and even thousands, of users to assume character roles and interact with each other. These games are known by a variety of names, such as **MUDs** (multiuser dungeons), **MOOs** (MUD object-oriented), and **MMOGs** (massively multiuser online games).

QUICK TIP
An **avatar** is an online character that a game player uses to represent him or herself.

FIGURE A-1: Web page on the NASA Web site on the Internet

FIGURE A-2: Blogger Web site

Internet

How Has the Internet Impacted Society?

In just over 30 years, the Internet has become one of the most amazing technological and social accomplishments of the last hundred years. Many people born after 1990 cannot even conceive of a world without the Internet. The World Wide Web has made the information on the Internet so accessible that users can access this information without the need to know much about computers and how they work. This ease of access has shrunk our world, opened international borders, and enabled people to connect and share information on an unprecedented scale. You continue your research for Roland by investigating some of the ways the Internet has changed society.

DETAILS

The following are some of the ways in which the Internet has impacted society:

QUICK TIP

Information seekers need to evaluate the sources of the information they find to make sure the person or company who provides the information is a reliable and knowledgeable source.

- **Finding Information Is Easier**

  The Internet has made an enormous bank of information readily available to people. Research on a topic is no longer limited to the books, encyclopedias, and periodicals available at a local library. For example, patients can research their illnesses and educate themselves so they can discuss treatments with their doctors, and interested citizens of almost any country can read headlines and news reports from other countries around the globe. Although the information has always been available, the Internet makes it accessible to anyone willing to spend a little time electronically searching. Figure A-3 shows a page of a Web site called "Lifehacker." The figure shows the topics available in the Clever Uses category.

QUICK TIP

The Internet has also allowed families and friends scattered across the globe to stay in touch.

- **Shrinking Borders**

  The Internet allows businesses to send and receive electronic documents and other files from people working in the next office or halfway around the world. For example, a publishing company in Boston can send manuscript files to a compositor in India, who can then send completed book pages back to the publisher, all without incurring any printing or shipping costs. Employees can save commuting time by working from home, communicating with colleagues, and sending and receiving files over the Internet.

- **Developing New Social Relationships**

  Electronic message forums, email, instant messages, and blogs have allowed people to build and maintain friendships and business connections with an ease never before possible. The Internet has also broadened the world for many people with physical disabilities and limited mobility by allowing them to easily communicate with others without needing to leave their homes.

- **Maximizing the Workday**

  Computers that store Web sites are never turned off, thereby allowing you to access the Internet 24 hours a day, seven days a week. People who use the Internet for business can work at night, and even communicate in real time with others in different time zones across the globe. However, this same 24/7 availability also makes it difficult for some people to confine their workday to a standard time frame of eight hours.

- **New Educational Possibilities**

  The Internet has opened new avenues for education. People can take college courses online; in fact, several colleges exist only in cyberspace. High school students can take courses online from teachers in other school systems. Elementary and middle school students can take having pen pals to a new level by using teleconferencing equipment. Figure A-4 shows information about online courses offered from the University of Massachusetts.

FIGURE A-3: Clever Uses page on the Lifehacker Web site

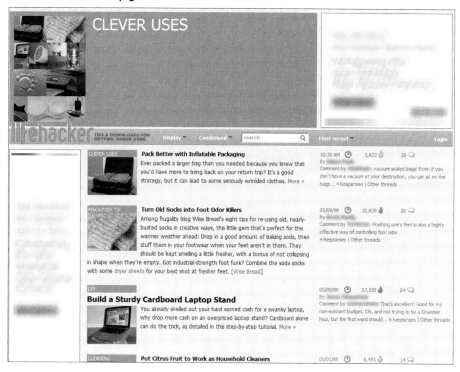

FIGURE A-4: University of Massachusetts Web page offering online courses

Legal issues created by the Internet

Although countries around the world have always had to work together to develop laws and procedures for handling international commerce, the Internet has created new issues. For example, some countries censor the news that their citizens receive, but the Internet makes news from all over the world available with a few mouse clicks.

Some countries, including the United States, restrict gambling, but with a credit card and an Internet connection, people in any country can gamble as much as they want. Individual countries are working to develop laws for their own citizens, and many countries are trying to work together to develop laws that cross international borders.

Who Invented the Internet?

No one person or group invented the Internet that we know today. It grew into its current form due to contributions made by many groups and people. The Internet began in the early 1960s when the U.S. Department of Defense (DOD) became concerned about the possible effects of nuclear attack on its computing facilities. The DOD created the **Defense Advanced Research Projects Agency (DARPA)**, which examined ways to connect its computers to one another and to weapons installations all over the world. When two or more computers are connected to each other, they form a **network**. A network allows computers to share resources, such as printers or programs. You decide to find out how the Internet developed from the activities of DARPA into the vast network of computers now available to anyone.

DETAILS

Here is how the Internet developed:

- **ARPANET**

    The **Advanced Research Projects Agency Network (ARPANET)** consisted of four computers networked together by DARPA researchers in 1969. These first four computers were located at the University of California at Los Angeles, SRI International, the University of California at Santa Barbara, and the University of Utah. Figure A-5 shows a famous hand-drawn sketch of the Internet as it existed in 1969.

- **Packet Switching**

    The **circuit switching** method for data transmission (once commonly used by telephone companies) could not be easily secured, so DARPA developed the **packet switching** method, which breaks down files and messages into **data packets** (small chunks of data). Each data packet is labeled electronically with codes that describe its origin and destination. The destination computer collects the data packets and reassembles the original data.

- **Protocols**

    Transfer protocol is the set of rules that computers use to move files from one networked computer to another. Vinton Cerf, who is often referred to as the Father of the Internet, along with his colleague Robert Kahn, developed the **Transmission Control Protocol** and the **Internet Protocol** (referred to by their combined acronym **TCP/IP**). The **Transmission Control Protocol (TCP)** includes rules that computers on a network use to establish and break connections. The **Internet Protocol (IP)** includes rules for routing individual data packets. The TCP/IP suite of protocols includes a tool to facilitate file transfer and another to access computers that are not part of a user's immediate network over the Internet. The most common transfer protocol used on the Internet is the **hypertext transfer protocol (HTTP)**. **File Transfer Protocol (FTP)** enables users to transfer files between computers.

- **New Networks**

    By 1981, the ARPANET had expanded to include more than 200 networks, and in 1984, ARPANET was split into two: ARPANET would continue its advanced research activities, and **MILNET** (for **Military Network**) would be reserved for military uses that required greater security. In addition, a number of TCP/IP-based networks—independent of the ARPANET—were created in the late 1970s and early 1980s. The National Science Foundation (NSF) funded the **Computer Science Network (CSNET)** for educational and research institutions that did not have access to the ARPANET. The City University of New York started a network of computers called the **Because It's Time** (originally, **Because It's There**) **Network (BITNET)**. The **Joint Academic Network (Janet)** was established in the United Kingdom to link universities in that country.

- **Creating the Internet**

    By 1987, an increasing number of users on the limited-capacity leased telephone lines created congestion on the ARPANET. To reduce the traffic load on the ARPANET, a network run by the National Science Foundation, called **NSFnet**, merged with CSNET and BITNET to form one network that could carry much of the network traffic that had been carried by the ARPANET. By the late 1980s, many other TCP/IP networks had merged or established interconnections. Figure A-6 summarizes how the individual networks combined to become the Internet as it is known today.

QUICK TIP

The computers that move data packets along their path are called **routers**, and the programs they use to determine the best path for the packets are **routing algorithms**.

QUICK TIP

The term "Internet" was first used in 1974 in an article written by Cerf and Kahn about TCP.

QUICK TIP

By 1990, a network of networks, now known as the Internet, had grown from the four computers on the ARPANET to more than 300,000 computers on many interconnected networks.

FIGURE A-5: The Internet's humble beginning as ARPANET, 1969

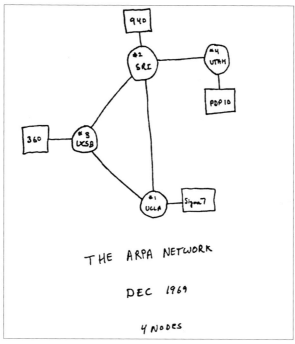

Courtesy of © Computer History Museum

FIGURE A-6: Networks that became the Internet

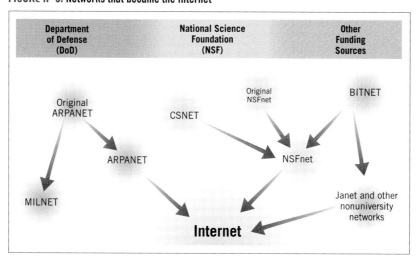

Open architecture philosophy

Open architecture philosophy ensured that each network connected to the ARPANET could continue using its own protocols and data-transmission methods internally. Four key points characterize this philosophy:

- Independent networks should not require internal changes to have a connection to the Internet.
- Data packets that do not arrive at their destinations must be retransmitted from their source network.
- Computers that route data packets do not retain information about the data packets they handle.
- No global control exists over the network.

This open architecture philosophy was revolutionary at the time. Most companies that built computer networking products at that time tried hard to make their networks incompatible with other networks. These manufacturers believed that they could lock out competitors by making their products difficult to connect with products made by other companies. The shift to an open architecture approach is what made the Internet of today possible.

Internet

How Did the Internet Grow into Its Current Form?

As personal computers (PCs) became more powerful, affordable, and available during the 1980s, companies increasingly used them to construct intranets. **Intranets** are networks that use the TCP/IP protocol but do not connect to computers or networks outside the company. Prior to 1989, most universities and businesses could not communicate with people outside their intranet. Because the National Science Foundation (NSF) prohibited commercial network traffic on the networks it funded, businesses that wanted to communicate outside their intranets turned to commercial email services. You want to learn more about how the Internet evolved from a resource used primarily by the academic community to one that became accessible to commercial services.

DETAILS

The growth of the Internet can be attributed to:

- **Email, Mailing Lists, and Bulletin Boards**

  In 1972, an ARPANET researcher named Ray Tomlinson wrote a program that could send and receive messages over the network. In this way, email was born and rapidly became widely used in the computer research community. Mailing lists (such as BITNET's **LISTSERV**) and information posting areas called **newsgroups** (such as the **User's News Network**, or **Usenet**) and **bulletin boards** appeared on the ARPANET. Email and these other communications facilities attracted many users in the education and research communities.

- **Development of Commercial Email Services**

  In 1989, the NSF permitted two commercial email services, MCI Mail and CompuServe, to establish limited connections to the Internet. These commercial providers allowed their subscribers to exchange email messages with members of the academic and research communities who were connected to the Internet. The NSF justified this limited commercial use of the Internet by describing it as a service that would primarily benefit the Internet's noncommercial users.

- **Commercialization of the Internet**

  In 1991, the NSF eased its restrictions on Internet commercial activity. When NSFnet was formed, they awarded a contract to Merit Network, Inc., IBM, Sprint, and the state of Michigan to upgrade and operate the main NSFnet backbone. A **network backbone** includes the long-distance lines and supporting technology that transports large amounts of data between major network nodes. As NSFnet converted the main traffic-carrying backbone portion of its network to private firms, it organized the network around four **network access points** (**NAPs**), which were operated by four telecommunications companies. These four companies and their successors sell access to the Internet through their NAPs to large organizations and businesses called **Internet access providers** (**IAPs**) or **Internet service providers** (**ISPs**). ISPs, in turn, provide Internet access to other businesses and individuals. Large ISPs that sell Internet access along with other services to businesses are often called **commerce service providers** (**CSPs**) because they help businesses conduct business activities (or commerce) on the Internet. The larger ISPs also sell Internet access to smaller ISPs, which in turn sell access and services to their own business and individual customers. This hierarchy of Internet service providers appears in Figure A-7.

- **Defining the Internet**

  A formal definition of the Internet, as shown in Figure A-8, was adopted in 1995 by the now-defunct Federal Networking Council (FNC). Many people find it interesting that a formal definition of the term did not appear until 1995. The Internet was a phenomenon that surprised the world.

FIGURE A-7: The hierarchy of Internet service providers

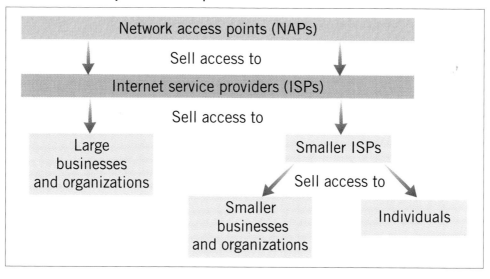

FIGURE A-8: The FNC's October 1995 resolution to define the term "Internet"

RESOLUTION: The Federal Networking Council (FNC) agrees that the following language reflects our definition of the term Internet. Internet refers to the global information system that

(i) is logically linked together by a globally unique address space based on the Internet Protocol (IP) or its subsequent extensions/follow-ons;

(ii) is able to support communications using the Transmission Control Protocol/Internet Protocol (TCP/IP) suite or its subsequent extensions/follow-ons, and/or other IP-compatible protocols; and

(iii) provides, uses or makes accessible, either publicly or privately, high level services layered on the communications and related infrastructure described herein.

Source: National Coordination Office for Networking and Information Technology Research and Development, Arlington, Virginia, USA

How Does the World Wide Web Work?

Many people use "the Web" and "the Internet" interchangeably, but they are not the same thing. The Internet is the entire system of networked computers, and the Web is a method used to access information contained on a subset of those networked computers. As you learned in the first lesson, documents formatted to be viewed on the Web are called Web pages, and a Web site is a collection of related Web pages stored on a computer. The development of the Web and its success have been instrumental factors in the phenomenal growth of the Internet. The Web's success is due to links that enable you to connect to any document on the Web, and user-friendly Web tools that enable users to view and search for Web pages with ease. In a short amount of time, the number of Web sites on the Internet has rapidly increased. Figure A-9 shows the fast growth of the Web during its short lifetime. As you continue your research about the Internet, you decide to learn more about how the Web was developed and how it makes information on the Internet more accessible.

DETAILS

The World Wide Web can be described using the following terms:

- **Hypertext Markup Language**

  In 1989, Tim Berners-Lee and Robert Calliau were working at CERN—the European Laboratory for Particle Physics—and each man independently proposed a hypertext development project to improve CERN's document-handling capabilities and allow the agency to display the complex graphics that were important parts of its theoretical models. Over the next two years, Berners-Lee developed the code for a hypertext server program and made it available on the Internet. A **hypertext server**, or a **Web server**, is a computer that stores files written in the hypertext markup language and lets other computers connect to it and read those files. **Hypertext Markup Language** (**HTML**) is a standard formatting language that marks text in a file with a set of **tags**, or codes, that define the structure and behavior of text, graphics, and other content on a Web page. For example, HTML includes a tag to create a header, a numbered list, or the placement of a graphic. When you view a Web page on the Internet, however, you do not see the HTML tags—you see just the resulting formatted Web page. A text file that contains HTML tags is called an **HTML document**.

- **Web Browser**

  A **Web browser** (or simply **browser**) is software that reads HTML documents. Web browsers let you read (or **browse**) HTML documents and move from one HTML document to another. This is sometimes referred to as "browsing the Web." You can use a Web browser to view any HTML document that resides on a computer connected to the Internet. Currently, the most widely used Web browser is Microsoft Internet Explorer. Another popular browser is Mozilla Firefox. Figure A-10 shows the home page of the U.S. Geological Survey Web site accessed using Internet Explorer. Web browsers use a **graphical user interface** (**GUI**, pronounced "gooey"), which uses text, pictures, icons, and other graphical elements to present information and allow users to perform a variety of tasks. For example, you could click the Print button, which looks like a picture of a printer, to print the Web page.

- **Links**

  Links (also called **hypertext links**, or **hyperlinks**) are text, graphics, or other Web page elements, that, when clicked, access additional data on the Web. On a Web page, a text link is often underlined, and the mouse pointer typically appears as ⏚ when positioned over a link. In Figure A-10, the text hyperlinks on this Web page are easy to identify because the Web browser software that displayed this page shows the hyperlinks as blue text. When you click a link, a new Web page, or another section of the same Web page, appears. This HTML document could be part of the Web site you are currently exploring or part of a Web site stored on a Web server halfway around the world. Hyperlinks can also lead to computer files that contain pictures, graphics, and media objects such as sound and video clips. Hyperlinks that connect to these types of files often are called **hypermedia links**.

FIGURE A-9: Growth of the World Wide Web

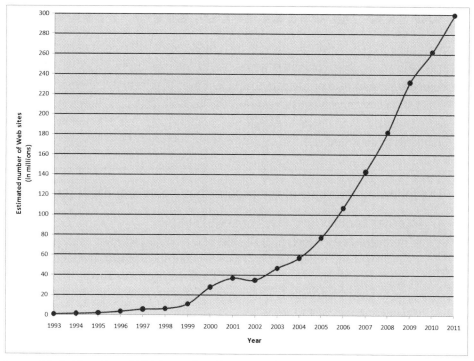

Source: Adapted from Netcraft Web Survey (http://www.netcraft.com)

FIGURE A-10: Example of a Web page in the Internet Explorer Web browser

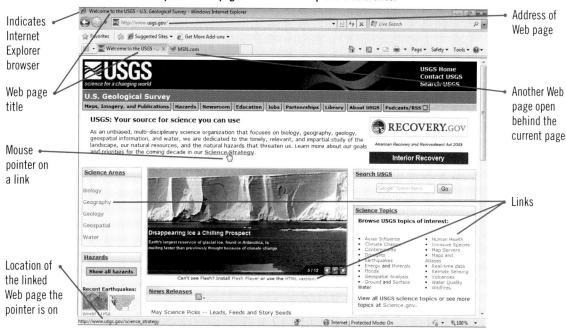

What is XML?

Another markup language that you might hear about is **XML**, which stands for **Extensible Markup Language**. XML was originally developed to meet the needs of large-scale electronic publishers, but today XML is becoming popular as a way of exchanging data between applications and organizations. While HTML uses predefined tags to describe how to format and display data, XML uses customized tags to describe data and its structure. The developer defines and uses the customized tags to describe the data in an XML document. For example, an XML document might define a product's ID number, style, name, and price using customized tags such as <product_id> and </product_id>, <style> and </style>, <name> and </name>, and <cost> and </cost>. These tags describe only the data contained within them; they do not describe how the data will look. XML also lets the developer define validation rules for data and hierarchical relationships of data.

Who Controls the Internet?

All of the Internet's activity occurs with no central coordination point or control. Companies and individuals who make their computers accessible to Internet users do so voluntarily. Although individual companies might read or use data that is sent over their network, there is no central organization that maintains a copy of all the data sent over the Internet. There are, however, several agencies that establish standards for the Internet. You continue your research and investigate the groups that set standards for the Internet.

DETAILS

The following are some of the groups that create standards for the Internet:

- **Internet Engineering Task Force (IETF)**

  As the Internet grew, people from all walks of life, not just scientists or academic researchers, started thinking of these networks as a global resource. Information systems professionals began to form volunteer groups. One such group is the **Internet Engineering Task Force (IETF)**, a self-organized group that makes technical contributions to the engineering of the Internet and its technologies and is the main body that develops new Internet standards.

- **World Wide Web Consortium (W3C)**

  The **World Wide Web Consortium (W3C)** is an international organization that establishes **specifications**, or sets of standards for the Web. Web site designers, Web site owners, and companies that develop hardware and software for the Web are not obligated to follow these specifications. However, if a company wants people to use its product or visit its Web site, they follow the W3C specifications to ensure that most people will have the appropriate technology to do so. Figure A-11 shows the W3C Web site.

- **Internet Society (ISOC)**

  The **Internet Society (ISOC)** was formed in 1992 as an international organization whose goal is to promote Internet standards so that people all over the world have access to the Internet. Its members work with the IETF to develop and promote Internet standards.

- **World Intellectual Property Organization (WIPO)**

  The **World Intellectual Property Organization (WIPO)** is an agency of the United Nations whose purpose is to develop international standards to protect the rights of intellectual property holders. **Intellectual property** is a general term that includes all products of the human mind. WIPO oversees arbitration and mediation hearings about possible thefts of a person's or company's intellectual property, including names used for domain names.

- **ICANN and IANA**

  Although no organization truly controls the Internet, some coordination is needed to avoid chaos, and each computer connected to the Internet needs a standard way of finding other computers connected to the Internet. The **Internet Corporation for Assigned Names and Numbers (ICANN)** is responsible for managing domain names, which are the equivalent of a computer's address on the Internet. ICANN was established in 1998 in California as a nonprofit organization chartered by the U.S. government. ICANN is different from the other organizations in this list because in order to establish a Web site, a Web site owner *must* register its domain name with an ICANN-approved registrar. The U.S. government is currently moving away from direct control of ICANN and ICANN is becoming a more international organization. Figure A-12 shows the ICANN Web site. The **Internet Assigned Numbers Authority (IANA)**, which is operated by ICANN, manages the actual **IP addresses**, the numeric system computers use to identify other computers on the Internet, as well as a few other duties crucial to keeping the Internet running.

FIGURE A-11: W3C Web site

FIGURE A-12: ICANN Web site

Courtesy of © 2009 Internet Corporation For Assigned Names and Numbers. Source: http://www.icann.org

How Are Networks Created?

The Internet is basically a giant network of networked computers. A **client/server network** is a network consisting of a server and client computers. A **server** is a computer that accepts requests from other computers that are connected to it and shares some or all of its resources, such as printers, files, or programs, with those connected computers. Each computer connected to a server is called a **client**. A **peer-to-peer network** is one in which all computers in the network are essentially equal; the computers share files and printers, but no computer acts as a server. Network connections create **communications circuits** through which data can travel. **Bandwidth** is a measure of the amount of data that can be transmitted simultaneously through a communications circuit. Different types of connections transmit data at different speeds. As you continue your research, you realize that Nostalgic Sweets has not updated its network in many years. You decide to learn more about networks so that you can recommend a specific upgrade plan.

DETAILS

The following terms describe networks and network connections:

- **Local Area Network (LAN)**

  A **local area network** (**LAN**) consists of a group of networked computers that are physically close to each other, usually in the same building. Figure A-13 shows a typical client/server LAN setup in an office environment.

- **Wide Area Network (WAN)**

  A **wide area network** (**WAN**) consists of networked computers that are not located near each other. For example, a typical college has several computer labs scattered throughout its many buildings. Each computer lab is a client/server LAN. The LANs in the college are interconnected to form the WAN.

- **Network Interface Card**

  A **network interface card** (**NIC**), or **network card**, is a removable circuit board that is used to connect a computer to a network. After inserting a NIC into a computer, you can connect it to a network by running a cable from the NIC to the server or to another client.

- **Cable Connections**

  Computers in a network are often connected using cables. **Twisted-pair cable** consists of two or more insulated copper wires twisted around each other and enclosed in a layer of plastic insulation. Telephone companies have used one type of twisted-pair cable, called **Category 1 cable**, for years. **Coaxial cable** is an insulated copper wire encased in a metal shield enclosed with plastic insulation that resists electrical interference better than twisted-pair cable. Coaxial cable carries signals about 20 times faster than Category 1 cable. Newer types of twisted-pair cables, called **Category 5 cable**, **Category 5e cable**, and **Category 6 cable**, are faster than coaxial cable and are used in computer networks. Category 5 cable transmits information 10 to 100 times faster than coaxial cable, and Category 5e and Category 6 cable transmit data up to 10 times faster than Category 5 cable. **Fiber-optic cable** transmits information by pulsing beams of light through very thin strands of glass instead of an electrical signal. Fiber-optic cable transmits signals much faster than coaxial cable.

- **Wireless Connections**

  Wireless networks use radio frequency technology to link computers. **Wireless fidelity** (**Wi-Fi**) is the term used to describe a short-range wireless network that connects a wireless access point to wireless devices located approximately 200 to 900 feet of each other. **Wireless LANs** (**WLANs**) are well suited to organizations and households in which cables are difficult to install. **Wireless wide area networks** (**WWANs**) are WANs connected using newer technologies that allow faster data transfer over longer distances. **WiMAX** (Worldwide Interoperability for Microwave Access) has a range of up to 31 miles, creating a way to make wireless broadband network access available in metropolitan areas. Cell phones use networks operated by individual providers, and these networks are referred to as second- or third-generation networks, or more commonly, 2G or 3G networks. The 2G standard allows data transfers of up to 14.4 Kbps, while the 3G standard allows transfers of up to 10 Mbps (10,000 Kbps). Figure A-14 depicts a wireless home network that includes two desktop PCs, two laptop PCs, and a shared printer.

QUICK TIP

The software that runs on the server is called a **network operating system**. This software coordinates how information flows among its various clients.

QUICK TIP

Because fiber-optic cable does not use electricity, it is completely immune to electrical interference. It is also lighter and more durable than coaxial cable.

FIGURE A-13: A client/server LAN

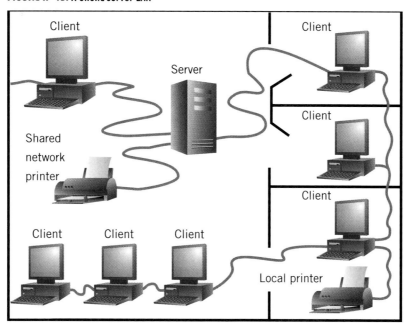

FIGURE A-14: A wireless home network

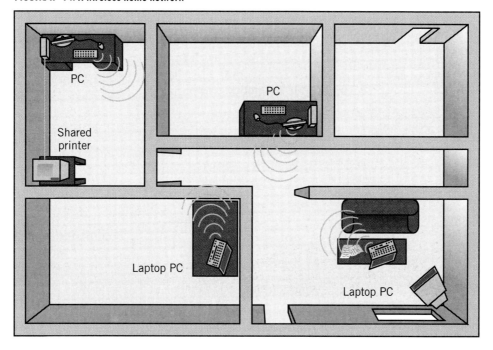

Pocket wireless connectivity

A new type of WLAN is MiFi, a small, pocket-sized device from a company called Novatel that provides a battery-operated personal hotspot that you can use to connect your Wi-Fi devices to the Internet. It works by producing a mobile hotspot that carries the 3G signal with you as you move around. It uses a rechargeable battery that operates for up to four hours or up to forty hours on standby. The hotspot created by MiFi is password-protected and connects up to five Wi-Fi devices, with a range of approximately thirty feet. To create a MiFi network, you must first purchase the device, and then subscribe to the 3G service through a cellular phone provider.

How Do Computers Connect to the Internet?

To connect your computer to the Internet, you need to be part of a communications network that can connect to a network access point (NAP). As you learned in an earlier lesson, to connect to a NAP, a business or an individual must contract with an Internet access provider (IAP) or an Internet service provider (ISP). Individuals can also sometimes access the Internet through an account with a school or employer. No matter how you connect to the Internet, in order to transmit and receive data, the computer used to connect to the Internet needs additional equipment. You investigate exactly what is needed in order for Nostalgic Sweets to connect its computers to the Internet.

DETAILS

In order to connect to the Internet, you need:

- ISPs

  Most IAPs call themselves ISPs because they offer more than just simple access to the Internet. At minimum, ISPs provide access to a NAP so individuals and businesses can connect to the Internet. In addition, they usually provide their customers with the software they need to connect to the ISP, view Web pages, send and receive email messages, and perform other Internet-related functions such as file transfer and remote login to other computers. ISPs also often provide network consulting services to their customers and help them design Web sites and manage networks.

- School or Employer Connection

  One of the easiest ways to connect to the Internet is through your school or employer, if it already has an Internet connection. Such a connection is generally free or very reasonably priced. Most schools and employers have an **acceptable use policy** (**AUP**) that specifies the conditions under which you can use their Internet connection. For example, many AUPs expressly prohibit you from engaging in commercial activities. In such cases, you could not use a school or employer connection to start a business on the Web. When using your school's or employer's Internet connection, the school or employer generally retains the right to examine any files or email messages you transmit. You need to consider carefully whether the limitations placed on your use of the Internet are greater than the benefits of the low cost of this access option.

- Modem

  To connect to the Internet, you usually need a **modem**, which is a device that converts signals between a computer and the transmission line. The term modem is short for **modulator-demodulator**. When you connect your computer, which communicates using digital signals, to another computer through a twisted-pair or coaxial cable, which uses analog signals, the signal must be converted. Converting a digital signal to an analog signal is called **modulation**; converting that analog signal back into digital form is called **demodulation**. A modem performs both functions; that is, it acts as a modulator-demodulator. The general term "modem" usually refers to a device used with a telephone line; most computers sold today include this variety of modem. Other methods of connecting to the Internet require different types of modems. For example, a cable connection through a cable television company requires a **cable modem**, and a DSL connection requires a **DSL modem**. Figure A-15 shows a DSL modem.

- WLAN Card

  To connect a device to the Internet without cables, you need a **WLAN card** (sometimes called a **wireless LAN PC card**) or a Wi-Fi-compatible device, and you must be within range of a wireless access point that is connected to the Internet. Most laptop computers have a built-in Wi-Fi-compatible device that can connect to a wireless access point. You can also purchase a WLAN card with a broadband network provider, such as a cell phone provider, to connect to the Internet from locations where there are no wireless access points. Figure A-16 shows a WLAN card.

FIGURE A-15: DSL modem

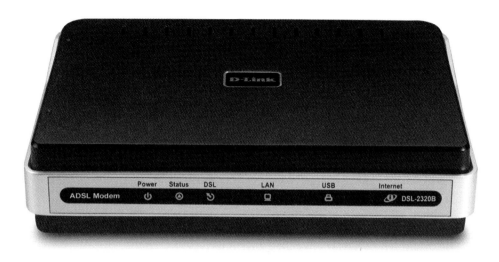

FIGURE A-16: Wireless LAN PC card

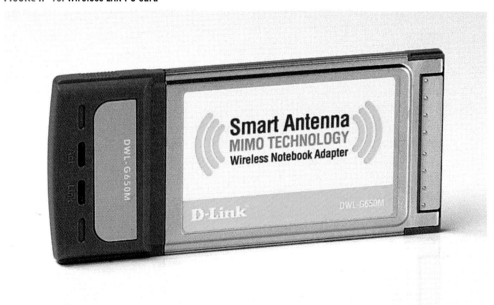

Public-access Internet service

Although many options exist for setting up Internet service in your home, some people find that they can meet their Internet access needs for free using public facilities. Many public libraries offer free Internet access to library card holders or to the general public. You might find it unnecessary to maintain Internet service at home if you have minimal Internet access requirements and such public access is available in a convenient location.

What Are the Types of Internet Connections?

When people or businesses set up accounts with ISPs, they must decide what type of connection they want to use to access the Internet. Common types of connections include the following: telephone service connection (sometimes referred to as **POTS**, or **plain old telephone service**); **Digital Subscriber Line (DSL)**; **T1** and **T3 connections**; **cable**; **satellite**; and **wireless**. Table A-1 summarizes the most popular types of connections currently used to connect to the Internet. Most ISPs offer only one way to connect to the Internet, but some offer more than one of these options. ▓▒▒▓ As your research continues, you evaluate the various connection options to determine which option you will recommend for Nostalgic Sweets.

DETAILS

The ways you can connect are listed below:

QUICK TIP

Some companies and research organizations estimate the number of regular users of the Internet today to be more than 800 million, but no one knows how many individual email messages or files travel on the Internet, and no one really knows how many people use the Internet today.

- **Telephone Line Connection**

  In major metropolitan areas, many ISPs offering dial-in and DSL services compete for customers and, therefore, connection fees are often very reasonable. In addition, some companies offer free Internet access in exchange for displaying advertising on your computer screen each time you connect. T1 and T3 connections are telephone company connections with a higher bandwidth, and they are much more expensive than POTS or DSL connections; therefore, they are usually used by organizations that require the greater bandwidth of T1 and T3 connections to link hundreds or thousands of individual users to WANs or to the Internet. Smaller firms can save money by renting access to a partial T1 connection from a telephone company. In a partial T1 rental, the connection is shared with other companies.

- **Cable Connection**

  A cable modem allows you to connect to the Internet through your cable television company, or another fiber-optic cable provider. A cable connection can provide downloads to your computer from the Internet as much as 350 times faster than a telephone line connection. Although the cost of a cable connection is usually higher than the cost of a telephone line connection, you save the cost of a second telephone line. The greatest disadvantage for most people is that the cable connection might not be available yet in their area. NAPs often use **optical carrier** (**OC**) connections. OC connections are available in a variety of bandwidths ranging from OC3, approximately 15 times faster than a fast connection provided by a cable television company, to OC192, approximately 1,000 times faster than a fast connection provided by a cable television company.

- **Satellite Connection**

  Many rural areas in the United States do not have cable television service and never will because their low population density makes it too expensive. A cable company simply cannot afford to run miles of cable to reach one or two isolated customers. People in these areas often buy satellite receivers to obtain television signals and Internet connections. The major advantage of a satellite connection is speed. Although the speeds are not as high as those offered by cable modems, they are approximately 5 to 10 times higher than those achieved with telephone connections. For users in remote areas, this technology often offers the best connection solution.

- **Hotspot**

  A **hotspot** is a wireless access point to a LAN that offers Internet access to the public. Some hotspot locations charge a fee, but many do not. Your computer or other device must have the necessary hardware to be compatible with the access point and to connect to a hotspot. Figure A-17 shows a customer using a hotspot connection.

FIGURE A-17: Customer using a hotspot connection

TABLE A-1: Types of Internet connections

type of service	description	speed in Kilobytes per second
Telephone service	Available through regular phone lines; used by individuals and small businesses to connect an ISP	28.8 to 56 Kbps
T1 line	Offers a higher grade of service for connecting to the Internet than telephone service does; used by large companies and organizations that must link hundreds or thousands of individual users to the Internet; more expensive than telephone service connections	1544 Kbps
T3 line	Same as T1 line, but faster	44,700 Kbps
Digital Subscriber Line (DSL)	Creates a high-speed connection using the customer's telephone wiring; used by individuals and businesses	100 to 9000 Kbps
Cable	Uses the customer's television cable or fiber-optic cable to connect to the Internet; used by individuals and businesses	300 to 20,000 Kbps
Satellite	Uses a satellite dish receiver; particularly useful for people in remote areas	125 to 500 Kbps
Wireless	Uses high-frequency radio waves to connect to a network access point	722 to 54,000 Kbps
OC3	Fiber-optic cable connections used by NAPs	156,000 Kbps
OC192	Same as OC3, but faster	10,000,000 Kbps

Connecting to the Internet with a wireless device

Wireless devices such as cell phones and personal digital assistants (PDAs) can upload and download email, transfer files, and access the Web. Some wireless devices, such as cell phones, connect to the wireless provider's network and these services automatically when they are within range of the cellular network. Other wireless devices, such as personal digital assistants (PDAs), might access the wireless provider's network using a connection to the cellular network or by being within range of a hotspot.

Internet

Practice

▼ CONCEPTS REVIEW

For current SAM information including versions and content details, visit SAM Central (http://samcentral.course. com). If you have a SAM user profile, you may have access to hands-on instruction, practice, and assessment of the skills covered in this unit. Since we support various versions of SAM throughout the life of this text, you will want to check with your instructor for instructions and the correct URI./Web site to access those assignments.

Match each term with the statement that best describes it.

1. Internet
2. ARPANET
3. TCP/IP
4. FTP
5. HTML
6. Links
7. IETF
8. Server
9. LAN
10. ISP

a. Clickable text, graphics, or other Web page elements that point to additional data on the Web

b. A protocol used to transfer files between computers

c. The formatting language used to create a Web page

d. An organization responsible for developing new Internet standards

e. Four computers networked together by DARPA in 1969

f. A network of computers located close together

g. Protocols used by all computers connected to the Internet

h. A business that offers an Internet connection to your home or office

i. A worldwide collection of interconnected networks

j. A computer that accepts requests from computers connected to it and shares resources with those computers

Select the best answer from the list of choices.

11. **The long-distance lines and supporting technology that transport large amounts of data between major network nodes are called a(n):**
    a. network backbone.
    b. IAP.
    c. T1 line.
    d. network access point.

12. **The type of cable used in telephone connections is called:**
    a. twisted-pair cable.
    b. TCP/IP cable.
    c. fiber-optic cable.
    d. coaxial cable.

13. **Which of the following methods is the switching method used by the Internet?**
    a. Circuit switching
    b. Cable switching
    c. Transmission switching
    d. Packet switching

14. **Which of the following is the term for the collection of rules that computers follow when formatting, ordering, and error-checking data sent across a network?**
    a. Open architecture
    b. Protocol
    c. Router
    d. ARPANET

15. **Which of the following terms is used to describe computer networks that use the TCP/IP protocol but do not connect to sites outside the firm?**
    a. Internet
    b. Intranet
    c. ARPANET
    d. World Wide Web

16. **Which of the following is a requirement for all home and business Internet connections?**
    a. An ISP
    b. DSL service
    c. A T1 line
    d. Cable television service

17. **The device that converts signals between a computer and the transmission line is a:**
    a. hotspot.
    b. WLAN.
    c. satellite connection.
    d. modem.

18. **A wireless access point to a LAN that offers Internet access to the public is a(n):**
    a. hotspot.
    b. WLAN.
    c. satellite connection.
    d. ISP.

19. **A collection of related Web pages stored on a computer is called a(n):**
    a. Web browser.
    b. Web address.
    c. Web site.
    d. intranet.

20. **A removable circuit board that is used to connect a computer to a network is a:**
    a. WLAN.
    b. server.
    c. communications circuit.
    d. NIC.

▼ INDEPENDENT CHALLENGE 1

As you learned in this unit, the Internet provides many and varied resources. If you are new to the Internet, you might be wondering how you can use the Internet in your life.

   a. List several topics that you are interested in exploring on the Internet. Think of your own hobbies and interests. Would you like to find travel information about Alaska? Gather information for a research paper on Mars? Learn new yoga techniques? Explore nuclear physics databases? Identify at least five topics that interest you, then list the Internet tools you would use to find more information about the topics.
   b. Describe three specific activities you want to engage in on the Internet. For example, you might want to send your resume to an employer across the country, write messages to a distant pen pal, view a clip of your favorite movie, chat in real time with friends, or listen to music performed by your favorite band. Briefly describe how you will perform these activities.

Internet

▼ INDEPENDENT CHALLENGE 2

Most companies and public institutions that offer Internet access require users to sign, or at least be aware of, an acceptable use policy (AUP).

a. Obtain a copy of your school's or employer's AUP.

b. Outline the main restrictions that the AUP places on student (or employee) activities.

c. Compare those restrictions with the limits that it places on faculty (or employer) activities.

d. Analyze and evaluate any differences in treatment; if there are no differences, discuss whether the policy should be rewritten to include differences.

e. If your school or employer has no policy, outline the key elements that you believe should be included in such a policy.

▼ INDEPENDENT CHALLENGE 3

Your school probably has a number of computer networks. At most schools, you can find information about computing facilities from the Department of Academic Computing, the school library, or the network administrator.

a. What LANs, WLANs, and WANs do you have on your campus?

b. Which of these networks are interconnected?

c. Are there any hotspots on campus?

d. Determine if the file server is a PC or a larger computer.

e. Which network operating system is used?

▼ REAL LIFE INDEPENDENT CHALLENGE

If you own a computer, you probably want to set up a connection to the Internet from your home. Before doing this, it is a good idea to determine which Internet service provider you should choose.

a. Find out the names of three ISPs in your area. If possible, include one ISP that provides Internet access via cable connection and one that provides a DSL connection. (*Hint*: If you have Internet access and know how to use a search engine, open your browser, then use a search engine to do your research.)

b. Create a table in a new word-processing document and list the following information about each of the three ISPs you have chosen:
1. What is the monthly base fee?
2. What are the upload and download speeds?
3. Is there a different price for faster service?
4. If the service is a dial-up service, is the telephone access number local or long distance?
5. What software is included?
6. What user-support services are available?
7. What is the best feature of the services provided by the ISP?
8. How many email accounts are included?

c. Identify which ISP you would choose based on your answers to the preceding questions.

Understanding Browser Basics

The Web consists of millions of Web sites, which are made up of millions of Web pages. To use the Web as an effective tool for both research and entertainment purposes, it is helpful to understand how the Web is structured and how to use a Web browser to find and view information.  Trinity Andrews, director of the Danville Animal Shelter, places ads on television and in newspapers to let the public know about specific pets available for adoption. You volunteer at the shelter, and you offer to help Trinity identify ways that the shelter can use the Internet to let the community know about the shelter and about specific pets available for adoption.

OBJECTIVES

Understand Web browsing

Understand Hypertext Markup
    Language (HTML)

Understand Web site addresses

Start a Web browser and open a
    new tab

Go to a Web site and work with tabs

Navigate through a Web site

Create and manage favorites in
    Internet Explorer

Create and manage bookmarks in
    Firefox

Save a Web page

Print a Web page

Copy text and graphics from a
    Web page

Understanding Web Browsing

Remember that HTML documents are text files that are marked with tags to display the content on a Web page in a specific manner, and that a Web browser is software that allows you to view HTML documents. **Browsing** is the term that describes using your computer, a browser, and an Internet connection to view these files. As you investigate how to use the Web for the Danville Animal Shelter, you begin by learning some common terms related to Web browsing.

DETAILS

The following terms are associated with Web browsing:

- **Worldwide Client/Server Network**

  When you use your Internet connection to become part of the Web, your computer becomes part of a worldwide client/server network. As a Web client, your computer makes requests of Web servers on the Internet. Figure B-1 shows how this client/server structure uses the Web to provide multiple interconnections among the various kinds of client and server computers.

- **Download**

  The term **download** means to request the files that contain the Web page you want to display in your browser window from the server, and then copy these files from the server to your computer. The process of the page appearing in the browser window is called **loading**.

- **Home Page**

  The term **home page** is commonly used when talking about the Web. It has three general meanings. In the second and third definitions it is sometimes called a **start page**.
  - A home page is the main Web page that all the Web pages on a Web site are organized around and link back to; it is typically the first Web page that opens when you visit a Web site. Figure B-2 shows the home page of the Atlanta Pet Rescue & Adoption Web site. Many of the links on this home page link to other Web pages included on the Atlanta Pet Rescue & Adoption Web site.
  - A home page is also a Web page that a Web browser displays the first time you use it. This Web page is typically the main Web page of the company or other organization that installed or created the Web browser software. This is also referred to as start page.
  - A home page is also the first Web page that opens when you start your Web browser. This type of home page, also sometimes called a start page, might be an HTML document stored on your own computer or the main Web page of a favorite Web site. If you are using a computer on your school's or employer's network, the Web browser might be configured to display the main Web page for the school or company.

- **Jumping**

  When a new page appears in the browser window as a result of the user clicking a link, it is referred to as **jumping** to that page.

FIGURE B-1: Client/server structure of the World Wide Web

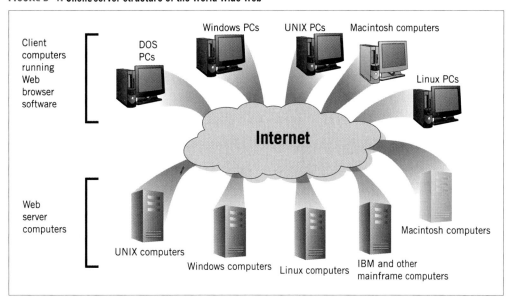

FIGURE B-2: Home page of the Atlanta Pet Rescue & Adoption Web site

Links to other pages on the Atlanta Pet Rescue & Adoption Web site

Link to a page with links to pages on other Web sites

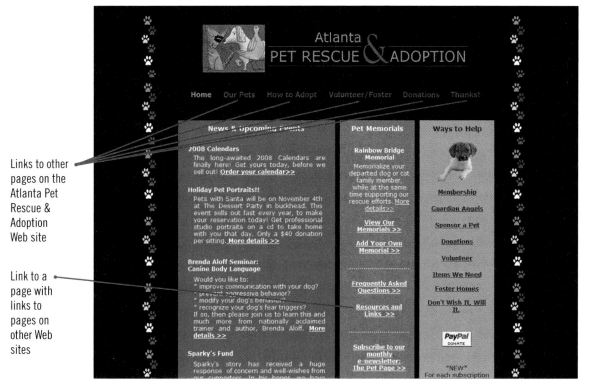

Internet

Understanding Hypertext Markup Language (HTML)

The public files on Web servers are ordinary text files that contain text and codes. The text and codes must follow a generally accepted standard so that Web browser software can read these files. As explained in Unit A, the standard used for formatting files viewed on the Web is Hypertext Markup Language (HTML). An HTML document is a text file that contains the Web page content and the instructions in HTML tags for formatting that content. A Web page is the result of a browser reading the tags in an HTML document and displaying the content by evaluating the tags. ░░░░ As you continue your research, you learn more about HTML and how links work.

DETAILS

The following terms are associated with formatting documents as Web pages:

QUICK TIP

To view the HTML document for a Web page in Internet Explorer, click the Page button on the Command bar, then click View Source. To view the HTML document for a Web page in Firefox, click View on the menu bar, then click Page Source.

• Hypertext Markup Language (HTML)

HTML uses tags to tell Web browser software how to display text and other elements contained in a document. Every Web page is created using HTML tags. When you view a Web page on the Internet, however, you do not see the HTML tags—you see just the resulting formatted Web page. Here is an example of a line of text that includes HTML tags:

<b>Welcome to the <i>Midland Pet Adoption Agency</i></b>

When the Web browser reads this line of HTML, it recognizes the <b> and </b> tags as instructions to display the enclosed text in bold and the <i> and </i> tags as instructions to display the enclosed text in italics. In a Web browser, the line of text would appear as follows:

Welcome to the *Midland Pet Adoption Agency*

• HTML Anchor Tag

An **HTML anchor tag** links multiple HTML documents together. Of all the HTML tags used to create a Web page, the HTML anchor tag is perhaps the most important because it enables you to easily open other Web pages that are relevant to the one you are viewing.

• Links

When Web page authors use an anchor tag to reference another HTML document, they create a link that points to other Web pages containing related information. As shown in Figure B-3, a Web page can link to other Web pages inside or outside a given Web site. Links often appear as underlined text in a color different from the other text on the Web page so that they are easily distinguishable. An image, such as a picture or company logo, can also contain a link to another Web page. Figure B-4 shows a Web page that contains several links. When you move the mouse pointer over a link in a Web browser, the mouse pointer changes to 🖑 .

FIGURE B-3: Linked Web pages

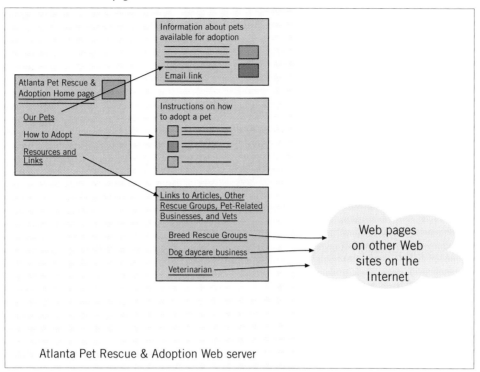

Atlanta Pet Rescue & Adoption Web server

FIGURE B-4: Web page with links

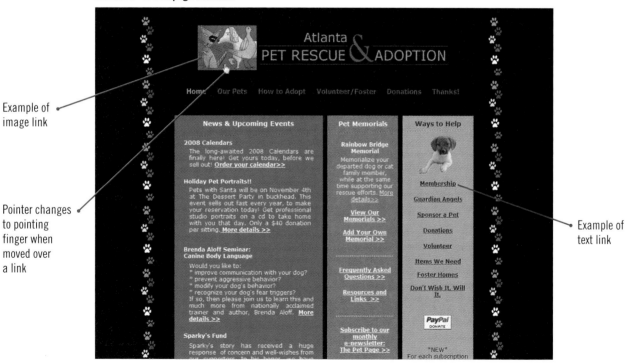

Example of image link

Pointer changes to pointing finger when moved over a link

Example of text link

Understanding Web Site Addresses

The Internet contains many servers answering requests for Web documents from many clients. To facilitate these interactions, each computer, whether client or server, is identified by a unique number called an **Internet Protocol address (IP address)**. Many servers as well as the individual Web sites on the servers can also be referenced by their **domain name**, which is the equivalent of an IP address that uses words and abbreviations. ▓▓▓▓ You decide to research terms that will help you understand the unique identification associated with each computer and each Web page.

DETAILS

The elements of Web site addresses are described below:

- **IP Addressing**

  An IP address consists of a four-part number. Each part is a number ranging from 0 to 255. For example, one possible IP address is 69.32.142.109.

QUICK TIP

Most companies register easy-to-remember domain names, such as www.disney.com or www.pepsi.com.

- **Domain Name Addressing**

  IP addresses can be difficult to remember, so most people use a domain name to identify a Web site. Domain names are identifiers made up of words and abbreviations that are associated with specific IP addresses. For example, the domain name gsb.uchicago.edu is an Internet server at the Graduate School of Business (gsb), which is an academic unit of the University of Chicago (uchicago), which is an educational institution (edu). No other computer on the Internet has the same domain name.

QUICK TIP

Post-secondary schools in the United Kingdom use ac as a second-level domain name.

- **Top-Level Domain**

  The last part of a domain name is called its **top-level domain** (**TLD**). In the example gsb.uchicago.edu, the top-level domain is "edu." Internet host computers outside the United States often use two-letter country domain names instead of, or in addition to, the TLD. For example, a nonprofit organization in Great Britain could have .uk as the last part of its domain name or .org.uk. Table B-1 shows the original seven top-level domains, some of the more popular country top-level domains, and newer top-level domains that were approved in 2000.

- **Uniform Resource Locators (URLs)**

  IP addresses and domain names identify particular computers on the Internet, but they do not identify where a Web page's HTML document resides on that computer. To find a specific Web page, you need to enter a **Uniform Resource Locator** (**URL**), which tells the Web browser the following information:

  - The transfer protocol to use when transporting the file (HTTP is the most common)
  - The domain name of the computer on which the file resides
  - The pathname of the folder or directory on the computer on which the file resides
  - The name of the file

  Figure B-5 shows an example of a URL. It uses HTTP as the protocol and points to a computer at the Scottish Council for Voluntary Organisations (scvo), which is a nonprofit organization (org) in the United Kingdom (uk). The pathname refers to the subfolders in which the text and graphics files that describe the SCVO organization are stored. Notice that the path includes two folder names. The second folder is stored within the first folder. The filename (AboutSCVOHome.aspx) is the file that contains the text and HTML codes for the Web page shown.

FIGURE B-5: Structure of a URL and its Web page in Internet Explorer

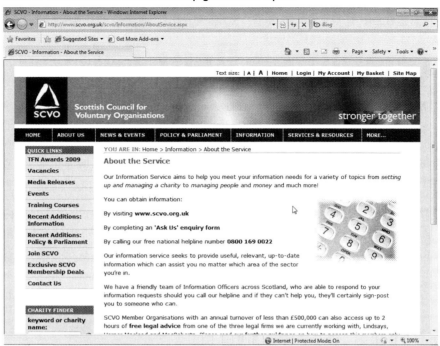

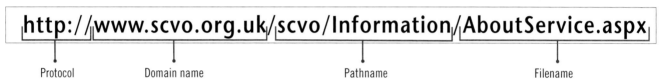

Protocol | Domain name | Pathname | Filename

TABLE B-1: Common top-level domains (TLDs)

Original General TLDs		Country TLDs		General TLDs Added Since 2000	
TLD	**use**	**TLD**	**country**	**TLD**	**use**
.com	U.S. commercial	.au	Australia	.asia	Companies, individuals, and organizations based in Asian-Pacific regions
.edu	U.S. four-year, post-secondary, educational institution	.ca	Canada	.biz	Businesses
.gov	U.S. federal government	.de	Germany	.info	General use
.mil	U.S. military	.fi	Finland	.int	International organizations and programs endorsed by a treaty between or among nations
.net	U.S. general use	.fr	France	.museum	Museums
.org	U.S. nonprofit organization	.jp	Japan	.name	Individual persons
.us	U.S. general use	.se	Sweden	.pro	Professionals (accountants, lawyers, physicians)
		.uk	Great Britain (United Kingdom)		

Internet

Starting a Web Browser and Opening a New Tab

The most popular Web browsers are Microsoft Internet Explorer and Mozilla Firefox. Both browsers display Web pages in tabs. **Tabs** allow you to display multiple Web pages in a single browser window, so that you can easily navigate from page to page by clicking the tab for the page you want to view. The tab on top is the **active tab**. You begin your research of Web sites devoted to pet adoptions by starting your Web browser.

STEPS

The steps in this book are written for Microsoft Internet Explorer 8 and Mozilla Firefox 3.5. If you use another browser, refer to the Appendix or ask your instructor for help.

TROUBLE
You may need to click a folder on the All Programs menu before you can click the name of your browser.

1. **Click the Start button on the taskbar, point to All Programs, click the name of the browser you are using, then click the Maximize button, if necessary**
   The browser starts and your start page appears in the browser window. The default start page for Internet Explorer is MSN.com. The default start page for Firefox is a Web page on Google that is a customized start page for Firefox users. The Web **page title** appears in the browser title bar. Figure B-6 shows the top part of the Internet Explorer and Firefox Web browser windows.

2. **If you are using Internet Explorer, point to the New Tab button to the right of the open tab so that the New Tab icon appears on it, then click ; if you are using Firefox, click the Open a new tab button to the right of the open tab**
   Figure B-7 shows the Internet Explorer browser window, and Figure B-8 shows the Firefox browser window.

3. **Find the following components in your browser window, then read their descriptions:**
   - **Title bar:** Shows the name of the open Web page and the Web browser's name and contains the Minimize, Restore Down/Maximize, and Close buttons.
   - **Command bar** or **Menu bar:** Contains the buttons and menus that allow you to access and use all the features of the browser.
   - **Address bar** or **Location bar:** Indicates the URL of the current Web page; you can type a new URL in this bar and press [Enter] or click the Go button next to the bar to go to another Web page.
   - **Tab:** Allows you to switch between multiple Web pages in the same Web browser window. This is known as **tabbed browsing**. The name of the displayed Web page appears on the page tab.
   - **Search box:** You can type keywords in the Search box, and then press [Enter] or click the Search button to search for Web pages that contain the keywords using your default search provider.
   - **Status bar:** Indicates the name of the Web page that is loading, the load status (partial or complete), and messages such as "Transferring data" or "Downloading images." When you point to a link, its URL appears in the status bar. Information about the security status of a page also might be indicated in the status bar.

QUICK TIP
ScreenTips sometimes identify the buttons with longer names. Point to each button to see its complete name.

4. **Find the following buttons in your Web browser window, then read their descriptions:**
   - **Back** and **Forward buttons:** Allow you to return to a previously viewed Web page. If you have just opened your Web browser, the Back and Forward buttons are dimmed, or inactive.
   - **Refresh** or **Reload button:** Allows you to load again the Web page that currently appears in your Web browser so that you can view the latest information (such as news headlines). In Internet Explorer, the Refresh button and the Go button occupy the same position to the right of the Address bar. The Go button appears when you start typing a URL in the Address bar.
   - **Home button:** Allows you to return to the start page for your Web browser.
   - **Stop button:** Allows you to stop loading the contents of a Web page. In Firefox, the Stop button is dimmed if you just started the program.

FIGURE B-6: Tops of browser windows

Web page title

New Tab button in Internet Explorer

Open a new tab button in Firefox

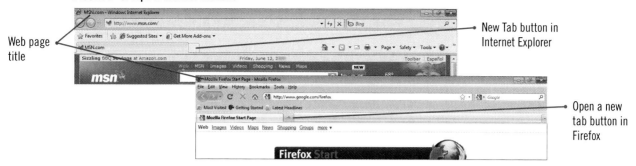

FIGURE B-7: Internet Explorer browser window with two tabs open

Back button

Forward button

Address bar

Title of start page for browser (yours might differ)

Tabs

New Tab button

Refresh button (changes to Go button when new text is typed in the Address bar)

Status bar

Search box

Stop button

Command bar

Home button

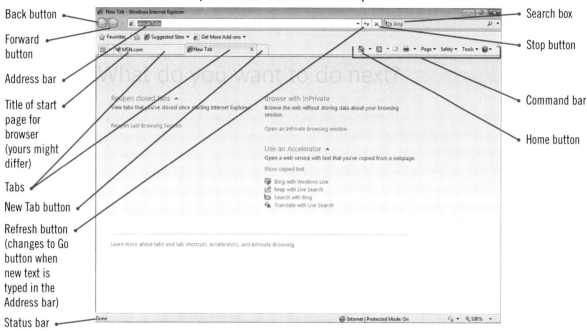

FIGURE B-8: Firefox browser window with two tabs open

Menu bar

Back button

Forward button

Refresh button

Title of start page for browser (yours might differ)

Stop button

Home button

Status bar

Search box

Go button

Location bar

Open a new tab button

Tabs

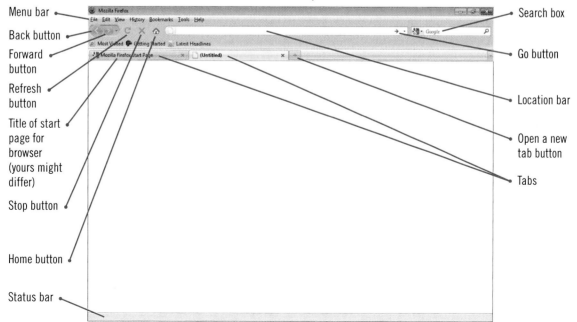

Internet

Going to a Web Site and Working with Tabs

After you start your Web browser, you can begin learning how to use it to find information on the Web. The fastest way to go to a specific Web site is to enter its URL in the Address bar in Internet Explorer or the Location bar in Firefox. ████████ You want to investigate the Web site of another agency that arranges pet adoptions. You will examine their home page to learn more about their services.

STEPS

1. **Click the left tab (the tab in which your start page is displayed)**
   Your browser's start page appears in the browser window. When multiple tabs are open, one way to switch between tabs is to click the tab you want to display.

2. **Click anywhere in the Address or Location bar in the browser window**
   The current URL in the Address or Location bar becomes highlighted, or selected. The selected URL in the Internet Explorer Address bar is shown in Figure B-9, and the selected URL in the Firefox Location bar is shown in Figure B-10.

   > **QUICK TIP**
   > You can click the Go button instead of pressing [Enter] to load the page whose URL is in the Address or Location bar. The Go button looks like an arrow pointing to the right and it is located to the right of the Address or Location bar.

3. **Type www.midlandpet.com**
   As soon as you start to type the new URL, the selected URL disappears. Even though a complete URL contains the protocol (such as http), followed by a colon and two slashes, most browsers add this prefix automatically, making it unnecessary to type it.

4. **Press [Enter]**
   The home page of the Midland Pet Adoption Agency Web site loads in your Web browser window.
   See Figure B-11. You can close a tab by clicking the Close Tab button on the tab. In Internet Explorer, you can click the Close Tab button only on the active tab. In Firefox, you can click the Close Tab button on any tab, even if the tab is not active.

   > **TROUBLE**
   > If you are using Firefox, skip Step 5.

5. **If you are using Internet Explorer, click the New Tab tab, point to the Close Tab button ☒ on the tab so that it changes to ☒, then click ☒**
   The blank tab closes.

   > **TROUBLE**
   > If you are using Internet Explorer, skip Step 6.

6. **If you are using Firefox, point to the Close Tab button ☒ on the (Untitled) tab, so that it changes to ☒, then click ☒**
   The blank tab closes.

FIGURE B-9: Selected URL in the Internet Explorer Address bar

Address bar

Click tab to make it the active tab

Close tab button

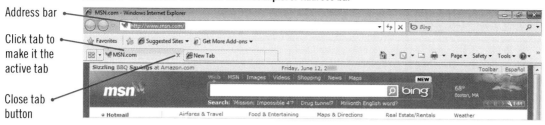

FIGURE B-10: Selected URL in the Firefox Location Bar

Click tab to make it the active tab

Close tab button

Location bar

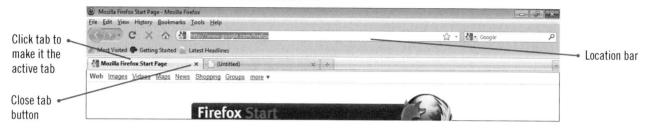

FIGURE B-11: Midland Pet Adoption Agency home page

Understanding error messages

Sometimes an error message appears in the browser window when you click a link. Common messages are "Server busy," "DNS entry not found," "File not found," and "Page cannot be displayed." These messages indicate that your Web browser cannot communicate with the Web server that stores the Web page you requested or cannot find the Web page because the server is busy, the Web page's location has changed permanently, or the Web page no longer exists on the Web. In Firefox, some of these errors result in a dialog box opening telling you that the connection was refused or the server timed out. Click OK in these dialog boxes to close them.

Navigating Through a Web Site

You can move from one Web page to a related one by clicking links. Links allow you to browse through a Web site in Paris, France one minute and then view a Web site in Tokyo, Japan the next minute. Most well-designed Web sites have a link to the Web site's home page on each of the other pages in the site. This is different from clicking the Home button in the browser, which opens the browser's defined start page. ████ You try another method of entering a URL, and then explore the Midland Pet Adoption Agency Web site by clicking several of the links on the site's home page.

STEPS

1. **If you are using Internet Explorer, click the Home button on the Command bar; if you are using Firefox, click the Home button to the left of the Location bar**
   The Home button looks like a house in most browsers. Your browser's start page appears.

2. **Select the URL in the Address or Location bar, then type www.mid**
   Because you typed this domain name previously, a list box appears below the Address or Location bar before you finish typing. The list box contains all URLs that you previously typed that start with "www.mid." In Internet Explorer, this list might also include pages in your history list (the list of all pages you have previously visited) and favorites (pages whose URL you have saved in a special folder) that contain these characters. You can click the URL in the list box instead of typing the full URL.

3. **Click http://www.midlandpet.com/ in the list box**
   The Midland Pet Adoption Agency home page appears again.

QUICK TIP
Note that the pointer does not always change to ⊕ when positioned on a link.

4. **Point to the Training Programs link near the top of the Web page**
   Notice that your mouse pointer changes to ⊕ and the URL of the link appears in the status bar in the browser window. Figure B-12 shows the pointer on the link in Internet Explorer.

5. **Click the Training Programs link**
   The Training Programs Web page appears in the current tab. This Web page contains information about the pet training programs offered by Midland Pet Adoption Agency.

TROUBLE
Be sure to click the Home link in the Web page and not the Home button on the Command bar or toolbar (which will display the start page for your Web browser). If you clicked the Home button, repeat Steps 2 through 6.

6. **Click the Home link near the top of the Web page**
   You return to the home page for Midland Pet Adoption Agency. Next, you will use the Back button to go back one page. The Back button looks slightly different in each browser, but it always is an arrow pointing to the left.

7. **Click the Back button on the toolbar to the left of the Address or Location bar**
   The Training Programs page reappears. Next, you will use the Forward button to move forward one page. The Forward button is an arrow pointing to the right.

8. **Click the Forward button on the toolbar to the left of the Address or Location bar**
   The Midland Pet Adoption Agency home page reappears. Next, you will open a link in a new tab.

9. **Right-click the Pets link**
   A shortcut menu opens offering commands for working with a link.

QUICK TIP
When you open a new tab from an existing tab in Internet Explorer, the new tab and the existing tab are colored with the same color to indicate that they are a tab group, a group of tabs that are related.

10. **If you are using Internet Explorer, click Open in New Tab on the shortcut menu; if you are using Firefox, click Open Link in New Tab on the shortcut menu**
    The Web page that lists the pets currently available for adoption opens in a new tab behind the current tab. Note that the Web page title appears in the tab as well as in the browser title bar. In Internet Explorer, you cannot see the entire page title in the tab because the default tab size is too small; point to the tab to see a ScreenTip that contains the page title as well as the complete URL of the page. In Firefox, you can see the complete page title, although if you open many tabs in Firefox, the tabs shrink in size. Figure B-13 shows the Pets page open in a tab behind the Midland Pet Adoption Agency home page in Firefox.

FIGURE B-12: Pointing to a link in Internet Explorer

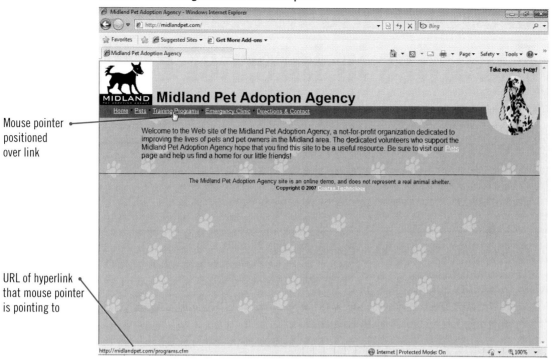

Mouse pointer positioned over link

URL of hyperlink that mouse pointer is pointing to

FIGURE B-13: Pets page open in a tab behind the home page in Firefox

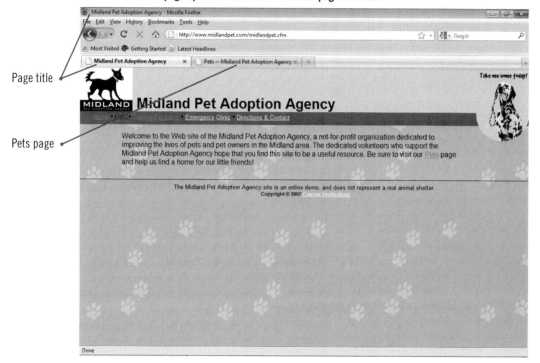

Page title

Pets page

Using the History feature

In addition to using the Back and Forward buttons to move to and from previously visited Web pages, most browsers include a History feature. The **History feature** is a list of Web sites you have visited over the past days or weeks, and it can help you locate Web sites you have visited in previous browsing sessions on the Web. To access the History list in Internet Explorer, click the Favorites button on the Favorites Bar, just below the Back button, and then click the History tab in the pane that opens. To access the History list in Firefox, click History on the menu bar, and then click Show All History to open the Library window. You can click links in the pane or the window to return to Web sites you have visited in the past.

Creating and Managing Favorites in Internet Explorer

In Internet Explorer, you can create a customized menu containing shortcuts to Web sites you specify. These shortcuts are called **favorites** in Internet Explorer. You use favorites to store and organize the URLs of Web pages that you have visited so you can return to them easily. If you do not think you will be visiting the page again, you can delete favorites you have added so that you do not have to weed through a long list searching for the one you want. You decide to save the home page of the Midland Pet Adoption Agency Web site as a favorite so you can easily return to it later.

STEPS

🛑 *If you are using Firefox, skip to the next lesson.*

QUICK TIP

To save all open tabs as favorites in a folder, click the Favorites button, click the Add to Favorites list button, click Add Current Tabs to Favorites, type a folder name in the Folder Name text box, then click Add.

1. **Make sure the home page of the Midland Pet Adoption Agency Web site is displayed in the current tab, click the Favorites button on the Favorites Bar (just below the Back button), then click Add to Favorites**

   The Add a Favorite dialog box opens with the title of the current Web page in the Name text box. See Figure B-14. It can be helpful to organize favorites into folders.

2. **Click New Folder**

   The Create a Folder dialog box opens.

3. **Type Pet Adoption Agencies in the Folder Name text box, make sure Favorites is listed in the Create in list box to select the folder in which the new folder will be stored, then click Create**

   The Create a Folder dialog box closes, and the Pet Adoption Agencies folder appears in the Create in list box in the Add a Favorite dialog box.

QUICK TIP

To add the current Web page as a Favorite to the Favorites Bar, click the Add to Favorites Bar button ⭐ on the Favorites Bar.

4. **Click Add**

   The dialog box closes and the favorite is saved in the selected folder. You will test the favorite you saved.

5. **Click the Home button on the Command bar, click the Favorites button on the Favorites Bar, then click the Favorites tab at the top of the pane that opens, if necessary**

   The pane that opens is called the **Favorites Center**, and the list of favorites on your computer appears in the Favorites tab in the Favorites Center.

6. **Click the Pet Adoption Agencies folder in the Favorites Center**

   The favorite you added—the Midland Pet Adoption Agency home page—appears in the Pet Adoption Agencies folder in the Favorites list. See Figure B-15.

QUICK TIP

To make the Favorites Center visible all the time, pin it into place by clicking the Pin the Favorites Center button 📌 at the top of the Favorites Center.

7. **Click Midland Pet Adoption Agency**

   The home page of Midland Pet Adoption Agency appears in the browser window again, and the Favorites Center closes. Sometimes you will want to delete a favorite.

8. **Click the Favorites button on the Favorites Bar, right-click the Pet Adoption Agencies folder in the list in the Favorites Center, then click Delete on the shortcut menu, as shown in Figure B-16**

   The Favorites Center closes and the Delete Folder dialog box opens asking if you are sure you want to move the folder to the Recycle Bin.

9. **Click Yes**

   The Pet Adoption Agencies folder and its contents are deleted.

10. **Click the Favorites button on the Favorites Bar to confirm that the folder is no longer in the list of favorites, then click the Favorites button again to close the Favorites Center**

FIGURE B-14: Add a Favorite dialog box in Internet Explorer

Web page title
appears here

Click to add to list
of favorites

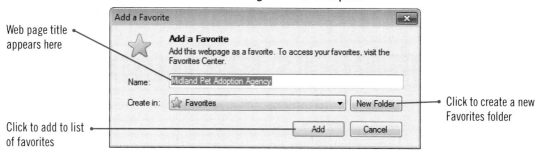

Click to create a new
Favorites folder

FIGURE B-15: Pet Adoption Agencies folder in Favorites Center

Favorites button

Add to Favorites button

List in Favorites Center on
your screen might differ

Favorite you added

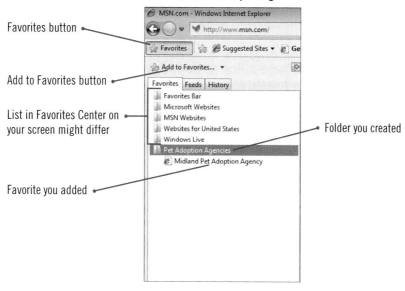

Folder you created

FIGURE B-16: Deleting a folder from the Favorites Center

Delete command
on shortcut menu

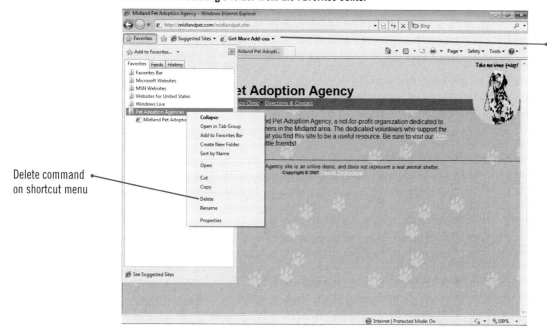

Favorites Bar

Internet

Creating and Managing Bookmarks in Firefox

In Firefox, you can create a customized menu containing shortcuts to Web sites you specify. These shortcuts are called **bookmarks** in Firefox. You use bookmarks to store and organize the URLs of Web pages that you have visited so you can return to them easily. If you do not think you will be visiting the page again, you can delete bookmarks you have added so that you do not have to weed through a long list searching for the one you want. Firefox also allows you to add **tags**, which are one- or two-word descriptions, to bookmarks to make it easier to search for specific types of bookmarks later. You decide to save the home page of the Midland Pet Adoption Agency Web site as a bookmark so you can easily return to it later.

STEPS

STOP *If you are using Internet Explorer, skip to the next lesson.*

QUICK TIP
To save all open tabs as bookmarks in a folder, click Bookmarks on the menu bar, click Bookmark All Tabs, type a folder name in the Name text box, then click Add Bookmarks.

1. **Make sure the home page of the Midland Pet Adoption Agency Web site is displayed in the current tab, click Bookmarks on the menu bar, then click Bookmark This Page**

   The Page Bookmarked pane opens with the name of the Web page in the Name text box. It can be helpful to organize favorites into folders.

2. **Click the Show all the bookmarks folders list arrow ▾ in the Page Bookmarked pane**

   The Page Bookmarked pane expands to list the subfolders in the Bookmarks folder and the list arrow you clicked changes to the Hide list arrow ▴. See Figure B-17.

TROUBLE
If the New Folder does not appear, click the Hide list arrow, repeat Steps 2 and 3.

3. **Click Bookmarks Menu in the list box, if necessary, to select the folder in which the new folder will be stored, then click New Folder**

   A new folder titled "New Folder" appears in the folder list in the Page Bookmarked pane. The folder name is selected.

4. **Type Pet Adoption Agencies**

   The text you typed replaces the temporary folder name, and the Pet Adoption Agencies folder appears in the folder list in the Page Bookmarked pane. You need to select the Pet Adoption Agencies as the current folder.

5. **Click Pet Adoption Agencies in the list box to select it, if necessary, then click Done**

   The Page Bookmarked pane closes and the bookmark is saved in the selected folder. You will test the bookmark you saved.

QUICK TIP
To quickly bookmark a page, click the Bookmark Star on the right end of the Location bar so that it changes to yellow.

6. **Click the Home button on the toolbar, click Bookmarks on the menu bar, then point to Pet Adoption Agencies**

   The bookmark you added—the Midland Pet Adoption Agency home page—appears on the Pet Adoption Agencies submenu on the Bookmarks menu. See Figure B-18.

QUICK TIP
To add a bookmark to the Bookmarks Toolbar, click the Folders list arrow in the Page Bookmarked pane that opens, then click Bookmarks Toolbar.

7. **Click Midland Pet Adoption Agency**

   The home page of Midland Pet Adoption Agency appears in the browser window again. Sometimes you will want to delete a bookmark.

8. **Click Bookmarks on the menu bar, click Organize Bookmarks to open the Library window, then click Bookmarks Menu in the list on the left**

   The Library window appears, as shown in Figure B-19.

9. **Click the Pet Adoption Agencies folder in the Bookmarks list on the right, click the Organize button on the toolbar in the Library window, then click Delete**

   The Pet Adoption Agencies folder and its contents are deleted.

10. **Click the Close button in the Library window**

   The Library window closes.

FIGURE B-17: Page Bookmarked pane in Firefox

Bookmarks Toolbar

Folders in Bookmarks folder; list on your screen might differ

Click to create a new Bookmarks folder

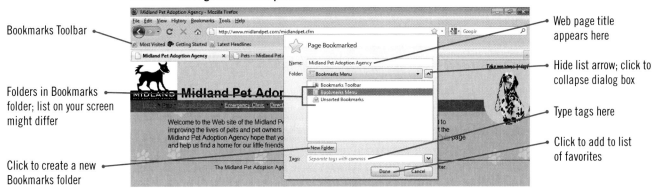

Web page title appears here

Hide list arrow; click to collapse dialog box

Type tags here

Click to add to list of favorites

FIGURE B-18: Pet Adoption Agencies subfolder on Bookmarks menu

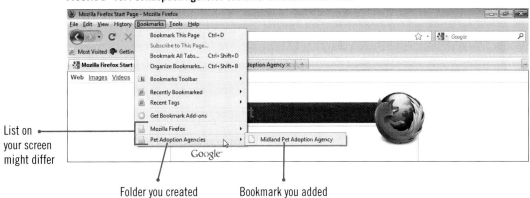

List on your screen might differ

Folder you created

Bookmark you added

FIGURE B-19: Library window

Organize button

Close button

Click to expand folder to see bookmarks stored in it

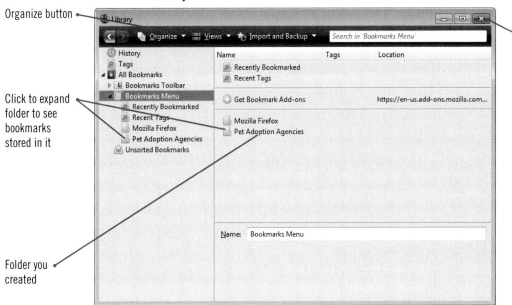

Folder you created

Internet

Saving a Web Page

If you are concerned that a Web page might change and you want to show it to someone in its current state, you can save the Web page to a disk. Sometimes when you save a Web page and open it later, you find that not all of the images were saved. This happens when the file that contains the image is not actually stored on the Web server that holds the files for the Web site you are viewing. When images on a page are stored on another Web server, the image will not be saved when you save the complete Web page. If you want to save the image that is missing, you can save the image in its own file on a disk. You will learn more about saving images in the lesson titled "Copying Text and Graphics from a Web Page" later in this unit. ◆◆◆◆◆ You decide to save the home page of Midland Pet Adoption Agency so Trinity can view it in its current form whenever she wishes.

STEPS

1. **Make sure the home page of the Midland Pet Adoption Agency Web site is displayed in the current tab**

2. **If you are using Internet Explorer, click the Page button on the Command bar, then click Save As; if you are using Firefox, click File on the menu bar, then click Save Page As**
   A dialog box similar to the standard Save As dialog box opens.

3. **Navigate to the drive and folder where your Data Files are stored, select the text in the File name text box if necessary, then type MidlandHomePage**

4. **If you are using Internet Explorer, make sure the Save as type is Web archive, single file (*.mht); if you are using Firefox, click the Save as type list arrow, then click Web Page, complete**
   Note in the Save as type text box that the file will be saved as a single-file Web archive file in Internet Explorer or a complete Web page file in Firefox. This means the file will be saved as an HTML file and the graphics and other components that are built into the page will be saved as well. Figure B-20 shows the Save Webpage dialog box in Internet Explorer, and Figure B-21 shows the Save As dialog box in Firefox.

TROUBLE
If a dialog box titled Downloads or something similar opens, click the Close button in its title bar.

5. **Click Save**
   The Save As dialog box closes and the Web page is saved in its current state. You decide to try opening it to make sure it saved as you expected.

6. **If you are using Internet Explorer, click the Home button on the Command bar; if you are using Firefox, click the Home button to the left of the Location bar**
   The start page for your browser appears in the browser window.

7. **Click the Start button on the taskbar, then click Documents**
   The Documents window opens on your desktop.

TROUBLE
If you are using Internet Explorer, you might see a yellow bar at the top of the window telling you that Intranet settings are turned off. This is a security setting. This presents no problems.

8. **Navigate to the drive and folder where your Data Files are stored, then locate the MidlandHomePage file**
   If you saved the Web page in Internet Explorer, the filename extension of the saved file is .mht. If you saved the Web page in Firefox, the filename extension of the saved file is .htm.

9. **Double-click the MidlandHomePage file**
   The Midland Pet Adoption Agency home page appears in a new tab in the browser window. Notice that the path and filename of the saved Web page appears in the Address or Location bar instead of the URL of the page on the Web.

10. **Close the tab or browser window that you just opened, click the Pets -- Midland Pet Adoption Agency tab (the second tab), if necessary, to display the Pets page on the Midland Pet Adoption Agency Web site, click the Documents window taskbar button, then close the Documents window**

FIGURE B-20: Save Webpage dialog box in Internet Explorer

Enter filename here

File type of saved Web page

Click to display available folders

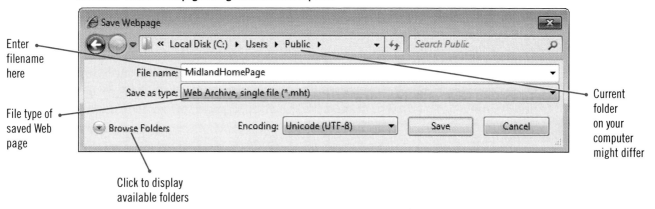

Current folder on your computer might differ

FIGURE B-21: Save As dialog box in Firefox

Enter filename here

File type of saved Web page

Click to display available folders

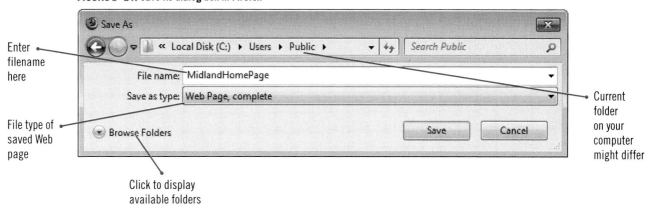

Current folder on your computer might differ

Saved Web page formats

In both Internet Explorer and Firefox, you can save a Web page as a complete Web page, HTML only, or a text file. When you save a Web page as a **complete Web page**, you save the page and all of its individual associated files. These files are automatically stored in a folder with the same name as the file you saved, followed by an underscore and the word "files"; for example, the folder associated with the Web page you saved in this lesson is called "MidlandHomePage_files." When you save a Web page as HTML only, you save the HTML formatted text on the Web page, but you do not save any graphics, sounds, videos, or other files. Saving a Web page as a text file saves the unformatted text only. In addition to these file types, in Internet Explorer, you also have the option to save a Web page as a **single-file Web page**, which means that all of the supporting elements, including text, graphics, and links, are stored in a single file.

Internet

Printing a Web Page

You can easily print the contents of a Web page so that you can view the information when you are not at your computer. When you print a Web page, the Web site source and the date on which the Web page was printed also appear. ▓▓▓▓ In addition to the saved version of the Midland Pet Adoption Agency home page, you decide to print a copy of the Pets page so you will have it to reference later.

STEPS

TROUBLE

If you are using Internet Explorer, and you do not see a menu when you click the Print button list arrow and the page is sent to the printer, you clicked the Print button itself, not the list arrow. Repeat Step 1.

1. **If you are using Internet Explorer, click the** Print button list arrow 🖨 ▾ **on the Command bar; if you are using Firefox, click** File **on the menu bar**

2. **Click** Page Setup

   The Page Setup dialog box opens. The Page Setup dialog box for Internet Explorer is shown in Figure B-22, and the Page Setup dialog box for Firefox is shown in Figure B-23. This dialog box allows you to set options for paper, headers and footers, page orientation, and margins.

3. **If you are using Internet Explorer, examine the settings in the dialog box; if you are using Firefox, click the** Format & Options tab **if necessary to view the settings on this tab, then click the** Margins & Header/Footer tab

4. **After examining the settings available in the Page Setup dialog box, click** Cancel

   You can preview the page to see how it will look when printed.

5. **If you are using Internet Explorer, click the** Print button list arrow 🖨 ▾ **on the Command bar; if you are using Firefox, click** File **on the menu bar**

6. **Click** Print Preview

   The Web page appears in the Print Preview window. The Internet Explorer Print Preview window is shown in Figure B-24, and the Firefox Print Preview window is shown in Figure B-25. The current page number and the total number of pages appear in the status bar in Internet Explorer and on the toolbar in Firefox, and you can see the header and footer that will appear on the page. (You might need to scroll to see the footer.)

QUICK TIP

If you are using Internet Explorer, you can simply click the Print button to open the Print dialog box.

7. **If you are using Internet Explorer, click the** Close button **on the title bar, and if you are using Firefox, click** Close **on the Print Preview toolbar**

   Print Preview closes and you are returned to the Web page.

8. **If you are using Internet Explorer, click the** Print button list arrow 🖨 ▾ **on the Command bar; if you are using Firefox, click** File **on the menu bar**

QUICK TIP

You can print directly from the Print Preview window by clicking Print on the Print Preview toolbar.

9. **Click** Print

   The Print dialog box opens. You want to print only one page.

10. **Click the** Pages option button, **type** 1 **in the** Pages text box **in Internet Explorer if necessary, or type** 1 **in both the** from **and** to text boxes **in Firefox, then click** Print **or** OK **in the Print dialog box**

    The Print dialog box closes and the Web page prints.

Making Web pages printer-friendly

Sometimes a Web page is wider than a standard sheet of paper. On some Web pages, most of the space is occupied by Web site navigation elements, with the main page content occupying only a narrow column in the center of the Web page. This can cause part of the Web page to be cut off on the printout, which can result in the use of many sheets of paper for a relatively small amount of information. To make Web page printouts as practical as possible, some Web pages include a **printer-friendly link**, which opens a Web page containing the same information as on the original Web page, but formatted like a printed page rather than a Web browser window. You should get in the habit of looking for a printer-friendly link on Web pages you want to print to ensure that you get a useful printout.

FIGURE B-22: Page Setup dialog box in Internet Explorer

Click to set paper size

Options to change the page orientation

Default margin settings

Default header includes the page title and number of pages

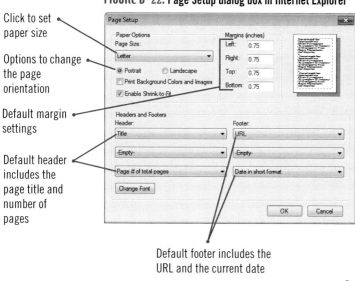

FIGURE B-23: Page Setup dialog box in Firefox

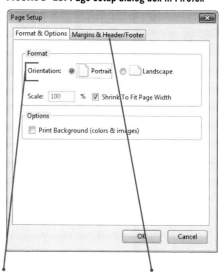

Default footer includes the URL and the current date

Options to change the page orientation

Default header on this tab includes codes to print Web page title and the URL; default footer includes codes to print the number of pages and the current date and time

FIGURE B-24: Print Preview in Internet Explorer

Print Preview toolbar

Total number of pages

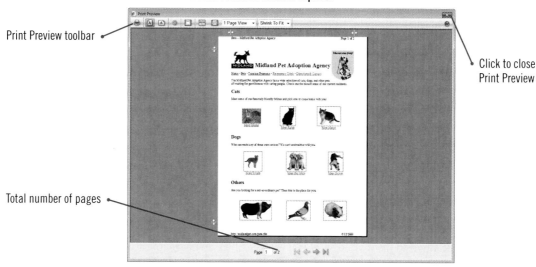

Click to close Print Preview

FIGURE B-25: Print Preview in Firefox

Print Preview toolbar

Total number of pages

Click to close Print Preview

Copying Text and Graphics from a Web Page

You can save portions of Web page's text to a file, so that you can use the text in other programs. One way to save the text is to copy it into a word-processing or text editor document. You can also save images from a Web page to a file. This is useful if you do not need to save the entire Web page or if you want to use the image in another document. ▓▓▓▓▓ Trinity would like to visit Midland Pet Adoption Agency so that she can meet with the director and learn more about how they developed their Web site. You can copy the agency's address and telephone number from the Web site to the Clipboard, and then paste it into a word-processing document such as a WordPad document. You can also copy the street map image from the Web site, which shows the location of the agency, to the Clipboard, or you can save the image to a disk so that you give it to Trinity.

STEPS

1. **Click the Directions & Contact link on the Pets – Midland Pet Adoption Agency page**
   The page with the address, phone number, and map opens.

2. **Drag the mouse pointer over the address and telephone number to select them**
   See Figure B-26.

3. **Right-click the selection, then click Copy on the shortcut menu**
   The selected text is copied to the Clipboard. You want to paste the text into a WordPad document.

4. **Click the Start button on the taskbar, point to All Programs, click Accessories, then click WordPad**
   The WordPad program starts with a new document open in the WordPad window.

TROUBLE
If a menu appeared instead of the text being pasted, you clicked the bottom part of the button. Click Paste on the menu that opened.

5. **On the Ribbon at the top of the window, on the Home tab, in the Clipboard group, click the Paste button**
   The text you copied from the Web page is pasted into the WordPad document.

6. **In the title bar of the WordPad window, click the Save button 🖫 to open the Save As dialog box, navigate to the drive and folder where your Data Files are stored, select the text in the File name text box, type MidlandAddressPhone, then click Save**
   The WordPad file is saved. Now you will save the map image to a disk.

7. **Click the Close button on the WordPad title bar to exit WordPad and switch back to your browser window, then right-click the map image to open a shortcut menu**
   The image shortcut menu in Internet Explorer is shown in Figure B-27. The image shortcut menu in Firefox is similar.

8. **Click Save Picture As or Save Image As on the shortcut menu**
   The Save Picture or Save Image dialog box opens.

TROUBLE
If the Downloads dialog box appears, click the Close button in the dialog box.

9. **Navigate to the drive and folder where your Data Files are stored, select the text in the File name text box, type MidlandMap, then click Save**
   The image is saved in a file.

10. **Click the Close button in the browser window title bar, then, if you are using Internet Explorer and a dialog box opens asking if you are sure you want to close more than one tab, click Close all tabs, or if you are using Firefox and a dialog box opens asking if you want Firefox to save your tabs for the next time it starts, click Quit**
    Your Web browser closes.

FIGURE B-26: Selecting text on a Web page

Selected text in Internet Explorer

Selected text in Firefox

FIGURE B-27: Saving the map image to a disk in Internet Explorer

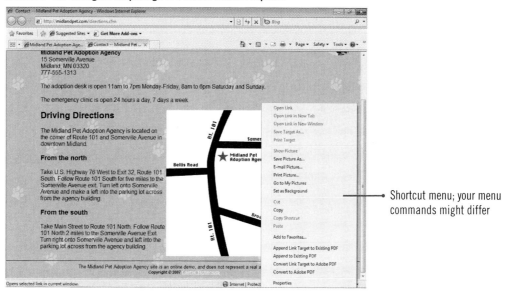

Shortcut menu; your menu commands might differ

Using Accelerators in Internet Explorer

An **Accelerator** is a type of add-on program that is actually a shortcut to another Web site. The Accelerators installed with Internet Explorer 8 by default include Map with Live Search and Search with Bing. To use an Accelerator, you select text or objects on a Web page to display the Accelerator icon, click the Accelerator icon to see a list of installed Accelerators, and then click the Accelerator you want to use. When you point to some Accelerators on the menu, such as Map with Live Search, a small window opens on top of the browser window displaying the result, as shown in Figure B-28. Other Accelerators require that you click them to open a new tab displaying the Accelerator's Web site.

FIGURE B-28: Map displayed using Map with Live Search Accelerator

Selected text

Accelerator icon

Installed Accelerators

Result of using Map with Live Search Accelerator

Internet

Practice

For current SAM information including versions and content details, visit SAM Central (http://samcentral.course.com). If you have a SAM user profile, you may have access to hands-on instruction, practice, and assessment of the skills covered in this unit. Since we support various versions of SAM throughout the life of this text, you will want to check with your instructor for instructions and the correct URL/Web site to access those assignments.

If you are using Internet Explorer, identify each element of the Internet Explorer window shown in Figure B-29. If you are using Firefox, identify each element of the Firefox window shown in Figure B-30.

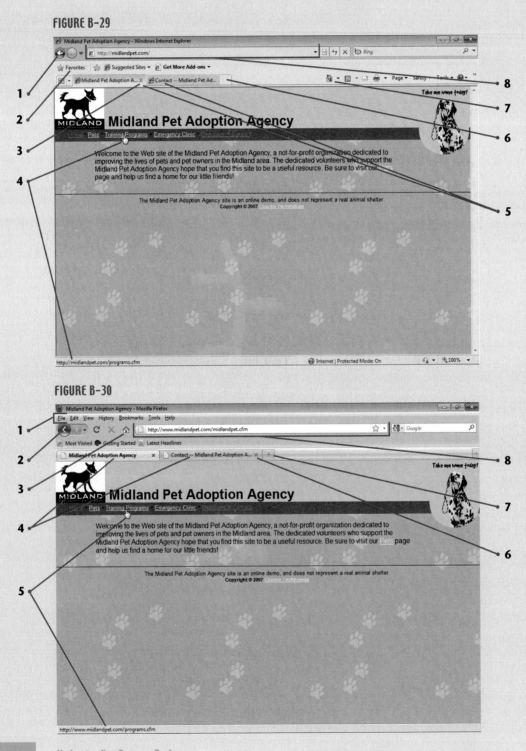

FIGURE B-29

FIGURE B-30

Match each term with the statement that best describes it.

9. **Web browser**
10. **Start page**
11. **Anchor tag**
12. **URL**
13. **Web site**
14. **Domain name**

a. The four-part addressing scheme that identifies the location of a Web page
b. The software that lets you view HTML documents
c. A tag that links multiple HTML documents together
d. The first Web page that opens when a Web browser starts
e. A collection of linked Web pages that has a common theme or focus
f. The equivalent of an IP address

Select the best answer from the list of choices.

15. **Web page authors link HTML documents using:**
    a. Netscape.
    b. HTML anchor tags.
    c. encryption.
    d. Internet Explorer.

16. **The numerical address that identifies each computer on the Internet is called the:**
    a. hierarchical address.
    b. URL.
    c. IP address.
    d. domain name address.

17. **The unique identifier composed of words or abbreviations that you can use to reference a server or Web site on a server is called the:**
    a. Web client.
    b. IP address.
    c. top-level domain.
    d. domain name.

18. **Which of the following is not a common top-level domain name?**
    a. .com
    b. .coop
    c. .ca
    d. .int

19. **If you want to view a Web page when you are not connected to the Internet, you can:**
    a. save the page as a favorite or bookmark.
    b. use the Back button.
    c. create a favorite or bookmark folder.
    d. save the page to a disk.

▼ SKILLS REVIEW

1. **Start a Web browser.**
   a. Start your Web browser.
   b. Wait for the home page to load.
   c. Open a new blank tab.
   d. Click the tab displaying the start page of your browser.
   e. Follow links on the home page to two or three Web sites that interest you. (*Note*: If there are no links on your home page, go to *www.course.com* and follow links on that page.)
   f. Make a list of the Web pages you visited. Include the URL of each Web site and provide a brief description of each Web site.

2. Go to a Web site and work with tabs.

  a. Select the current URL in the Address or Location bar, type the URL for Course Technology, www.course.com, then press the Enter key.

  b. On the Course Technology Web site, move the mouse pointer around the Web page to identify links.

  c. Consider these questions: How are the links identified on the Web page? Are there any links that surprised you because they did not look like links until you placed the mouse pointer over them?

  d. Follow one link.

  e. What link did you follow? How did you identify the link on the Web page? Did the linked content relate to the link you followed?

  f. Close the blank tab you opened in Step 1c.

3. Navigate through a Web site.

  a. Go to the Online Companion page for Unit B, then click the American Kennel Club link under Skills Review 3.

  b. Follow links to the page about breeds.

  c. Click the Home button to go to your browser's home page.

  d. Click the Back button to go back to the breed page on the American Kennel Club Web site, then click the Back button again to go back to the home page on the American Kennel Club Web site.

  e. Click the Forward button to go forward to the breed page on the American Kennel Club Web site.

  f. Open any link in a new tab.

4. Create and manage favorites or bookmarks.

  a. Go to the Online Companion page for Unit B, then click The New York Times link under Skills Review 4.

  b. Create a favorites or bookmarks folder called Newspapers.

  c. Add The New York Times Web site to the Newspapers folder in your list of favorites or bookmarks.

  d. Switch to the other open tab.

  e. Return to the Online Companion page for Unit B, then click The Boston Globe link under Skills Review 4.

  f. Add The Boston Globe home page to your list of favorites or bookmarks in the Newspapers folder.

  g. Go to your Web browser's home page in the current tab.

  h. Test the favorites or bookmarks you created to make sure they open to the correct Web pages.

  i. Delete the Favorites or Bookmarks Newspapers folder.

5. Save a Web page.

  a. Go to the Online Companion page for Unit B, then click the American Kennel Club Breed Rescue link under Skills Review 5.

  b. Save the Breed Rescue Web page as BreedRescue to the drive and folder where your Data Files are stored.

  c. Display your Web browser's home page in the current tab.

  d. Open the BreedRescue Web page file you saved.

  e. If you opened a window in Windows Explorer, close it.

6. Print a Web page.

  a. Make sure the BreedRescue Web page is still open in your browser.

  b. View the page in Print Preview.

  c. Set the print options to print only one page.

  d. Print one page.

  e. Close the tab displaying the stored Breed Rescue page.

7. Copy text and graphics from a Web page.

  a. Go to www.midlandpet.com, click the Pets link, then click the Meet Maxie link.

  b. Copy the paragraph describing Maxie to a WordPad document.

▼ SKILLS REVIEW (CONTINUED)

c. Save the document as **MaxieDescription** to the drive and folder where your Solution Files are stored.

d. Exit WordPad.

e. Save the picture of the cat as **MaxiePicture** to the drive and folder where your Solution Files are stored.

f. Exit your Web browser, closing all tabs.

▼ INDEPENDENT CHALLENGE 1

As part of your research for the Midland Pet Adoption Agency, you want to explore Web sites of pet rescue agencies.

a. Start your Web browser. Go to the Online Companion page for Unit B, then click the link under Independent Challenge 1. Use this link as a starting point for your search.

b. Find four pet adoption agencies in your state or neighboring states.

c. Create a favorites or bookmark folder called **Pet Rescue Agencies**.

d. Store the URLs of the four Web sites you have chosen in the Pet Rescue Agencies folder.

e. Test each favorite or bookmark you stored.

f. Save the home page of one of the Web sites you saved as a favorite or bookmark to the drive and folder where your Data Files are stored as **PetRescuePage**.

g. Print one page of the home page of another one of the sites you saved as a favorite or bookmark.

h. Delete the Pet Rescue Agencies favorites or bookmark folder and its contents, then close your Web browser.

▼ INDEPENDENT CHALLENGE 2

Business Web sites range from simple informational Web sites to comprehensive Web sites that offer information about the company's products or services, history, current employment openings, and financial information. An increasing number of businesses offer products or services for sale via their Web sites. You have just landed a position on the public relations staff of Value City Central, a large chain of television and appliance stores. Your first assignment is to research and report on the types of information that similar large firms offer on their Web sites.

a. Start your Web browser. Go to the Online Companion page for Unit B, then examine the links for Independent Challenge 2. There you will find a list of appliance retailers.

b. Choose two of the Web sites listed that you believe would be most relevant to your assignment.

c. Add each Web site to your list of favorites or bookmarks.

Advanced Challenge Exercise

■ Examine the properties for one of the bookmarks. (Right-click the favorite in the Internet Explorer Favorites Center, then click Properties on the shortcut menu, or open the list of bookmarks in the Library window in Firefox, then click a bookmark in the window to see the Properties listed at the bottom.)

■ Rename one of the favorites or bookmarks you created.

■ Create a folder named **Appliances** in the Favorites or Bookmarks folder, then move the favorites or bookmarks you created into this folder.

■ Close the Organize Favorites dialog box or the Library window, if necessary.

d. Copy a picture of an appliance from one of the Web sites you chose and save it as **ApplianceImage** to the drive and folder where your Data Files are stored.

e. Spend about 10 minutes exploring each of the two Web sites you have chosen, then write a paragraph comparing the two Web sites in terms of the overall presentation of the corporate image (is it clear? easy to understand? effective? attractive?) and the description of products or services offered (are the descriptions easy to follow? engaging? non-threatening?). In your comparison, indicate which of the two Web sites you believe projects its image most effectively. Which of the two Web sites would encourage you to purchase the company's products? Why?

f. Delete the favorites or bookmarks you created, then close your Web browser.

Internet

▼ INDEPENDENT CHALLENGE 3

The Columbus Suburban Area Council is a charitable organization devoted to maintaining and improving the general welfare of people living in Columbus-area suburbs. As the director of the council, you are interested in encouraging donations and other support from area citizens and want to stay informed of grant opportunities that might benefit the council. You are especially interested in developing an informative and attractive presence on the Web.

a. Start your Web browser. Go to the Online Companion page for Unit B, then examine the links for Independent Challenge 3. There you will find a list of charitable organizations.

b. Follow the links to charitable organizations to find out more about what other organizations are doing with their Web sites.

c. Add at least four Web pages to a favorites or bookmark folder named Charities. For each Web site, record a list of its contents. Note if each Web site includes financial information and if the Web site discloses how much the organization spent on administrative or non-program activities.

Advanced Challenge Exercise

- Use the History feature to select two of the Web sites you visited.
- Change the sort order of the items in the History so they are sorted by site or location.
- Delete one of the pages you visited today from the History list.
- On a page that lists a location, drag the pointer over the text that identifies the location, then use the Map with Live Search Accelerator to display a map of the location.

d. Identify which Web site you believe would be a good model for the council's new Web site. Explain why the Web site you chose would be the best example to follow.

e. Delete the Charities favorites or bookmark folder and its contents, then close your Web browser.

▼ REAL LIFE INDEPENDENT CHALLENGE

Many businesses register for an easy domain name—one that is easy for customers to remember; for example, the URL for the Web site of the Walt Disney Company is *www.disney.com* and the URL for the Pepsi-Cola Company is *www.pepsi.com*. See if you can find well-known organizations with which you are familiar that use such domains.

   a. Make a list of at least five large organizations that you would expect to have Web sites. Then list two possible easy domain names for each. For example, you might expect United Airlines to have a Web site at united.com or ual.com.

   b. Start your Web browser. Enter each of your guesses in your Web browser's Address bar or Location Bar.

   c. Record the correct domain name for each organization, or write "not found" if your guesses were unsuccessful.

   d. Identify a subject in which you are interested, then try entering an easy domain name that might lead to a Web site connected with your interests. For example, if you are interested in skiing, see whether a Web site exists at www.skiing.com. If you are interested in Beethoven, check out www.beethoven.com. You will know the domain name is invalid if your Web browser requires more than 10 or 20 seconds to find the Web site, or if the message appears in a Web page telling you that the browser could not find any results for the URL you typed or that the URL you typed did not match any documents. If the Web browser takes too long, just click the Stop button and try another domain name.

   e. Record the names of at least three subject-based domain names that produced the resources you were seeking.

   f. Close your Web browser.

▼ VISUAL WORKSHOP

Many organizations update their Web sites on a daily basis. In this Visual Workshop, you will analyze the changes made to a Web site. Start your browser, then type www.nasa.gov in the Address or Location bar. (If you have any difficulty, go to the Online Companion page for Unit B, then click the link for NASA under Visual Workshop.) Find at least four differences between the Web page on your screen and the Web page shown in Figure B-31. Make a list of these differences.

FIGURE B-31

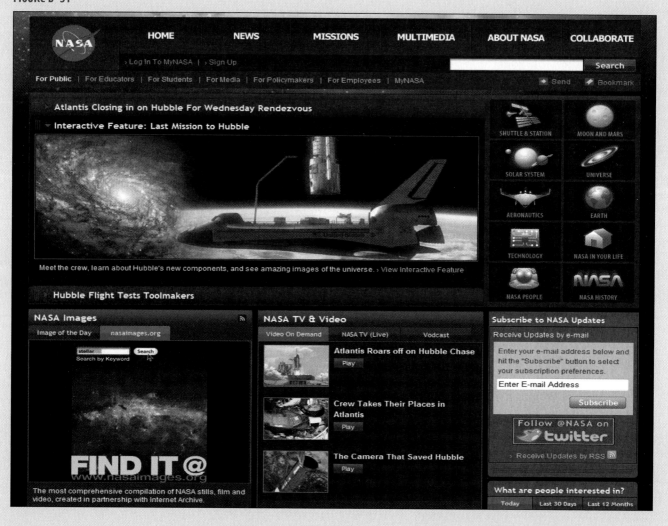

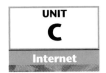

Using Email

Email is one of the most prevalent forms of business communication and the most popular way individuals use the Internet. Whether for business or recreational use, people rely on email as an indispensable way of sending messages and data to one another. Several programs for managing email are currently available. You can use any of these programs to send email to people who use the same or different email programs. The recipients can read your email just as you can read the email you receive from other people, regardless of the email programs they use. Kikukawa Air is an air charter service based in Maui, Hawaii, which offers service to all of the Hawaiian Islands. Sharon Kikukawa, one of the owners, wants to use email as the company's primary means of communication to save on long distance phone bills. She asked you to find out more about email.

OBJECTIVES

Understand email

Start Windows Live Mail and explore the
  mail window

Connect to your Hotmail account and explore
  the mail window

Send an email message

Check incoming email

Attach a file to an email message

Save an email attachment in Windows Live Mail

Save an email attachment in Hotmail

Reply to an email message

Forward an email message

Organize email messages

Delete email messages

Maintain a contact list in Windows Live Mail

Maintain a contact list in Hotmail

Create a category in Windows Live Mail

Create a category in Hotmail

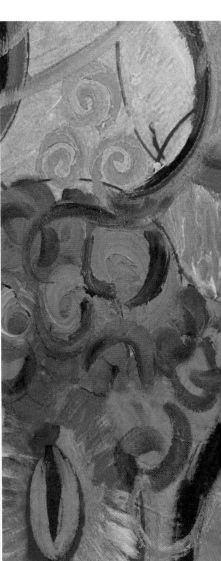

Understanding Email

As you learned in an earlier unit, **electronic mail**, or **email**, is a form of communication in which electronic messages are created and transferred between two or more devices connected to a network. Although similar to other forms of correspondence, including letters and memos, email has the added advantage of being fast and inexpensive. You begin your research for Sharon by learning some basic email concepts.

DETAILS

The following are some basic email concepts:

QUICK TIP

Windows Mail comes installed with Windows Vista. It is the predecessor to Windows Live Mail. You can upgrade to Windows Live Mail if you want.

- **Email Programs**

    You can send and receive email messages in two ways:
    - **Mail client software** lets you send and receive email and store email on your computer, which means that you can read email that you've received even after disconnecting from the Internet. Popular email client programs are Windows Live Mail, which you can freely download and install from the Microsoft Web site, and Thunderbird, which is part of the Mozilla family of products. Figure C-1 shows the Windows Live Mail program window.
    - A **Web-based email service** (often called **Webmail**) allows you to send and receive email by using a Web browser and the service's Web site. This service lets you read your stored email messages from different computers (for example, at home, work, or school); however, you can only access your stored email messages when you're connected to the Internet. Most Webmail is free. Many Webmail services cancel your account if you don't use it for a specified amount of time. Popular Webmail services include Windows Live Hotmail, Google's Gmail, and Yahoo! Mail. Figure C-2 shows the Windows Live Hotmail window.

- **Email Addresses**

    Email addresses uniquely identify an individual or organization connected to the Internet. An email address includes the **user name** (the name your ISP uses to identify you), the at sign (@), and the **domain name** (the computer that stores the email). For example, the email address of a Kikukawa Air employee named Chris Breed might be chrisbreed@kikukawaair.com, where "chrisbreed" is the user name and "kikukawaair.com" is the domain name.

- **Mail Server**

    When you send an email message to a particular addressee, the message is sent to a **mail server**, which is a server that runs special software for handling email tasks. Based on the recipient's email address, the mail server determines which of several electronic routes it will use to send your message. Each mail server on the route determines the next route for your message until it finally arrives at the recipient's electronic mailbox.

- **Message Header**

    The **message header** in an email contains all the information about the message—the recipient's email address (To), the sender's email address (From), and a subject line (Subject), which indicates the topic of the message. In addition, the message header can list other people who have received copies of the message and sometimes, the filename of an **attachment** (a separate file sent with an email message).

- **Message Body**

    The **message body** contains the actual message. It appears in the **message body pane** in a message window. Figure C-3 shows a sample email message in Windows Live Mail.

- **Junk Email**

    Junk emails, also called **spam**, are unsolicited emails usually selling an item or service. Some email programs include a **Junk e-mail** or **Spam folder** to which messages that the program thinks might be junk emails are automatically filed when they are copied from the server. Other email programs allow you to block mail from specific people or domains, or with certain words in the subject. Some Webmail services and ISPs block suspected junk email before it ever reaches you.

FIGURE C-1: Windows Live Mail program window

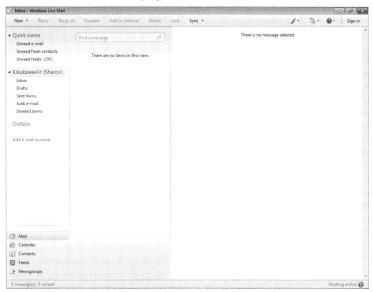

FIGURE C-2: Windows Live Hotmail window

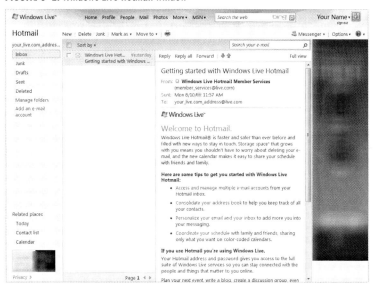

FIGURE C-3: Sample email message in Windows Live Mail message window

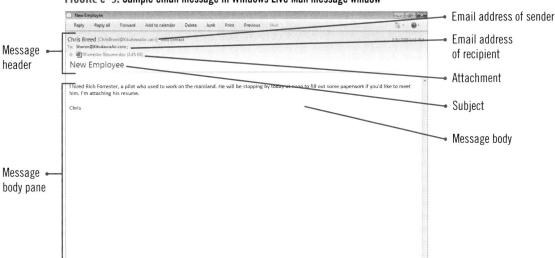

Message header

Message body pane

Email address of sender

Email address of recipient

Attachment

Subject

Message body

Starting Windows Live Mail and Exploring the Mail Window

Windows Live Mail is the mail client software that Microsoft makes available for free by allowing Windows users to download it from the Microsoft Web site. Before you can send email, you need to start your email program. The mail window is the interface in an email program that allows you to compose, send, receive, and manage your emails. You decide to get started with email.

STEPS

 The steps for using mail client software in this unit are written for Windows Live Mail Version 2009. If you have Windows Vista and use Windows Mail Version 6, use Thunderbird, or if you have Windows XP and you use Outlook Express, refer to Appendix A. If you have not set up your Windows Live Mail program yet, see the Clues box on the next page. If you are using Windows Live Hotmail or another Webmail program, skip to the next lesson.

1. **Click Start on the menu bar, point to All Programs, click Windows Live, then click Windows Live Mail**

   Windows Live Mail starts. Windows Live Mail is usually also listed as one of the programs near the top of the Start menu.

> **TROUBLE**
> If you are prompted for logon information, see your instructor or technical support person for help.

2. **If a dialog box opens telling you that Windows Live Mail is not your default email program, decide if you want it to be the default email program, then click Yes or No**

3. **Click Inbox in the list on the left, if necessary**

   See Figure C-4.

4. **If the reading pane is not open on the right side of the window, as shown in Figure C-4, click the Menus button on the right end of the toolbar, click Layout, click Reading pane (Mail) at the top of the Layout dialog box if necessary, click the Show the reading pane check box to select it if necessary, click the To the right of the message list option button, then click OK**

> **TROUBLE**
> Because you can customize the mail window by resizing, hiding, and displaying different panes and their individual elements, your screen might look different from Figure C-4.

5. **Examine Figure C-4 to locate the following elements of the Windows Live Mail program window:**
   - **Toolbar**, which changes depending on the purpose of the current window and contains commands for creating, sending, and organizing email messages.
   - **Folder list**, which consists of the following default folders:
     - **Inbox folder**, which stores messages that you have received.
     - **Drafts folder**, which contains saved messages that you are not yet ready to send.
     - **Sent items folder**, which contains copies of messages you sent.
     - **Junk e-mail folder**, to which possible junk emails are automatically sent when they arrive in the Inbox.
     - **Deleted items folder**, which stores messages you delete until you permanently delete them.
   - **Outbox**, which stores messages waiting to be sent.
   - **Message list**, which displays the message headers of the messages stored in the selected folder.
   - **Reading pane**, which displays the contents of the selected message in the message list.

FIGURE C-4: Windows Live Mail program window

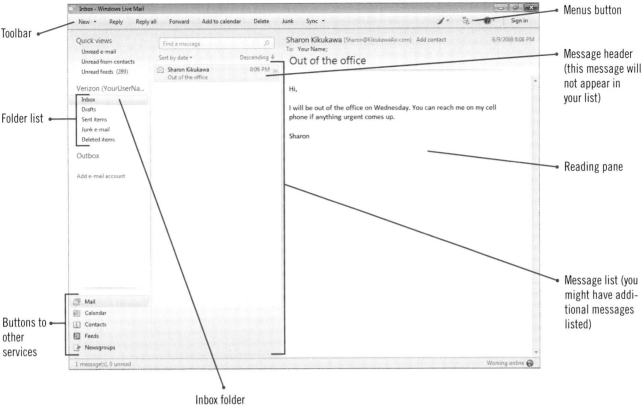

Toolbar

Menus button

Folder list

Message header (this message will not appear in your list)

Reading pane

Message list (you might have additional messages listed)

Buttons to other services

Inbox folder

Installing Windows Live Mail and setting up an account

If you are using Windows 7, and Windows Live Mail is not already installed on your computer, you need to download and install it. Go to the Online Companion page for Unit C and click the Windows Live Mail link. (You can also go to the Microsoft Web site and search for Windows Live Mail.) Click Download on the page that loads, click Run in the File Download – Security Warning dialog box that opens, click Run in the Download Complete dialog box if necessary, and then click Yes in the User Account Control dialog box that opens. In the Windows Live window that opens, select the Mail check box, and deselect the check boxes next to any other Windows Live program that you do not want to install to deselect them, and then click Install.

Select the options you want and click Continue as needed in the next few windows, and then click Close in the final window. If you are using Windows Vista, Windows Mail is installed on your computer. See Appendix A for information on how to use Windows Mail. The first time you start Windows Live Mail, the Add an E-mail Account dialog box opens. To set up your Windows Live Mail account, type your email address, password, and display name, click Next, and then continue following the directions in the dialog boxes to finish setting up your Windows Live Mail account. If the Add an E-mail Account dialog box does not appear automatically, click the Add e-mail account link in the pane on the left.

Connecting to Your Hotmail Account and Exploring the Mail Window

Windows Live Hotmail, or simply, Hotmail, is the Webmail service available from Microsoft. Before you can send email, you need to connect to your Webmail account. The mail window is the interface in a Webmail program that allows you to compose, send, receive, and manage your emails. You decide to get started with email.

STEPS

 The steps for using a Webmail program in this unit are written for Hotmail. If you use Gmail or Thunderbird, refer to Appendix A. If you have not registered for a Hotmail account, see the Clues box on the next page. If you are using Windows Live Mail, skip to the next lesson.

1. **Start your browser, go to the Online Companion page for Unit C, then click the Windows Live Hotmail link**

    The sign-in page for Hotmail appears.

2. **Type the email address you used when you registered with Hotmail in the Windows Live ID text box, press [Tab], type your password, then click Sign in**

    The Today page in your Hotmail account appears.

3. **Click Inbox in the pane on the left, then click a message in the message list, if necessary, to display it in the reading pane**

    The Mail window appears with Inbox selected at the top of the pane on the left. See Figure C-5.

4. **If the reading pane is not open on the right side of the window, as shown in Figure C-5, click the Options button on the toolbar, then click Right**

5. **Examine Figure C-5 to locate the following elements of the Hotmail Mail window:**
    *   **Toolbar**, which changes depending on the purpose of the current window and contains buttons for creating, sending, and organizing email messages.
    *   **Folders list**, which consists of the following default folders:
        *   **Inbox folder**, which stores messages that you have received.
        *   **Junk folder**, to which possible junk emails are automatically sent when they arrive in the Inbox.
        *   **Drafts folder**, which contains saved messages that you are not yet ready to send.
        *   **Sent folder**, which contains copies of messages you have sent in the past 30 days.
        *   **Deleted folder**, which stores messages you delete until you permanently delete them.
    *   **Message list**, which displays the message headers of the messages stored in the selected folder.
    *   **Reading pane**, which displays the contents of the selected message.
    *   Links, which provide access to different Hotmail services accessible in the following four windows:
        *   **Today**, which appears when you first sign into your Hotmail account. It displays the total number of messages in your Inbox and the percentage of your storage space on the Hotmail server that you have used.
        *   **Contact list**, which lists the names of the people stored in the Contact list. The **Contact list** stores people's names and email addresses, as well as other contact information.
        *   **Calendar**, which provides you with an electronic calendar that you can use to track appointments and to-do lists. You can also allow anyone with Internet access to view your calendar.

FIGURE C-5: Mail window in Hotmail

Toolbar

Folders list

Links to other services

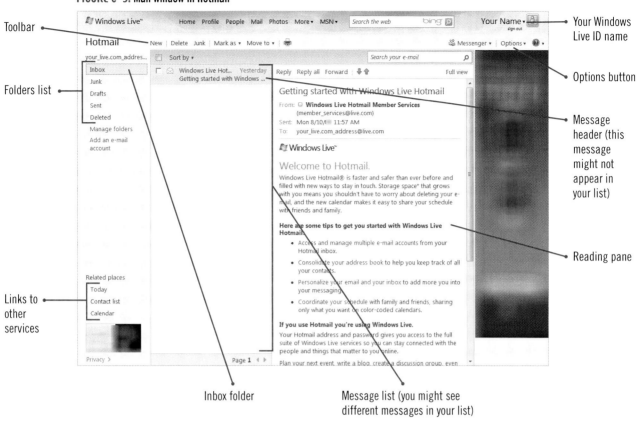

Your Windows Live ID name

Options button

Message header (this message might not appear in your list)

Reading pane

Inbox folder

Message list (you might see different messages in your list)

Signing up for a Hotmail account

Hotmail, like most Webmail services, provides free email service to anyone with an Internet connection. Before you can use it, you need to establish a user account. To do this, go to the Online Companion page for Unit C, and then click the Windows Live Hotmail link. This brings you to the sign-in page for Windows Live. In order to sign up for a Hotmail account, you need to get a Windows Live ID. (If you already have a Windows Live ID but do not have a Hotmail account, type your ID and password in the appropriate text boxes on the Sign In side of

the page, and then click Sign In.) To obtain a Windows Live ID, click Sign up, and then enter the required information (your name, country, birth date, and so on). When you sign up for a Windows Live ID, you can choose live.com or hotmail.com as the domain name. Both will allow you to send and receive email using Hotmail. When you are finished, the Hotmail Today page for your account will appear on the screen.

UNIT
C

Internet

Sending an Email Message

When you send an email message, you enter the recipient's email address in the **To** text box. You can use the **Cc** (carbon or courtesy copy) text box to send a copy of the message to recipients. You can also use the **Bcc** (Blind carbon copy) text box to send a copy to recipients without the knowledge of the other addressee(s). You can enter multiple email addresses in each of these text boxes. The **From** text box may not appear in the message window; your name, your email address, or both are automatically entered in this box. The **Subject** text box is where you summarize the main topic of an email message. You enter the message content in the message body pane. When you click the Send button, the message is transferred to your mail server for delivery to the email recipient(s). You need to send an email message to Sharon. You will also send a copy of the message to your own email address so that you can verify that the message is sent correctly.

STEPS

STOP *This lesson is written for both Windows Live Mail and Hotmail users. Read each step carefully and perform only those steps that apply to your email program.*

1. **Click the** New button **on the toolbar**

   A new message window opens with the insertion point in the To text box.

> **QUICK TIP**
> Messages sent to this email address are deleted without being opened or read, so do not send important messages to this address.

2. **If you are using Windows Live Mail, click the** Maximize button **in the New Message window title bar, if necessary**

3. **Type** sharon@kikukawaair.com **in the To text box**

4. **Click the** Show Cc & Bcc link **on the right side of the message window**

   The Cc and Bcc boxes appear below the To text box in the message window.

> **QUICK TIP**
> A drop-down list might appear with your name and email address in it. You can click this to add your email address to the Cc text box.

5. **Click in the** Cc text box, **then type your email address**

6. **If you are using Windows Live Mail, press** [Tab] **twice, and if you are using Hotmail, press** [Tab] **three times to move the insertion point to the** Subject text box, **then type** Practice

   The information in the Subject text box will appear in the message header in the recipient's Inbox. In most email programs, it also becomes part of the title of the message window in the window's title bar.

7. **Click in the** message body pane, **type** Sharon, **press** [Enter] **twice, type** I'm testing email. Please let me know that this message arrived., **press** [Enter] **twice, type** Thanks, **press** [Enter] **twice, then type your name**

   If you are using Windows Live Mail, your screen should look similar to Figure C-6; if you are using Hotmail, your screen should look similar to Figure C-7.

> **TROUBLE**
> If you are using Windows Live Mail and a dialog box opens asking you to enter your user name and password, type this information, then click OK. If you are using Hotmail and a yellow Information bar appears asking you to verify your account, click the verify your account link in the bar, follow the instructions in the window that opens, then repeat Step 9.

8. **If you are using Windows Live Mail and you are working on a shared computer, check the email address in the From list box near the top right of the window under the toolbar; if it is not your email address, click the** From list arrow, **then click your email address**

9. **Click the** Send button **on the toolbar in the message window**

   The message window closes, and the message is sent to the mail server for delivery to Sharon and to you, and copied to the Sent items folder. If you are using Windows Live Mail, the mail window appears again. If you are using Hotmail, a window appears with the notification that your message has been sent.

10. **If you are using Hotmail, click the** Return to inbox link

    The Mail window appears with Inbox selected in the pane on the left.

Using Email

FIGURE C-6: Completed message window in Windows Live Mail

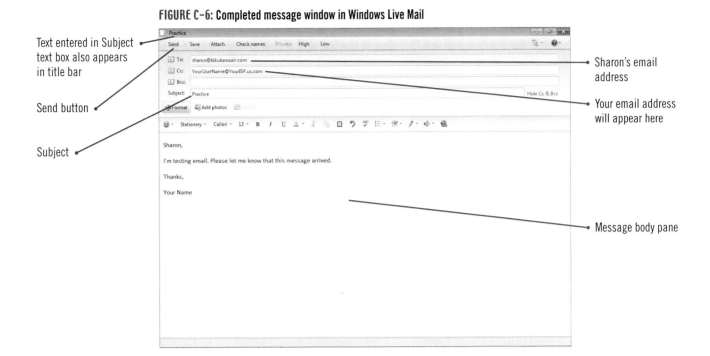

Text entered in Subject text box also appears in title bar

Send button

Subject

Sharon's email address

Your email address will appear here

Message body pane

FIGURE C-7: Completed message window in Hotmail

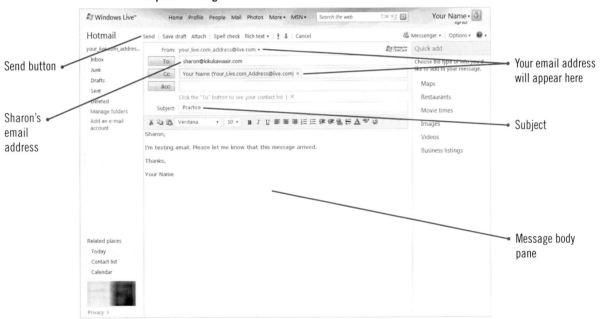

Send button

Sharon's email address

Your email address will appear here

Subject

Message body pane

Correcting your email message content

If you notice a typing error before sending an email message, you can select the error with your mouse pointer and then make the required correction. You can move the insertion point between the text boxes by pressing [Tab] to move forward or [Shift][Tab] to move backward, or by clicking in the desired text boxes. In Windows Live Mail, you can check the spelling of your email message by clicking the Check spelling button on the toolbar above the message pane; in Hotmail, click the Spell check button on the toolbar. In Windows Live Mail, you can turn on automatic spell checking for a message by clicking the Menus button on the toolbar in the main program window, clicking Options, clicking the Spelling tab, and then clicking the Always check spelling before sending check box to select it.

Checking Incoming Email

Email messages sent to you are held on the mail server until you use your email program to retrieve them. You receive incoming email messages in your Inbox folder (also called the Inbox). When the Inbox contains unread messages, the word "Inbox" and the number of unread messages appear in bold in the folders list. A closed envelope icon appears in the message header for an unread message, and the message header summary appears in bold. An open envelope icon appears next to the message header summary for each message you have read, and the message header summary is not bold. When you sent the message to Sharon, you copied the message to yourself by typing your email address in the Cc text box. You check your email to see if you received the copy of the message you sent to Sharon.

STEPS

🛑 *This lesson is written for both Windows Live Mail and Hotmail users. Read each step carefully and perform only those steps that apply to your email program.*

1. View the list of messages in your Inbox

If you are using Windows Live Mail and you have set your options to check for new messages periodically, the Practice message might already appear in the message list in your Inbox. If you are using Hotmail, the Practice message should appear in the message list.

TROUBLE

If a dialog box opens asking for your password, type your password, then click OK.

2. If the message is not in your Inbox, click the Sync button on the toolbar if you are using Windows Live Mail, or click Inbox in the Folders list on the left if you are using Hotmail

Within a few moments, your mail server transfers all new email to your Inbox. The message that you copied to yourself when you emailed the message to Sharon appears in the message list. See Figure C-8.

TROUBLE

If you do not see the Practice message in your Inbox, you might be looking in the wrong folder. Be sure "Inbox" is selected in the Folders list. If you still do not see the Practice message in the message list, wait a few minutes, then repeat Steps 2 and 3.

3. Click the Practice message in the message list

The selected message appears in the reading pane to the right of the message list, as shown in Figure C-9; if you are using Hotmail, the selected message appears in the reading pane, as shown in Figure C-10.

4. Double-click Practice in the message list

If you are using Windows Live Mail, the Practice message appears in a new window; if you are using Hotmail, the Mail window changes to display the contents of the Practice message.

QUICK TIP

In Hotmail, you can also click Inbox in the Folders list.

5. If you are using Windows Live Mail, click the Close button in the Practice message window title bar; if you are using Hotmail, click the Close message button in the upper-right corner of the message pane

If you are using Windows Live Mail, the message window closes and the mail window appears with your account selected and the contents of the Inbox listed in the message list. If you are using Hotmail, the Inbox in the Mail window appears.

Saving drafts of messages

If you compose an email message but you are not ready to send it yet, you can file it in the Drafts folder. To save a draft in Windows Live Mail, click the Save button on the toolbar at the top of the window in a New Message window. If a dialog box opens telling you that the message was saved in your 'Drafts,' folder, click OK. To save a draft in Hotmail, click the Save draft button on the toolbar in the message window.

FIGURE C-8: Windows Live Mail and Hotmail Mail windows containing new message

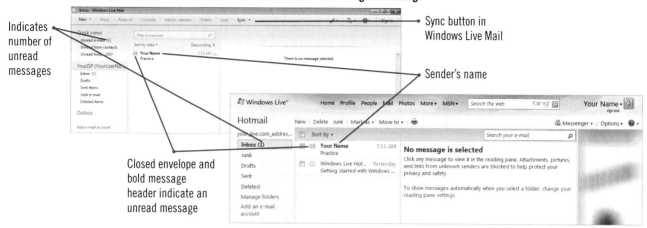

Indicates number of unread messages

Sync button in Windows Live Mail

Sender's name

Closed envelope and bold message header indicate an unread message

FIGURE C-9: Practice message in Windows Live Mail reading pane

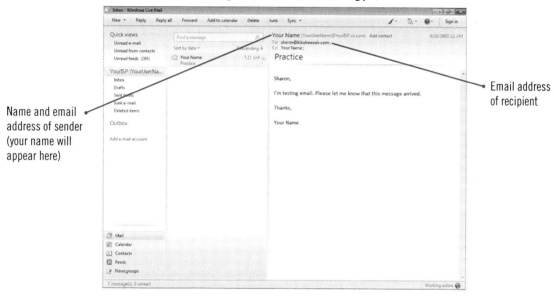

Name and email address of sender (your name will appear here)

Email address of recipient

FIGURE C-10: Practice message in Hotmail message window

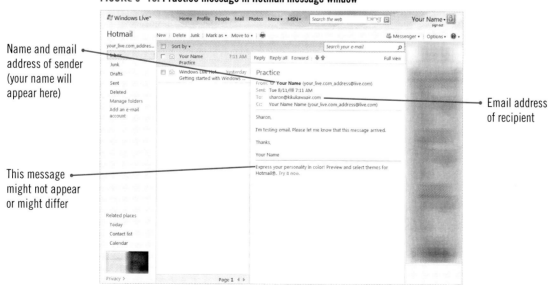

Name and email address of sender (your name will appear here)

Email address of recipient

This message might not appear or might differ

Internet

Attaching a File to an Email Message

You might want to send an email message that includes a file, such as a document created in a word-processing program or a spreadsheet program, or a picture. You can send any type of file over the Internet by attaching it to an email message. A file linked to an email message is called an **attachment**. Because emailing attachments between employees of Kikukawa Air would be useful for sharing information, such as maintenance schedules, you decide to explore how the attachment feature works by attaching a memo reminding pilots to get their annual physicals.

STEPS

🛑 *This lesson is written for both Windows Live Mail and Hotmail users. Read each step carefully and perform only those steps that apply to your email program.*

1. **Open a new message window**

2. **Type your email address in the To text box**

3. **Click in the Subject text box, then type Annual physical reminder**

4. **Press [Tab], then type Please see the file attached to this message. in the message body pane**

5. **Press [Enter] twice, then type your name**

TROUBLE

If you are using Hotmail and Firefox, click Browse, which appears below the Subject text box, to open the File Upload dialog box.

6. **Click the Attach button on the toolbar at the top of the message window**

   If you are using Windows Live Mail, the Open dialog box appears. If you are using Hotmail, the Choose File to Upload dialog box appears.

7. **Navigate to the drive and folder where you store your Data Files, then double-click the file Physicals.rtf**

   The message window changes to show the file Physicals.rtf listed as attached to the message. See Figure C-11 if you are using Windows Live Mail; see Figure C-12 if you are using Hotmail.

QUICK TIP

Most Webmail services and ISPs restrict the size of file attachments; in some cases, an email message with file attachments over two megabytes in size might be rejected and returned to the sender.

8. **Click the Send button on the toolbar in the message window, then, if you are using Hotmail, click the Return to inbox link**

   The message is sent to the mail server for delivery, and the Inbox appears in the mail window.

FIGURE C-11: Windows Live Mail email message with attachment

Attach button

Filename of attached file

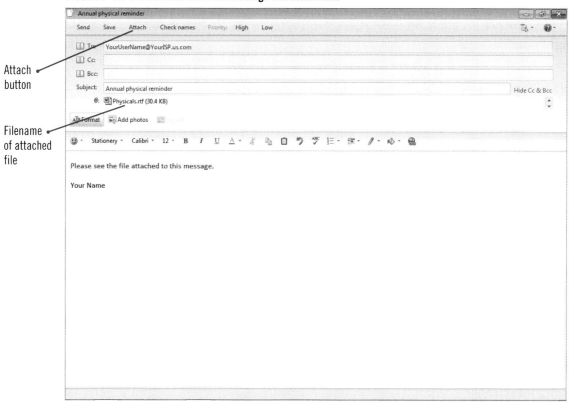

FIGURE C-12: Hotmail email message with attachment

Attach button

Filename of attached file

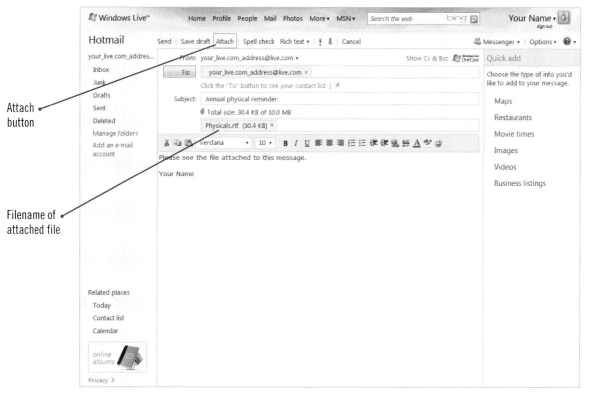

Internet

Saving an Email Attachment in Windows Live Mail

When you receive an email message with a file attached, you can open the attachment or you can save it to view later. You decide to experiment with the options for working with an attached file. You save the attachment on your computer.

STEPS

(STOP) *If you are using Hotmail, skip to the next lesson.*

1. **If the Annual physical reminder message has not arrived in your Inbox yet, click the** Sync button **on the toolbar at the top of the program window**

   The Annual physical reminder message appears in the message list. The paper clip in the message header summary indicates that the message contains an attachment.

2. **Click** Annual physical reminder **in the message list**

   The message appears in the reading pane with the filename of the attachment next to a paper clip above the subject in the reading pane.

QUICK TIP

To open the file in the program in which it was created, double-click the filename in the reading pane, then click Open in the Mail Attachment dialog box, if necessary.

3. **Right-click** Physicals.rtf **in the reading pane**

   A menu appears. See Figure C-13. If you click Open, the file will open in the program in which it was created, and then you can use the Save As command in that program to change the filename to one that is more meaningful to you.

4. **Click** Save as **on the menu**

   The Save Attachment As dialog box opens. See Figure C-14.

5. **Navigate to the drive and folder where you store your Data Files, click in the** File name text box, **change the filename to** Downloaded Physicals.rtf, **then click** Save

   The dialog box closes and the attachment is saved.

FIGURE C-13: Saving an attachment in Windows Live Mail

Indicates an
attachment

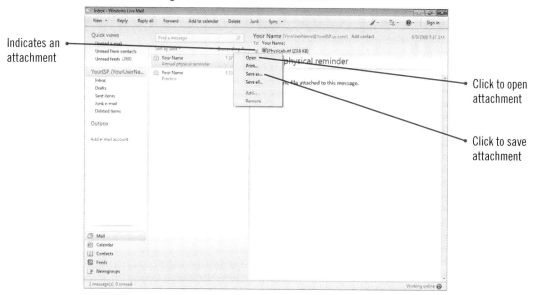

Click to open
attachment

Click to save
attachment

FIGURE C-14: Save Attachment As dialog box in Windows Live Mail

Your path
might differ

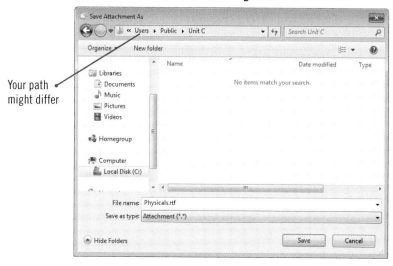

Understanding email viruses, worms, and Trojan horses

Email can carry malicious programs, such as viruses, worms, and Trojan horses. A computer **virus** is a piece of software that runs without your permission and performs undesired tasks, such as deleting the contents of your hard disk. Viruses **self-replicate**, meaning that they create, and in some cases distribute, copies of themselves to infect more computers. **Worms** and **Trojan horses** are variations on this idea, and they are of special concern to email users because they reproduce by using email programs on infected computers to send out copies of themselves as attachments to automatically generated email messages to everyone in the victim's email contacts list. However, you can take a couple of simple steps to protect yourself and those with whom you exchange email. The most important precaution you can take is not opening a file attachment from a sender you do not know, because the attachment might contain a worm or Trojan horse. If you receive an email message from an email address that you recognize, make sure the accompanying email message makes sense and is specific to you. If it is not, it might be the product of a worm. You can also install **antivirus software**, which is software that protects your computer from these malicious programs. Some email programs have built-in virus detection, and many schools and colleges distribute antivirus software for free to students, staff, and faculty; check with your instructor, system administrator, or computing services center to see if this software is available to you.

Internet

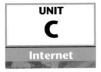

Saving an Email Attachment in Hotmail

When you receive an email message with a file attached, you can open the attachment or save it to view later. You decide to experiment with the options for working with an attached file. You save the attachment on your computer.

STEPS

🛑 *If you are using Windows Live Mail, skip to the next lesson.*

1. **If the Annual physical reminder message has not arrived in your Inbox yet, click Inbox in the Folders list on the left**

   The Annual physical reminder message appears in the message list. The paper clip next to the Annual physical reminder message header indicates that the message contains an attachment. See Figure C-15.

2. **Display the Annual physical reminder message in the reading pane, if necessary**

   The attachment is listed as a link next to a paper clip below the message header in the reading pane. See Figure C-16.

3. **Click the Physicals.rtf link below the paper clip in the reading pane**

   If you are using Internet Explorer, the File Download dialog box opens; if you are using Firefox, the Opening Physicals.rtf dialog box appears.

4. **If you are using Internet Explorer, click Save; if you are using Firefox, click the Save File option button, then click OK**

   If you are using Internet Explorer, the Save As dialog box opens. If you are using Firefox, the Enter name of file to save to dialog box opens.

5. **Navigate to the drive and folder where you store your Data Files, click in the File name text box, change the filename to Downloaded Physicals.rtf, then click Save**

   The attachment is saved.

6. **If you are using Internet Explorer and the File Download box changes to the Download complete dialog box, click Close; if you are using Firefox and the Downloads dialog box is open, click its Close button**

   The Mail window appears with the Inbox selected.

TROUBLE

If you are using Firefox and the Enter name of file to save to dialog box does not open, then Firefox is configured to save files to a pre-determined location. Click Tools on the menu bar, click Options, click the Main button on the toolbar, then look at the path in the Downloads section of the dialog box next to the Save files to option button. Use Windows Explorer to locate this folder and the Physicals.rtf file, move the file to the drive and folder where your Data Files are stored, then skip Step 5.

FIGURE C-15: Message with attachment in the Hotmail message list

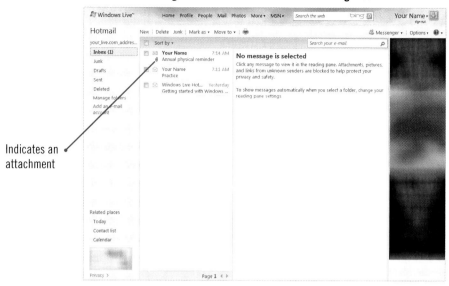

Indicates an attachment

FIGURE C-16: Attachment in reading pane for selected message in Hotmail

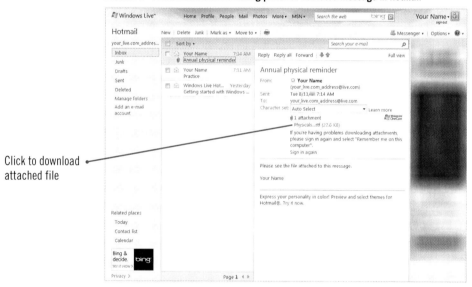

Click to download attached file

Understanding email viruses, worms, and Trojan horses

Email can carry malicious programs, such as viruses, worms, and Trojan horses. A computer **virus** is a piece of software that runs without your permission and performs undesired tasks, such as deleting the contents of your hard disk. Viruses **self-replicate**, meaning that they create, and in some cases distribute, copies of themselves to infect more computers. **Worms** and **Trojan horses** are variations on this idea, and they are of special concern to email users because they reproduce by using email programs on infected computers to send out copies of themselves as attachments to automatically generated email messages to everyone in the victim's email contacts list. However, you can take a couple of simple steps to protect yourself and those with whom you exchange email. The most important precaution you can take is not opening a file attachment from a sender you do not know, because the attachment might contain a worm or Trojan horse. If you receive an email message from an email address that you recognize, make sure the accompanying email message makes sense and is specific to you. If it is not, it might be the product of a worm. You can also install **antivirus software**, which is software that protects your computer from these malicious programs. Some email programs have built-in virus detection, and many schools and colleges distribute antivirus software for free to students, staff, and faculty; check with your instructor, system administrator, or computing services center to see if this software is available to you.

Replying to an Email Message

You can use your email program's Reply option to respond to the sender of a message quickly and efficiently. When you reply to an email message, the sender's name is automatically placed in the To text box, and the text of the original message appears in the body of the new message for reference. You practice using the Reply option by replying to the copy of the email message you sent to Sharon.

STEPS

This lesson is written for both Windows Live Mail and Hotmail users. Read each step carefully and perform only those steps that apply to your email program.

1. **Click the Practice message in the message list, if necessary**

   The Practice message is selected.

QUICK TIP

If the original sender sent the message to multiple recipients, you can reply to the sender and all recipients of the original message by clicking the Reply all button.

2. **Click the Reply button on the toolbar (if you are using Hotmail, the toolbar is at the top of the reading pane)**

   A new message window opens. The original sender's email address or name appears in the To text box (in this case, this is your name). "Re:" appears at the beginning of the original subject text, indicating that this message is a response to the original message. The insertion point appears in the message body pane above the original message. In Windows Live Mail, the headings in the message header in the original message are bold. In Hotmail, a gray horizontal line appears above the header and body of the original message. See Figure C-17.

3. **Type I created this message using the Reply button. in the message body pane, press [Enter] twice, then type your name**

4. **Click the Send button on the message window toolbar, then, if you are using Hotmail, click Inbox in the Folders list on the left**

   The message is sent to the mail server for delivery to you, and the mail window appears.

5. **If the Re: Practice message is not in your Inbox, click the Sync button on the toolbar if you are using Windows Live Mail, or click the Inbox in the Folders list on the left if you are using Hotmail**

   The Re: Practice message appears in your Inbox.

6. **Click the Re: Practice message in the message list**

   See Figure C-18 if you are using Windows Live Mail; see Figure C-19 if you are using Hotmail.

Learning about netiquette

Netiquette, a term coined from the phrase "Internet etiquette," is the set of commonly accepted rules that represent proper behavior on the Internet. Email has its own set of rules, which have evolved over time and will continue to evolve as it gains new users. The generally accepted rules for email messages are:

- Avoid writing your messages in ALL CAPITAL LETTERS BECAUSE IT LOOKS LIKE YOU ARE SHOUTING.
- Keep your messages simple, short, and focused on their topics.
- Include a descriptive subject in the Subject line, so the recipient knows the content of your message.
- Avoid sending unsolicited messages, especially those with attachments.
- Use a spell checker and read your message and correct any spelling or grammatical errors before sending it.

- Use common courtesy, politeness, and respect.
- Use caution when attempting sarcasm or humor in your messages, as the recipient might not appreciate the attempt at humor and might actually misunderstand your intentions. Without the sender's body language and tone of voice, some written statements are subject to misinterpretation.
- Do not assume that all your mail is delivered and read. If you suspect that an important message did not arrive in the recipient's mailbox, either resend the message with an appropriate addition stating that you think that the message was not received, or call the person and follow up by phone. Another way to check your account is to send a message to yourself; if you do not receive it, you can suspect a problem.

FIGURE C-17: Re: Practice message windows in Windows Live Mail and Hotmail

"Re:" automatically added to the Subject box

Bold headings in message header in Windows Live Mail

Original message appears under horizontal line in Hotmail

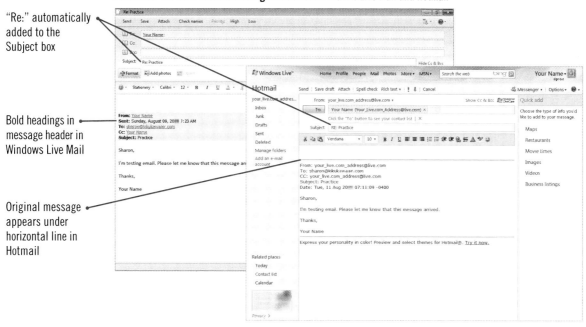

FIGURE C-18: Re: Practice message selected in Windows Live Mail

Reply button

Reply all button

Message selected in list

Reading pane

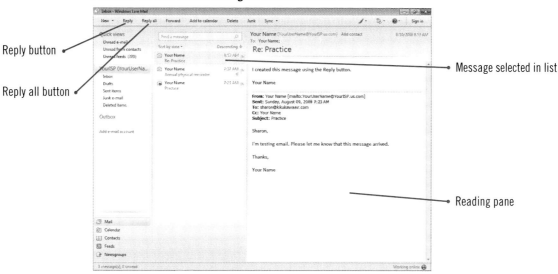

FIGURE C-19: RE: Practice message selected in Hotmail

Message selected in list

Reply button

Reply all button

Reading pane

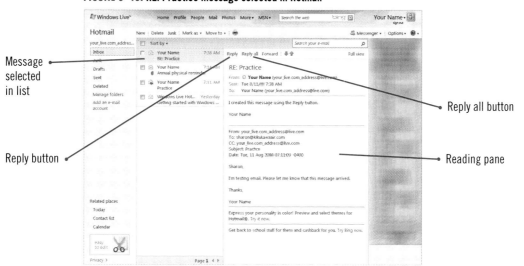

Forwarding an Email Message

You can send any message you receive to someone else, which is called **forwarding**. When you use the Forward option, the original message appears in the new message window. Forwarding is similar to replying, except that a forwarded message is not automatically addressed to the original sender; you must address the message to the desired recipients. To practice forwarding messages and to see how they look to recipients, you forward the Practice message to yourself and to Sharon.

STEPS

 This lesson is written for both Windows Live Mail and Hotmail users. Read each step carefully and perform only those steps that apply to your email program.

1. **Click the Practice message in the message list**

   The Practice message is selected.

2. **Click the Forward button on the toolbar (if you are using Hotmail, the toolbar is at the top of the reading pane)**

   A new message window opens and displays the text of the message to forward. Notice that the Subject text box includes "Fw:" and the original subject text. "Fw:" indicates that the message is being forwarded. In Windows Live Mail, the original message is in the message body pane under a heading identifying it as the original message. In Hotmail, a gray horizontal line appears above the header and body of the original message. The insertion point appears in the To text box.

3. **Type sharon@kikukawaair.com in the To text box**

4. **Click the Show Cc & Bcc link, if necessary**

5. **Click in the Cc text box, then type your email address**

6. **Click in the message body pane above the original message line, type Sharon, press [Enter] twice, type I used the Forward command to send this message., press [Enter] twice, then type your name**

7. **Click the Send button on the toolbar, then, if you are using Hotmail, click Inbox in the list on the left**

   The message is sent to the mail server for delivery to you, and the mail window appears.

8. **If the Fw: Practice message is not in your Inbox, click the Sync button on the toolbar if you are using Windows Live Mail, or Inbox in the Folders list on the left if you are using Hotmail**

   The Fw: Practice message appears in your Inbox.

9. **Click the Fw: Practice message in the message list**

   See Figure C-20 if you are using Windows Live Mail; see Figure C-21 if you are using Hotmail.

FIGURE C-20: Fw: Practice message in the reading pane in Windows Live Mail

Message selected in list

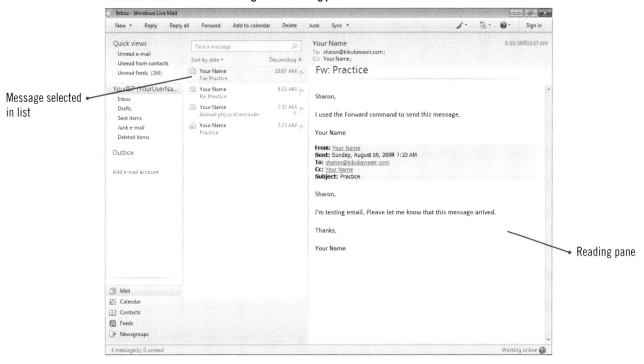

Reading pane

FIGURE C-21: FW: Practice message in the reading pane in Hotmail

Message selected in list

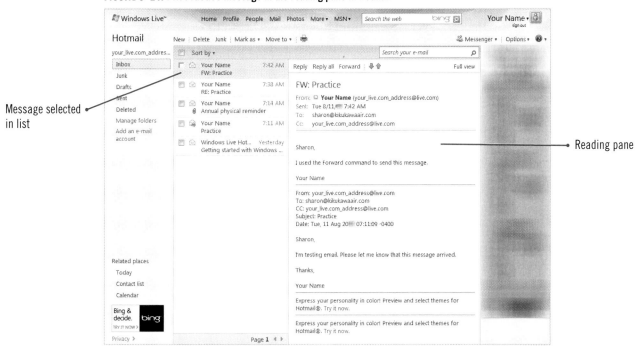

Reading pane

Using emoticons

Email can be an impersonal form of communication, and as a result some writers use emoticons to express emotion. An **emoticon** is a form of electronic body language expressed by a group of keyboard characters that represent a human expression when viewed together. To see the emotion the writer is expressing, tilt your head to the left. Some examples of emoticons are :-) (the **smiley**), :-((a frown), ;-) (a smiley with a wink), and :-o (fear or surprise).

Organizing Email Messages

You can organize your email messages by using email folders to file your messages. For example, you might file messages from friends in one folder and file messages concerning a certain project in a different folder. When you file a message, you move it from the Inbox to another folder. If you are using Windows Live Mail, you can also make copies of a message to store it in multiple folders. Sharon wants you to show employees of Kikukawa Air how they can organize their email, so you decide to try creating a folder to hold all messages relating to Kikukawa Air, and then copy a few messages into it.

STEPS

 This lesson is written for both Windows Live Mail and Hotmail users. Read each step carefully and perform only those steps that apply to your email program.

1. **If you are using Windows Live Mail, click the** New button list arrow **on the toolbar, then click** Folder**; if you are using Hotmail, click the** Manage folders link **in the Folders list on the left, then click the** New button **on the toolbar**

   If you are using Windows Live Mail, the Create Folder dialog box opens, as shown in Figure C-22; if you are using Hotmail, the New folder window appears in the Mail window, as shown in Figure C-23.

2. **Type** Kikukawa **in the Folder name text box**

3. **If you are using Windows Live Mail, click your account name in the list in the dialog box, then click** OK**; if you are using Hotmail, click the** Save button **on the toolbar**

   The new Kikukawa folder you created appears in the folder list. See Figure C-24.

4. **If you are using Hotmail, click** Inbox **in the Folders list on the left**

5. **Drag the** Practice message **from the message list to the Kikukawa folder in the Folders list**

   The Practice message disappears from the Inbox message list.

6. **Click** Kikukawa **in the Folders list**

   The message list displays the contents of the Kikukawa folder. The only message in it is the message you moved from the Inbox, Practice.

7. **Click** Inbox **in the Folders list**

   You want to move the other three messages you sent in this unit as well. You can move all three of them at once.

8. **If you are using Windows Live Mail, click** Fw:Practice**, press and hold [Ctrl], click** Re: Practice**, click** Annual physical reminder**, then release [Ctrl]; if you are using Hotmail, click the** FW: Practice**,** RE: Practice**, and** Annual physical reminder check boxes

   All three messages are selected.

9. **Drag the selected messages to the Kikukawa folder**

   The messages disappear from the Inbox message list.

10. **Click** Kikukawa **in the Folders list**

    The four messages you moved appear in the message list.

FIGURE C-22: Create Folder dialog box in Windows Live Mail

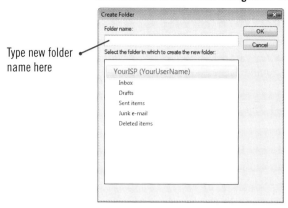

Type new folder
name here

FIGURE C-23: New folder window in Hotmail

Type new folder
name here

Manage folders
link

FIGURE C-24: Kikukawa folder in Folders list in Windows Live Mail and Hotmail

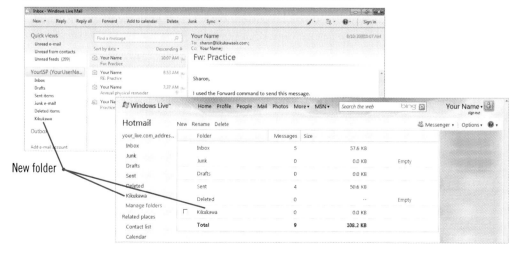

New folder

Deleting Email Messages

Just as you can delete unnecessary files from your computer, you can also delete email messages that you no longer need. When you delete a message, the message moves to the Deleted items folder in Windows Live Mail and the Deleted folder in Hotmail. To permanently delete messages from these folders, you need to empty the folder. You practice deleting email by removing the messages you have received.

STEPS

> **(STOP)** *This lesson is written for both Windows Live Mail and Hotmail users. Read each step carefully and perform only those steps that apply to your email program.*

1. **Click the Practice message in the Kikukawa folder message list, if necessary, to select it**
   The Practice message is selected.

TROUBLE
If you accidentally delete the wrong message, click Deleted items or Deleted in the folder list, then drag the message back to the Kikukawa folder.

2. **Click the Delete button on the toolbar**
   The Practice message is moved from the Kikukawa folder to the Deleted items folder in Windows Live Mail and to the Deleted folder in Hotmail.

3. **If you are using Windows Live Mail, click Deleted items in the folder list; if you are using Hotmail, click Deleted in the Folders list**
   The Practice message you deleted appears in the Deleted items or Deleted folder message list. Figure C-25 shows the contents of the Deleted items in Windows Live Mail, and Figure C-26 shows the contents of the Deleted folder in Hotmail. You do not need to view the contents of the Deleted items or Deleted folder before you delete its contents, but opening this folder before emptying it allows you to verify that you are not about to permanently delete a message you want to keep.

4. **If you are using Windows Live Mail, click the Empty this folder button to the right of Deleted items in the folder list; if you are using Hotmail, click the Empty button on the toolbar**
   A warning dialog box opens asking if you are sure you want to permanently delete or empty the contents of the folder.

5. **If you are using Windows Live Mail, click Yes; if you are using Hotmail, click OK**
   The email message no longer appears in the Deleted items or Deleted folder message list. When you empty this folder, the message is permanently deleted. Now you will delete the Kikukawa folder you created and its contents.

6. **If you are using Windows Live Mail, right-click Kikukawa in the folder list, then click Delete on the shortcut menu; if you are using Hotmail, click the Manage folders link in the Folders list, click the Kikukawa check box, then click the Delete button on the toolbar**
   A warning dialog box opens asking if you are sure you want to delete the folder.

7. **If you are using Windows Live Mail, click Yes; if you are using Hotmail, click OK**
   The Kikukawa folder and its contents are moved to the Deleted items or Deleted folder.

QUICK TIP
In Hotmail, you can click the check box in the blue bar at the top of the message list to select all the messages in the list.

8. **Click Sent items or Sent in the folder list, then delete the four messages you sent in this unit**
   You should check this folder periodically and delete unneeded messages to avoid this file growing too large.

9. **Permanently delete the messages in the Deleted items or the Deleted folder**

FIGURE C-25: Viewing the contents of the Deleted items folder in Windows Live Mail

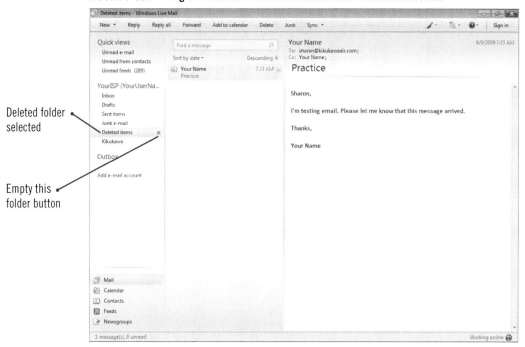

Deleted folder selected

Empty this folder button

FIGURE C-26: Viewing the contents of the Deleted folder in Hotmail

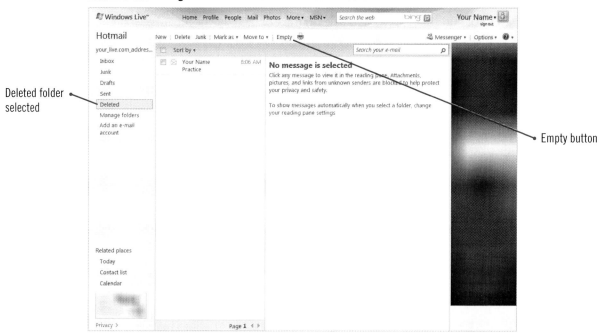

Deleted folder selected

Empty button

Copying messages in Windows Live Mail

If you are using Windows Live Mail, you can copy a message from one folder to another instead of moving them, so that the message appears in both folders. Select the messages you want to copy. Press and hold [Ctrl], drag the selected messages to the folder, and then release [Ctrl]. A copy of the selected message is placed in the folder to which you dragged the messages, while leaving the original messages in their current location. Notice that the messages remain in the message list of the current folder. Click the folder to which you copied the messages. The messages appear in that folder as well.

Maintaining a Contact List in Windows Live Mail

You can save email addresses and contact information, such as phone numbers and postal addresses, in a **contact list**. Each person that you add is called a **contact**, and the information about that person is collected on a **contact card**. You can type the full name in the To, Cc, or Bcc boxes to enter that person's email address, or you can click the To button and click the person's name in the list of contacts. You begin to create a contact list for employees of Kikukawa Air.

STEPS

(STOP) *If you are using Hotmail, skip to the next lesson.*

1. **At the bottom of the pane on the left, click the Contacts button, then maximize the window that opens**

   The Windows Live Contacts window opens displaying a list of your contacts in the middle pane in the window. See Figure C-27.

2. **Click the New button on the toolbar in the Windows Live Contacts window**

   The Add a Contact dialog box opens with Quick add selected in the list on the left.

QUICK TIP
To add additional contact information for the contact, click the other categories in the list on the left in the Add a Contact dialog box, then add the contact's phone numbers, physical address, and other information. To edit information of an existing contact, double-click the contact icon to open the Edit Contact dialog box for that contact.

3. **Type Sharon in the First name text box, press [Tab], type Kikukawa in the Last name text box, click in the Personal e-mail text box, then type sharon@kikukawaair.com**

   Figure C-28 shows the completed Add a Contact dialog box for Sharon.

4. **Click Add contact, create entries in the Contacts list for the following Kikukawa Air employees, then add yourself as a contact if you are not already listed:**

first name	last name	email address
Chris	Breed	chrisbreed@kikukawaair.com
Jennifer	Mahala	jenmahala@kikukawaair.com
Richard	Forrester	richardforrester@kikukawaair.com

   Figure C-29 shows the Windows Live Contacts window with the new contacts entered and the contact Sharon Kikukawa selected.

QUICK TIP
To delete an address from your list of contacts, select it, then click the Delete button on the Contacts window toolbar.

5. **Click the Close button on the Contacts window title bar, click the New button on the toolbar in the mail window, then click the To button to the left of the To text box**

   A dialog box listing your contacts opens.

6. **Click Sharon Kikukawa, then click the To button at the bottom of the dialog box**

   Sharon Kikukawa's name appears in the To text box.

7. **Click your name in the dialog box, click the Cc button at the bottom of the window, then click OK**

   Sharon's name appears in the To text box in the New Message window, and your name appears in the Cc text box.

8. **Click in the Subject text box, type Contact list test, click in the message body pane, type I'm testing the Contacts list feature in Windows Live Mail., press [Enter] twice, type your name, then click the Send button on the message window toolbar**

   The message is sent to Sharon and arrives in your Inbox.

TROUBLE
If the Contact list test message is not in your Inbox, click the Sync button on the toolbar.

9. **Delete the Contact list test message from your Inbox, delete it from the Sent items folder, then empty the Deleted items folder**

FIGURE C-27: Windows Live Contacts window

Click to add a
new contact

If there are contacts
in your contact list,
they will be listed
here instead of this
message

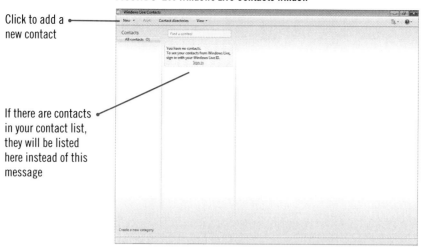

FIGURE C-27: Windows Live Contacts window

FIGURE C-28: Add a Contact dialog box for Sharon Kikukawa

FIGURE C-29: Windows Live Contacts window with new contacts added

Selected
contact

Completed
contact list

Details of
selected contact

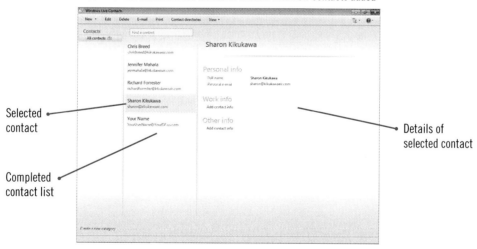

Updating the Windows Live Contacts list

You can quickly add a sender's email address to the Windows Live contact list. When you receive a message from someone who is not in your list of contacts, right-click the person's name in the message header summary in the message list, and then click Add Sender to Contacts on the shortcut menu; or open the message in its message window, right-click the sender's name in the message header, and then click Add to Contacts on the shortcut menu.

Maintaining a Contact List in Hotmail

You can save email addresses and contact information, such as phone numbers and postal addresses, in a **contact list**. Each person that you add is called a **contact**, and the information about that person is collected on a **contact card**. When you add a name to a list of contacts, you also create a **nickname**, which is a shortened name for the contact. You can type the full name or the nickname in the To, Cc, or Bcc boxes to enter that person's email address, or you can click the To button and click the person's name in the list of contacts. You begin to create a Contact list for employees of Kikukawa Air.

STEPS

(STOP) *If you are using Windows Live Mail, skip to the next lesson.*

> **QUICK TIP**
> After you send a message, you can quickly add a recipient's name to your contact list by clicking Add to contacts in the window that appears after the message is sent.

1. **Click the** Contact list link **at the bottom of the pane on the left**
   The All contacts window opens in Hotmail, as shown in Figure C-30.

2. **Click the** New button **on the toolbar in the All contacts window**
   A new contact card opens in the window. You use this window to add email addresses to your list of contacts.

3. **Type** Sharon **in the First name text box, press [Tab], type** Kikukawa **in the Last name text box, press [Tab], type** Shar **in the Nickname text box, press [Tab], then type** sharon@kikukawaair.com
   Figure C-31 shows the completed contact card for Sharon.

> **QUICK TIP**
> To edit information of an existing contact, click the contact in the All contacts window to open the contact card, then click the Edit button on the toolbar.

4. **Click the** Save button **on the toolbar, then click the** Go to contact list link **in the pane on the left**
   The All contacts window appears again and Sharon's contact card appears in the list.

5. **Create contact cards for the following Kikukawa Air employees, add yourself as a contact (including a nickname) if you are not already listed, then return to the All contacts window:**

first name	last name	nickname	email address
Chris	Breed	Chris	chrisbreed@kikukawaair.com
Jennifer	Mahala	Jen	jenmahala@kikukawaair.com
Richard	Forrester	Rich	richardforrester@kikukawaair.com

> **QUICK TIP**
> To delete an address from your list of contacts, select its check box in the All contacts window, then click the Delete button on the toolbar.

6. **Click** Inbox **near the bottom of the list on the left, click the** New button **on the toolbar, then click the** To button **to the left of the To text box**
   Your contacts appear in a list below the To text box. See Figure C-32. Notice that the list has three tabs, and the People tab is selected.

7. **Click the** Sharon Kikukawa check box **in the list**
   Sharon's name and email address appear in the To text box in a blue shaded box. You can continue clicking names in the contact list, or you can type nicknames in the To, Cc, or Bcc text boxes.

8. **Click in the** To text box **after the blue shaded box, type your nickname, then press [Enter]**
   Your name and email address appear below Sharon's in the list of recipients.

9. **Click in the** Subject text box, **type** Contact list test, **click in the message body pane, type** I'm testing the Contact list feature in Hotmail., **press [Enter] twice, type your name, click the** Send button **on the message window toolbar, then click the** Return to inbox link
   The message arrives in your Inbox.

10. **Delete the** Contact list test message **from your Inbox, delete it from the Sent folder, then empty the Deleted folder**

FIGURE C-30: All contacts window in Hotmail

Click to add new contact

Your list might contain names

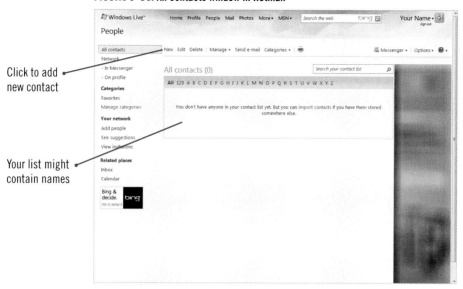

FIGURE C-31: Contact card for Sharon Kikukawa in Hotmail

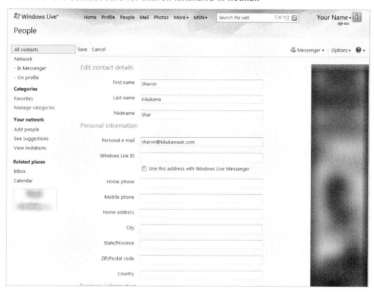

FIGURE C-32: Using the contact list to add a name to the To text box

People tab selected

Names in your list of contacts

Creating a Category in Windows Live Mail

You can quickly send an email message to a group of people by creating a **category** (sometimes called a **group** or **mailing list**), which is a collection of two or more email addresses. You create a category in Windows Live Mail by creating a name for the category, and then assigning email addresses to that category. When you want to send an email message to the contacts in a category, simply insert the category name in the To text box to send a single message to all the category members simultaneously. Because Kikukawa Air, like many companies, is organized into departments such as Personnel, Marketing, and Operations, you realize that categories would be useful when you want to send messages to all the employees in a particular department. You start by creating a category for the Personnel Department.

STEPS

 If you are using Hotmail, skip to the next lesson.

QUICK TIP
You can also click the Create a new category link at the bottom of the pane on the left.

1. **Open the Windows Live Contacts window, click the New button list arrow on the Windows Live Contacts window toolbar, then click Category**

   The Create a new category dialog box opens, as shown in Figure C-33.

2. **Type Personnel in the Enter a category name text box**

   Next, you can select the contacts you want to add to the category.

3. **Click Chris Breed in the list, then click Jennifer Mahala**

   The names you clicked appear in the text box at the bottom of the dialog box.

4. **Click Save**

   The Create a new category dialog box closes and Personnel appears in the list on the left, as shown in Figure C-34. The number 2 appears between parentheses after the category name to indicate that there are two contacts in this category. You can add additional members to the category after you have created it.

5. **Drag Sharon Kikukawa to the Personnel category in the list on the left**

   The number after Personnel changes to 3.

6. **Click Personnel in the list on the left**

   The list of names in the Personnel category appears in the middle pane. Notice that the number after All contacts in the list on the left is still 5.

7. **Click the Close button in the Windows Live Contacts window title bar, open a New Message window, then click the To button**

   The Personnel category is listed in the list of contacts in the dialog box.

8. **Click Cancel in the dialog box, then click the Close button in the New Message window title bar**

9. **Open the Windows Live Contacts window, click Chris Breed, press and hold [Ctrl], click Jennifer Mahala, Richard Forrester, and Sharon Kikukawa, click the Delete button on the toolbar, then click OK**

   All of the contacts you added in this unit are deleted. Now you need to delete the category you created and exit the program.

10. **Right-click Personnel in the list on the left, click Delete Category on the shortcut menu, click OK, click the Close button in the Windows Live Contacts window title bar, then click the Close button in the Windows Live Mail window title bar to exit the Windows Live Mail program**

FIGURE C-33: Create a new category dialog box

Type category name here

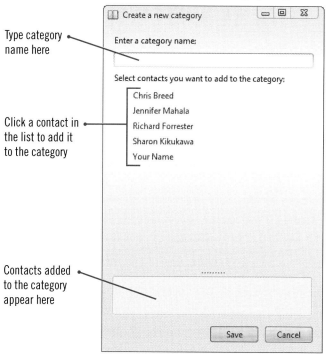

Click a contact in the list to add it to the category

Contacts added to the category appear here

FIGURE C-34: Windows Live Contacts window after creating the Personnel category

Personnel category added

Indicates that there are two contacts in this category

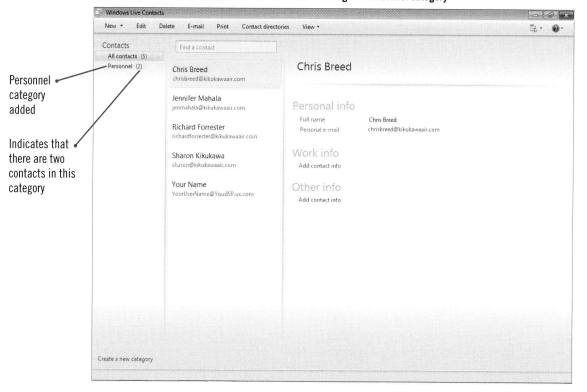

Creating a Category in Hotmail

You can quickly send an email message to a group of people by creating a **category** (sometimes called a **group** or **mailing list**), which is a collection of two or more email addresses. You create a category in Hotmail by creating a name for the category, and then assigning email addresses to the category. When you want to send an email message to the contacts in a category, simply insert the category name in the To text box to send a single message to all the category members simultaneously. Because Kikukawa Air, like many companies, is organized into departments such as Personnel, Marketing, and Operations, you realize that categories would be useful when you want to send messages to all the employees in a particular department. You start by creating a category for the Personnel Department.

STEPS

 If you are using Windows Live Mail, skip this lesson.

1. **Click** Contact list **in the pane on the left, click the** Manage categories link **in the list on the left, then click the** New button **on the toolbar**
   The New category window opens, as shown in Figure C-35.

2. **Type** Personnel **in the Name text box**

3. **Click in the** Members text box, **type** Chris, **then click** Chris Breed **in the list that appears at the bottom of the Members text box**
   Chris Breed's name appears in the Members list.

4. **Click** Save
   The Manage categories window appears with Personnel listed in the list in the window and in the list on the left.

5. **Click** All contacts **in the list on the left, click the** Jennifer Mahala **and** Sharon Kikukawa **check boxes in the All contacts window, click the** Categories button **on the toolbar, then click** Personnel
   Jennifer and Sharon are added to the Personnel category.

6. **Click** Personnel **in the pane on the left**
   The Personnel category is selected and the three names you added appear in the contact list for this category, as shown in Figure C-36.

7. **Return to the Inbox, open a new message window, click the** To button **to the left of the To text box, click the** Categories tab **at the top of the list of contacts that opens, then click the** Personnel check box **in the list**
   The category name appears in the To text box. If you sent this email message, it would go to all members of this category.

TROUBLE
If a dialog box opens, asking you to confirm that you want to cancel the email without sending, click OK.

8. **Click the** Cancel button **on the toolbar, click** OK **in the warning dialog box that opens, open the All contacts window, click the** Manage categories link **in the list on the left, click the** Personnel check box, **click the** Delete button **on the toolbar, then click** OK
   The message window closes without being sent or saved, and the Personnel category is deleted from the list of categories in the Manage categories window.

9. **Click** All contacts **at the top of the list on the left, click the** Chris Breed, Jennifer Mahala, Richard Forrester, **and** Sharon Kikukawa **check boxes, click the** Delete button **on the toolbar, then click** OK
   The selected contacts are deleted.

10. **Click the** Sign out link **in the upper right of the Hotmail window to sign out of your Hotmail account, then exit your browser**

FIGURE C-35: New category in Hotmail

Type category name here

Type contact names here

Click to save category and return to Manage categories window

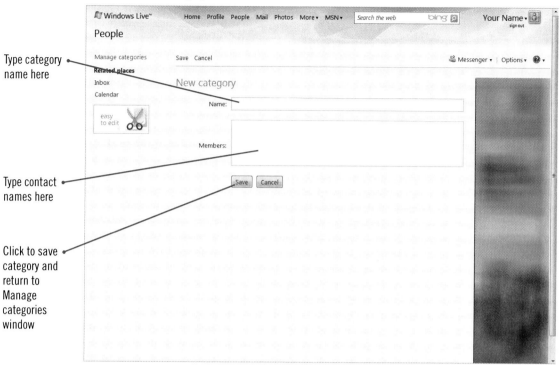

FIGURE C-36: Personnel category in Hotmail

Personnel category selected

Contacts in selected category

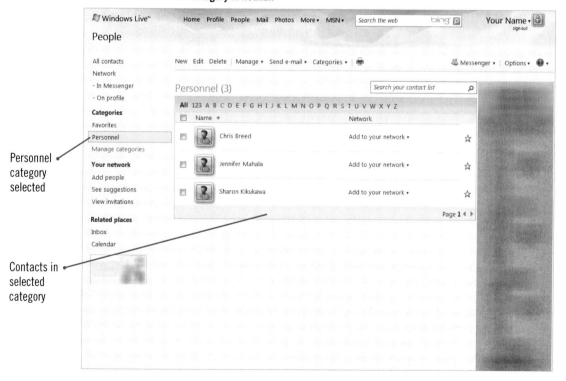

Practice

▼ CONCEPTS REVIEW

Identify the function of each element of the message window shown in Figure C-37 if you are using Windows Live Mail or in Figure C-38 if you are using Hotmail.

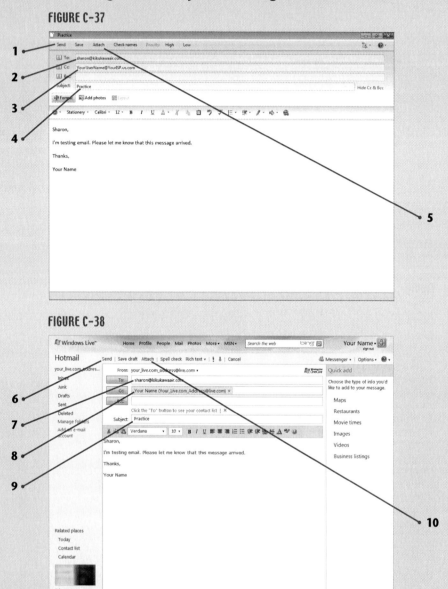

FIGURE C-37

FIGURE C-38

Match each term with the statement that best describes it.

11. **Attachment**
12. **Contact card**
13. **Inbox**
14. **Mail server**
15. **Message header**
16. **Subject text box**

a. The summary information about a message, including sender, subject, and date
b. A location where you type the main topic of an email message
c. Information about a person, including the email address, collected in one place
d. A server that runs special software for handling email tasks
e. A file that accompanies an email message
f. A folder that contains all incoming messages

Select the best answer from the list of choices.

17. Message headers are listed in the:
   a. message body list.
   b. mail window.
   c. message body pane.
   d. folders list.

18. Sending an email message you have received to a new recipient is called:
   a. forwarding.
   b. messaging.
   c. replying.
   d. copying.

19. You can organize your email by placing messages into:
   a. the Junk e-mail or Junk folder.
   b. the contact list.
   c. files.
   d. folders.

20. To send a copy of an email message to someone who is not the main recipient of the message, in which text box do you enter that person's email address?
   a. To
   b. Cc
   c. Subject
   d. Attachment

21. Email that lets you send and receive messages using a browser and the service's Web site is called:
   a. domain email.
   b. mail client software.
   c. browser email.
   d. Webmail.

22. The name your ISP uses to identify you is the:
   a. client name.
   b. user name.
   c. message name
   d. domain name.

23. A name and email address stored in your email program is a:
   a. user name.
   b. nickname.
   c. stored name.
   d. contact.

▼ SKILLS REVIEW

1. Send an email message.
a. Start your email program or sign into your Webmail account, then open a new message window.

b. Address the message to your instructor, a friend, or a colleague.

c. Cc the message to yourself.

d. Create the email message shown in Figure C-39.

e. Send the message.

FIGURE C-39

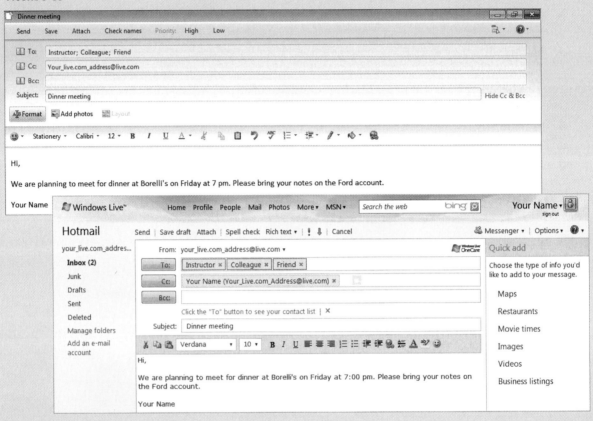

2. Check incoming email.
a. Retrieve your email.

b. Read the Dinner meeting message.

3. Attach a file to an email message.
a. Open a New Message window.

b. Address the message to your instructor, a friend, or a colleague.

c. Cc the message to yourself.

d. Type Follow-up on Dinner Meeting as the subject of your message.

    e. Type the following message:

        The list of the people we have invited to attend the meeting at Borelli's on Friday is attached. Please check the list and let me know if you think I need to add anyone to the list.

    f. Add your name to the end of the message.

    g. Attach the **Meeting Participants.rtf** file located in the drive and folder where you store your Data Files.

    h. Send the file with the attachment.

4. Save an email attachment.

    a. Retrieve your email.

    b. Save the **Meeting Participants.rtf** file attached to the Follow-up on Dinner Meeting message as **Downloaded Participants.rtf** in the location where you store your Data Files.

5. Reply to an email message.

    a. Reply to the sender of the Follow-up on Dinner Meeting message.

    b. Send a copy of the message to your instructor, a friend, or a colleague.

    c. Type the following message:

        I'd be delighted to attend the meeting on Friday.

    d. Add your name to the message.

    e. Send the message.

    f. Retrieve your email.

6. Forward an email message.

    a. Forward the Follow-up on Dinner Meeting message to your instructor, a friend, or a colleague.

    b. Cc the message to yourself.

    c. Type the following message:

        I think we should invite Mark Sanchez from Marketing to the dinner meeting on Friday.

    d. Add your name to the message.

    e. Send the message.

    f. Retrieve your email.

7. Organize email messages.

    a. Create a new email folder named **Meetings**.

    b. Move all four of the messages about dinner meetings to the Meetings folder.

    c. View the contents of the Meetings folder to verify that all four messages appear.

8. Delete email messages.

    a. Delete the Dinner meeting message in the Meetings folder.

    b. Delete the Meetings folder and all of its contents.

    c. Delete the four messages about the dinner meeting that you sent from the Sent items or Sent folder.

    d. Empty the contents of the Deleted items or Deleted folder.

9. Maintain a contact list.

    a. Create a new contact card for Loree Erickson at lerickson@kikukawaair.com. If you are using Hotmail, enter **Lo** as Loree's nickname.

    b. Create a new contact card for Robert Seale at rseale@kikukawaair.com. If you are using Hotmail, enter **Rob** as Robert's nickname.

    c. Create a new contact card for Consuela Martinez at cmartinez@kikukawaair.com. If you are using Hotmail, enter **Connie** as Consuela's nickname.

10. Create a category.

    a. Create a category called **Meetings**.

    b. Add Loree Erickson and Consuela Martinez to the category.

    c. Check the contact list for the Meetings entry.

    d. Delete the contacts and category that you added.

    e. If you are using Windows Live Mail, exit the program.

    f. If you are using Hotmail, sign out of the service and exit your browser.

▼ INDEPENDENT CHALLENGE 1

Your instructor has asked you to submit your next assignment via email. You are also asked to send a copy of the assignment to yourself.

a. Locate a file in one of the folders on your computer to include as an attachment with the email message to your instructor. Make sure the file contains a very short document that will not take up a great deal of disk space. For example, you could select a short essay that you completed for another course or a short letter you wrote to a friend. Alternately, you could use one of the Data Files from this unit. After you have determined which file you will attach to your email, start your email program or sign into your Webmail service.

b. Add your instructor's name and email address to the contact list. If you are using Hotmail, use an appropriate nickname.

c. Create a new message.

d. Type **Email Assignment** for the subject.

e. Address the email to your instructor.

f. In the Cc text box, type your email address.

g. Type the following message in the message body pane:

Here's a copy of <<describe the file>> as you requested. Please let me know as soon as you receive the file. Thanks.

h. Leave a blank line after the end of your message, then type your name, class name, class section, and email address on four separate lines.

i. Attach the file you have chosen to the message.

Advanced Challenge Exercise

- Format the file description in italics and a different color font.
- Mark the message as high priority by clicking the appropriate button on the toolbar.
- Check the spelling in the message by clicking the appropriate button on the toolbar.

j. Send the message, then check for new email to download your message.

k. Delete the Email Assignment message from the Inbox and the Sent items or Sent folders, if necessary, then empty your Deleted items or Deleted folder.

l. Exit your email program or sign out of your Webmail service and exit your browser.

▼ INDEPENDENT CHALLENGE 2

Bridgefield Engineering Company (BECO) is a small engineering firm in Somerville, New Jersey, that manufactures and distributes heavy industrial machinery for factories worldwide. Because BECO has trouble reaching its customers around the world in different time zones, the company has decided to implement an email system to facilitate contact between BECO employees and their customers. BECO hired you to help employees set up and use this email system. Your first task is to send a message to several of BECO's marketing staff located throughout the country.

a. Start your email program or sign into your Webmail service.

b. If necessary, add your instructor and two classmates to the contacts list.

c. Start a new message, and address the message to your instructor and your two classmates.

d. Send a copy (Cc) of the message to yourself.

e. Type an appropriate topic in the Subject text box.

f. Type the following message:

Please include the following at the end of all email messages you send to customers. "Bridgefield manufactures machines to your specifications, including borers, planers, and horn presses. Email us for further information."

g. Sign your name.

h. Send the message.

▼ INDEPENDENT CHALLENGE 2 (CONTINUED)

i. Retrieve the message.

j. Delete the message you just sent and received, empty the Deleted items or Deleted folder, then exit your email program or sign out of your Webmail service and exit your browser.

▼ INDEPENDENT CHALLENGE 3

You have recently set up office email at Fiona's Hat Shop where you work. Now that clients and vendors have begun sending you emails, you need to set up a way of organizing the email messages that you have received.

a. Start your email program or sign into your Webmail service.

b. Send brief messages to four classmates, and send copies of the messages to yourself. Include the name of the store, Fiona's Hat Shop, somewhere in the body of two of the messages.

c. Retrieve and view all email messages that you receive.

d. Create a folder named **Vendors** and a folder named **Clients**.

e. Move one email message into the Vendors folder, then move three messages into the Clients folder.

f. View the contents of both folders.

Advanced Challenge Exercise

■ If you are using Hotmail, create a rule or a filter to sort messages that contain the word "hat" in the Subject into the Clients folder as they arrive.

■ Edit the rule or filter to sort messages that contain the word "hat" into the Vendors folder as they arrive.

■ Test your rule by creating a new email message that you send to yourself. Type **Hat** as the subject.

■ Delete the rule or filter that you created.

g. Delete the messages you sent and received, delete the two folders you created, empty the Deleted items or Deleted folder, if necessary, then exit your email program or sign out of your Webmail service and exit your browser.

▼ REAL LIFE INDEPENDENT CHALLENGE

You regularly send email updates of what is going on in your life to several friends who do not live nearby. You want to create a category in your contact list to simplify addressing the updates.

a. Start your email program or sign into your Webmail service.

b. Add the names, appropriate nicknames if you are using Hotmail, and email addresses of three classmates to your list of contacts.

c. Add your instructor's full name, nickname if you are using Hotmail, and email address to your list of contacts, if necessary.

d. Create a new category named **Updates**, then add your classmates, your instructor, and yourself to the category.

e. Create a new email message with **Update Message** as the subject. Address the message to the Updates category.

f. Type a short message informing your classmates that your email message is testing the use of your new category.

g. Send the message.

h. Retrieve and open the message. (You should receive the message because you are included in the category.)

i. Delete the message you just sent and received, empty the Deleted items or Deleted folder, delete the contacts and category you added, then exit your email program or sign out of your Webmail service and exit your browser.

▼ VISUAL WORKSHOP

Use the skills you learned in this unit to create the message shown in Figure C-40 if you are using Windows Live Mail or in Figure C-41 if you are using Hotmail. The file attachment is located in the drive and folder where your Data Files are stored. When you have completed the message and attached the file, add the email address of your instructor to the To text box, then send the message.

FIGURE C-40

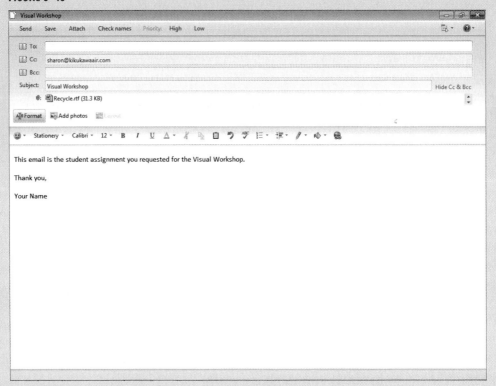

FIGURE C-41

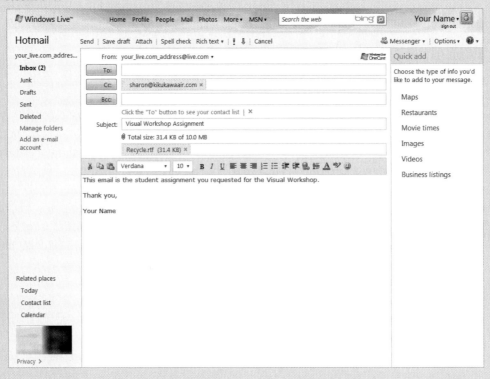

Searching the Web

Files You Will Need:

No files needed.

You can use the Web to access millions of Web pages, which contain information on a virtually unlimited number of topics. To find the information you want among all these Web pages, you need to learn searching methods and tools.  Nancy Shand and Ranjit Singh, staff writers at the *Georgetown Journal*, a top-rated daily newspaper that serves the Georgetown metropolitan area, have hired you as their assistant. They want you to use the Web to help them gather information for their stories.

OBJECTIVES

Define search engines

Develop a Web search strategy

Use a search engine

Use a Web directory

Use a metasearch engine

Use a subject guide

Understand advanced searching techniques

Conduct a search using the Advanced Search page

Conduct a search using Boolean operators

Defining Search Engines

A **search engine** is a Web site (or part of a Web site) that finds Web pages containing the word or phrase you specify and displays the pages as a list of links. For example, you could enter the word "Louisiana" into the appropriate location in a search engine, and then click the Search button to get a list of Web pages that might contain information about Louisiana. One of the most popular search engines is Google, but there are many others available. ████ Before you accept your first research assignment from Ranjit and Nancy, you decide to learn some of the terms associated with Web searching and search engines.

DETAILS

The following terms are associated with searching the Web:

- #### Search Expression and Keyword

  A **search expression** or **query** is the words or phrases you enter when you conduct a search. A search expression can be composed of one or several words; each word in a search expression is called a **keyword**.

QUICK TIP
Even the best search engine sites cannot keep their databases completely updated, so you will occasionally click a link in the list of results only to find that the page to which it is linked no longer exists.

- #### Search Engine Database

  A search engine does not search the Web to find a match to the search expression you enter; it searches only its own database of Web content that it has catalogued. Each search engine database indexes the information it collects from the Web differently. Some search engines store the entire content of every Web page they index; other search engines collect information only from a Web page's title, description, keywords, or HTML tags; and others read only a certain amount of the text in each Web page. If the terms you use in your search expression are not in the part of the Web page that the search engine stores in its database, the search engine will not return that page. Therefore, if you enter the same search expression into different search engines, you will get some results that are the same and some that are different because each search engine contains a different set of information in its database and each search engine uses different procedures to search its database.

QUICK TIP
Many search engines include information about their search engines, robots, and databases on their Help or About pages.

- #### Web Robot

  Most search engines use a Web robot to build their database. A **Web robot**, also called a **bot** or a **spider**, is a program that automatically searches the Web to find new Web sites and updates information about Web sites that are already in the database. A Web robot also deletes information in the database when a Web site no longer exists.

QUICK TIP
Most major search engines search for variants of keywords automatically; for example, if you search using the keywords *Canada travel guide*, most search engines will return hits that include the keywords "Canadian" and "guides" as well.

- #### Hit

  A **hit** is a Web page that is indexed in the search engine's database and contains text that matches your search expression.

- #### Results Pages

  All search engines provide a series of **results pages**, which include links to Web pages that match your search expression. Figure D-1 shows a results page using the AlltheWeb search engine for the search expression *modern art*; Figure D-2 shows search results for the same search expression in the Lycos search engine. Notice that suggested related search expressions are listed on the right. The Bing search engine does something similar by listing categories that you can click to narrow the search.

- #### Narrowing the Search Results

  Often, a search will yield millions of hits. To narrow your search results, create a search expression that contains more than one keyword; most search engines will search for pages that contain all of the words in your search expression, although in no particular order. If you want to search for pages that contain a specific phrase, enclose the phrase in quotation marks in the search expression. For example, a search for pages that contain the keyword *rice* returns over 96 million hits in one search engine, and the pages cover topics ranging from a page for Rice University to a page about someone whose last name is Rice to pages having something to do with rice, the grain. But a search using the search expression *brown rice* decreases the number of hits to about 21 million; and a search with *"brown rice"* (enclosed in quotation marks) decreases the number of hits to just under 2 million. Finally, if you add the keyword *recipe* so that the complete search expression is *"brown rice" recipe*, the number of hits decreases again to about 1 million, and all of the hits are about recipes with brown rice. You can refine the search further by adding additional ingredients to the search expression. You get the best results by using keywords that do not have multiple meanings and are not articles or prepositions.

FIGURE D-1: Results page for a search on keywords "modern" and "art" in the AlltheWeb search engine

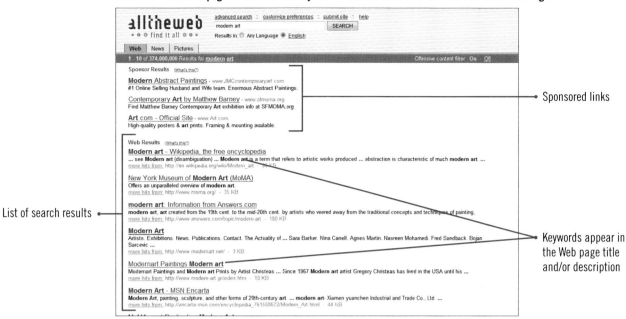

List of search results

Sponsored links

Keywords appear in the Web page title and/or description

Courtesy of Yahoo! Inc. ® 2009 by Yahoo! Inc. YAHOO! and the YAHOO! logo are trademarks of Yahoo! Inc.

FIGURE D-2: Results page for a search on keywords "modern" and "art" in the Lycos search engine

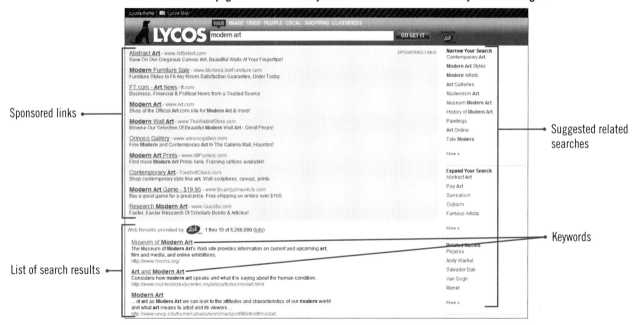

Sponsored links

List of search results

Suggested related searches

Keywords

How search engines are financed

The organizations that operate search engines often sell advertising space on the search engine Web site and on the results pages. Many search engine operators also sell paid placement links on results pages. For example, a car manufacturer might want to purchase rights to the keyword *car*. When you enter a search expression that includes the keyword *car*, the search engine creates a results page that has a link to that company's Web site at or near the top of the results page. Most, but not all, search engines label these paid placement links as **sponsored links**. If the advertising appears in a box on the page (usually at the top, but sometimes along the side or bottom of the page), it is called a **banner ad**. Search engine Web sites use the advertising revenue to cover the costs of maintaining the computer hardware and software required to search the Web and create and search the database, and to generate profit. The only price you pay for access to these tools is that you see advertising banners on many of the results pages, and you might have to scroll through some sponsored links at the top of results pages; otherwise, your usage is free.

Developing a Web Search Strategy

You can use the Web to quickly find answers to specific questions or as a resource to explore interesting concepts and ideas. Each of these question types, specific and exploratory, requires a different search strategy. Before you start accepting research requests from Nancy and Ranjit, you decide to familiarize yourself with a searching strategy.

DETAILS

Consider the following as you develop a search strategy:

- **Specific Question**

  A **specific question** is a question that you can phrase easily and has only one answer. Specific questions might require you to start with broad categories of information and then gradually narrow the search until you find the answer to your question. Figure D-4 shows this process of sequential, increasingly focused questioning. As you narrow your search, you might find results that do not lead you to the answer of your question. If that happens, you need to choose the result (or path) that will lead you to the correct answer, as shown in Figure D-4.

- **Exploratory Question**

  An **exploratory question** starts with a general, open-ended question that leads to other, less general questions, which result in multiple answers. The answers to the questions at each level should lead you to more information about the topic you are researching. This information then leads you to more questions and answers. Figure D-5 shows how this questioning process broadens the scope of results as you gather information pertinent to the exploratory question.

- **Conducting a Search**

  Once you determine the type of question you need to use in your search, you can begin the actual Web search process. After you carefully formulate and state your question, you select the appropriate tool or tools to use in your search, and then conduct the search.

- **Evaluating the Results**

  After obtaining your results from a Web search tool, you need to evaluate these results to determine if they answer your question. If they do not, you continue the search by refining or redefining your question and then selecting a different search tool to see if you get a different result. The determination of when your search process is completed is different for each type of question. For specific questions, you repeat this process as many times as necessary until you obtain the specific answer you seek; for exploratory questions, you repeat it until you have found a satisfactory range of information regarding your topic.

Asking for help from other people

Some search engines include a feature in which you can ask other people for the answer to a question. After you type your question and send it to the search engine, the question becomes available for anyone using the site to see. If people know the answer, they might reply and you will see the answer listed below your question. You need to remember, however, that not everyone who answers a question is an expert, and the answer might very well be wrong. On most of these sites, you need to sign up to be a registered user and then identify yourself as a user in order to ask or respond to a question. The Yahoo! Answers page is shown in Figure D-3.

FIGURE D-3: Yahoo! Answers page

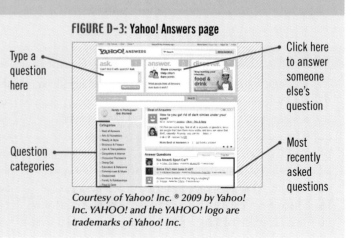

Type a question here

Question categories

Click here to answer someone else's question

Most recently asked questions

Courtesy of Yahoo! Inc. ® 2009 by Yahoo! Inc. YAHOO! and the YAHOO! logo are trademarks of Yahoo! Inc.

FIGURE D-4: Specific research question search process

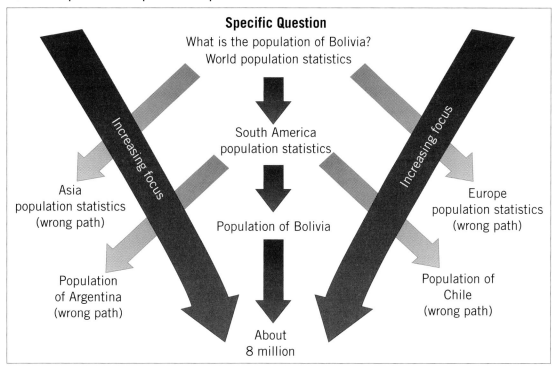

FIGURE D-5: Exploratory research question search process

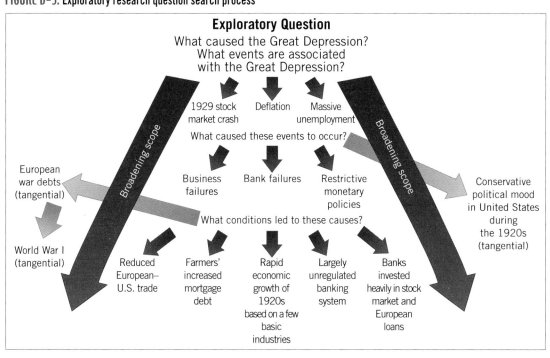

Internet

Using a Search Engine

No one knows how many Web pages exist on the Web, but the number is now in the billions. Each of these Web pages might contain thousands of words, images, or links to downloadable files. Unlike the content of a library, the content of the Web is not indexed in any standardized way. Fortunately, you can use search engines to help you find the information you need. ◼◼◼◼◼ Nancy needs to know the average temperature on Mars for a story that she is writing. This search question is a specific question, not an exploratory question, because you are looking for one specific answer—the average temperature on Mars.

STEPS

1. **Start your Web browser, go to the Online Companion page for Unit D, then click one of the links to a search engine under Lesson 3**

   Your browser opens the home page of the search engine you chose.

2. **Type Mars in the search expression text box**

   Figure D-6 shows *Mars*, the search expression, entered in the Search text box on the home page of the Google search engine. Notice the drop-down list below the Search box. Several search engines provide suggestions in a drop-down list in this manner to help you formulate your search expression. If you see your search expression in the list, you can click it to accept that suggestion.

3. **Press the Spacebar, then type average temperature**

> **TROUBLE**
>
> If the results page contains a message that the search engine could not find any results that matched your search expression, return to the Online Companion, choose a different search engine, then repeat Steps 2 through 4.

4. **Click the appropriate button to start the search (this button is usually labeled "Search," "Go," or "Find")**

   The search results appear on a new results page. The results page indicates that there are well over a million Web pages that might contain the answer to your query. Figure D-7 shows the results page in the Bing search engine.

> **TROUBLE**
>
> If you do not find any useful links on the first page of search results, click the numbers at the bottom of the results page to open additional results pages.

5. **Scroll down the results page, examine your search results, then click links until you find a Web page that provides the average temperature of Mars**

   The average temperature on Mars is –63° Celsius, –81° Fahrenheit. (Some Web sites might report a slightly different number.)

6. **Return to the Online Companion page for Unit D, then click a link to another of the search engines listed under Lesson 3**

   The home page of the search engine you chose opens.

7. **Type Mars average temperature in the search expression text box, then click the appropriate button to start the search**

   The search results appear on a new results page.

> **QUICK TIP**
>
> Both Internet Explorer and Firefox allow you to access a search engine from a search box on the Address bar.

8. **Scroll down the results page, examine your search results, then click links until you find the average temperature of Mars**

   Once again, you should find that the average temperature on Mars is –63° Celsius, –81° Fahrenheit. Your specific search was successful.

FIGURE D-6: Search expression entered in the Google search engine

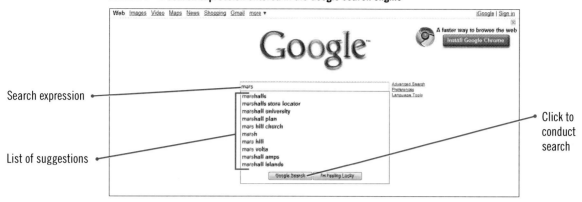

Search expression

List of suggestions

Click to conduct search

FIGURE D-7: Results page for "Mars average temperature" in the Bing search engine

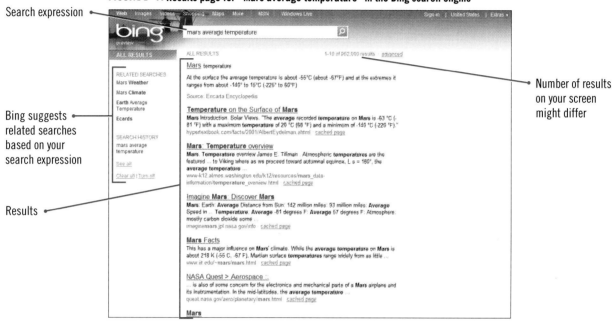

Search expression

Bing suggests related searches based on your search expression

Results

Number of results on your screen might differ

Using natural language queries

Some search engines have attempted to include natural language querying. A **natural language query** allows users to enter a question exactly as they would ask a person that question. The search engine analyzes the question using knowledge it has been given about the grammatical structure of questions and then uses that knowledge to convert the natural language question into a search query. Although no major search engine has been able to make a natural language query interface that has worked consistently, mathematical software company Wolfram has a Web site that offers a natural language interface to a database of collected facts. This site, Wolfram Alpha, is a computational engine and performs calculations using the information it extracts from its database. It lets users ask questions in natural language that relate to the facts in its database. Figure D-8 shows the results of the search using *Mars average temperature* as the search expression. The results page includes an interpretation of the search expression and returns the temperature in various units, including degrees Celsius, Fahrenheit, and kelvin. It also includes several scientific calculations using the search results.

FIGURE D-8: Wolfram Alpha natural language interface results

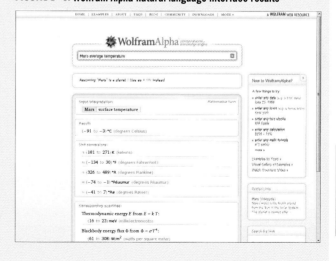

Using a Web Directory

A **Web directory** is a list of links to Web pages that is organized into hierarchical categories. Web directories and search engines both use a database of links to Web pages to enable users to search for information in different ways. Rather than using a database compiled by Web bots, however, a Web directory uses human editors or computers to decide which Web pages will be included in the directory and in which category to store the link to selected Web pages. Users can browse for information by general categories, rather than by using specific search terms. Many Web directories are one feature of larger search engines, and you need to click a link on the search engine's home page to view the directory. ▰▰▰ Ranjit wants to know the latest news and information about his profession. He asks you to provide him with a set of links to Web sites about the media industry. You use a directory to identify Web sites based on the category of information that Ranjit needs.

STEPS

1. **Go to the Online Companion page for Unit D, then click one of the links to a Web directory under Lesson 4**

   The directory you selected opens. The home page contains a list of categories into which the directory links are organized. The Gigablast directory is shown in Figure D-9.

   QUICK TIP

   A category that contains the term "Media," "Professions," "Jobs," or "Reference" would be a good choice.

2. **Examine the categories on the directory's home page and click a link that is likely to contain information about the journalism profession**

   The page you selected opens, showing links to lower levels in the hierarchy, links in the hierarchies of other categories, and, usually, some sponsored links.

3. **Examine the page that loads in your browser and search for links to subcategories that include words such as "industry news" or "industry updates"**

   You might need to search several levels down in the directory to find the information you are looking for. You also might need to try a different directory.

   QUICK TIP

   In some Web directories, you can enter a search expression and search within a category.

4. **When you find a link to a subcategory that seems like it contains information about the media industry, click it**

   The Yahoo! Web directory, after following the News & Media/Industry Information links, is shown in Figure D-10.

5. **Examine the links on the page that opens in your browser, then, if the category does not seem narrow enough or the links are not appropriate, click additional subcategories until you see links that might contain the information you are searching for**

6. **Click one of the links listed in the subcategory and examine the Web page**

   QUICK TIP

   Web directories that are part of Web sites that also include search engines are called **hybrid search engines**.

7. **Navigate back to the subcategory page, click a different subcategory link, then examine the Web page**

FIGURE D-9: Gigablast directory categories

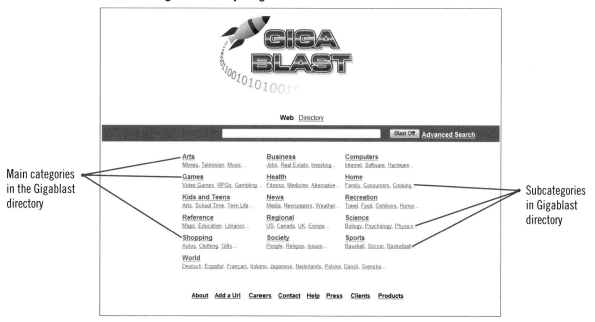

Main categories in the Gigablast directory

Subcategories in Gigablast directory

FIGURE D-10: Yahoo! News and Media Industry Information directory page

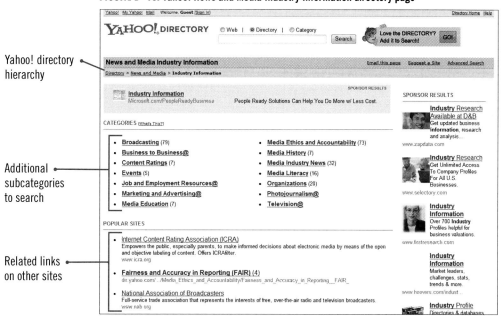

Yahoo! directory hierarchy

Additional subcategories to search

Related links on other sites

Courtesy of Yahoo! Inc. ® 2009 by Yahoo! Inc. YAHOO! and the YAHOO! logo are trademarks of Yahoo! Inc.

Examining About.com and the Open Directory Project

About.com hires content experts to create and manage its Web directory entries, and also identifies its experts for you. Each of the About.com experts, called Guides, hosts a page with hyperlinks to related Web pages, moderates discussion areas, and provides an online newsletter. This creates a community of interested persons from around the world that can participate in maintaining the Web directory. The Open Directory Project uses the services of more than 40,000 volunteer editors who maintain listings in their individual areas of interest.

The Open Directory Project offers the information in its Web directory to other Web directories and search engines at no charge. Many of the major Web directory, search engine, and metasearch engine sites regularly download and store the Open Directory Project's information in their databases. For example, AlltheWeb, AltaVista, Dogpile, and Google all include Open Directory Project information in their databases.

Using a Metasearch Engine

A **metasearch engine** is a tool that uses multiple search engines. Using a metasearch engine, you can search several search engines simultaneously, so you do not have to conduct the same search in different search engines. Most metasearch engines forward your queries to a number of major search engines and directories. After a metasearch engine sends your search expression to several search engines, the search engines compare the search expression against their databases of Web page information and return results to the results page of the metasearch engine for you to view. Some metasearch engines identify the search engine from which they retrieve the links; others do not. ▰▰▰▰ You want to learn how to use metasearch engines so that you can access information more quickly. You decide to use Nancy's question about the average temperature on Mars to test a metasearch engine.

STEPS

1. **Go to the Online Companion page for Unit D, then click one of the links under Lesson 5**

   The home page of the metasearch engine you chose opens.

QUICK TIP
Mamma.com was one of the first metasearch engines on the Web.

2. **Type Mars average temperature in the search expression text box**

3. **Click the appropriate button to start the search**

   A results page appears showing the hits for each search engine that the metasearch engine searched. If you used the Dogpile metasearch engine, you might see results similar to the results page shown in Figure D-11.

4. **Examine your search results, then click appropriate links to find the average temperature on Mars**

   As you scroll through the results pages in a metasearch engine, you might see a wide variation in the number and quality of the results provided by each search engine or directory. Although some of the Web pages returned by one search tool will not be returned by any other search tool, you also might notice duplicate hits.

FIGURE D-11: Dogpile metasearch engine results

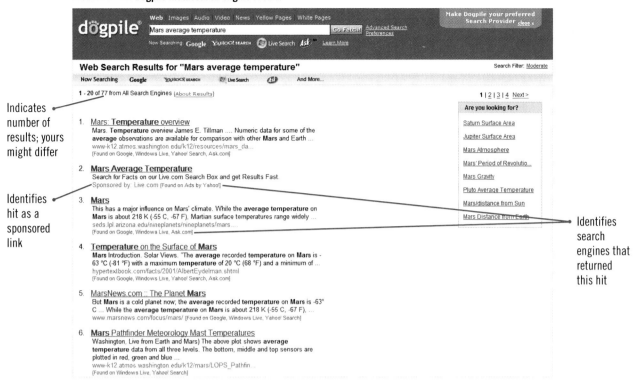

Indicates number of results; yours might differ

Identifies hit as a sponsored link

Identifies search engines that returned this hit

Examining the KartOO metaseach engine

Figure D-12 shows the results page from one of the more interesting metasearch engines, KartOO. KartOO presents results in a graphic format. (To see these graphical results, you need to click the button to the left of OPTIONS near the top of the KartOO window.) Each image is a link and the images are clustered around words that appear in the results pages. When you move the pointer over a word, the links appear as lines between the word and the images. The word you point to is added to the end of the search expression; the clustering of links based on that term are shown as orange lines. See Figure D-12. The list of links on the left side of the page also changes to reflect the addition of the term.

FIGURE D-12: KartOO metasearch graphic results

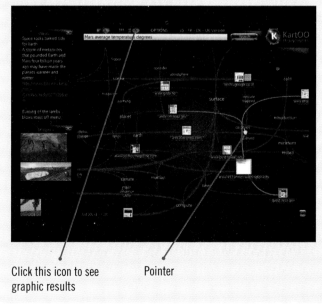

Click this icon to see graphic results

Pointer

Internet

Using a Subject Guide

A **subject guide** (also called a **Web bibliography**, **clearinghouse**, or **virtual library**) organizes references into categories and subcategories. In a subject guide, each reference is a link to a Web page. Some subject guides include **annotations** (summaries or reviews) of Web pages. This information can help you identify Web pages that fit your level of knowledge or interest. You can often find useful subject guides by entering the search term along with the words "subject guide" into a regular search engine. Ranjit needs information about the business and economic effects of current trends in biotechnology and the potential effects of genetic engineering research. He asks you to find some Web sites that he can explore to learn more about biotechnology trends in general and genetic engineering research in particular. You know that biotechnology is a branch of the biological sciences, so you identify three keywords, *biotechnology*, *genetic engineering*, and *biology*, to use as you browse the subject guide's categories. You decide to use a subject guide so that you can use the provided reviews to help you determine the best links to give to Ranjit.

STEPS

1. **Go to the Online Companion page for Unit D, click one of the links to a Web bibliography under Lesson 6, then scroll down the Web page and read the category links**
   Figure D-13 shows the home page for the Awesome Library Web site.

QUICK TIP
As with ordinary search engines, you can also enter a search term in the search expression text box on the site.

2. **Examine the page for links that might lead to information about biotechnology, genetic engineering, or biology, then click one of the links**
   A list of subcategories opens.

3. **Click an appropriate subcategory link, then click links as necessary to find the information that Ranjit requested; again, look for categories that mention biotechnology, genetic engineering, or biology**
   A list of links appears, or you might need to click additional subcategories. The list of links that appears after following the Science/Technology/Biotechnology links in the Librarians' Internet Index is shown in Figure D-14. Figure D-15 shows the links on the INFOMINE Web site after using the search function on that site with the keyword "biotechnology."

QUICK TIP
If you regularly do research in a specific field, it can be helpful to ask other researchers who work in that field if they know of useful Web bibliographies that specialize in relevant subjects.

4. **Open a new tab, go to the Online Companion page for Unit D, then click a link to another Web bibliography under Lesson 6**
   As you look at the links available on this Web site, note the similarities and differences to the first Web site you examined.

5. **Click category and subcategory links to find a list of reference links for biotechnology, genetic engineering, or biology**
   Compare the list of links on this page with the list of links open in the first tab.

6. **Close the second tab**

Subject guides vs. search engines

Subject guides are compiled by reference experts or experts in the categorized fields, so they naturally do not list as many references as a search engine would. So why would you want to use a subject guide when you are given fewer results in response to a search? Subject guides are useful when you want to obtain a broad overview or a basic understanding of a complex subject area. For example, using a search engine or directory to find information about quantum physics could give you millions of hits to technical papers and Web pages devoted to current research issues in quantum physics. In contrast, a subject guide page can offer hyperlinks to specific information about quantum physics at various levels so you can quickly find pages that give you a basic introduction to the subject or offer the latest news about the subject.

FIGURE D-13: Home page of the Awesome Library Web site

Categories of information

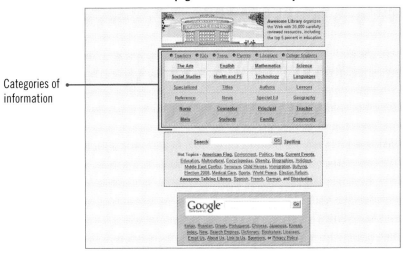

FIGURE D-14: Biotechnology subcategory on the Librarians' Internet Index Web site

URL of site listed

Description of site listed

Topics included on the site

Identifies date the data was added to the site

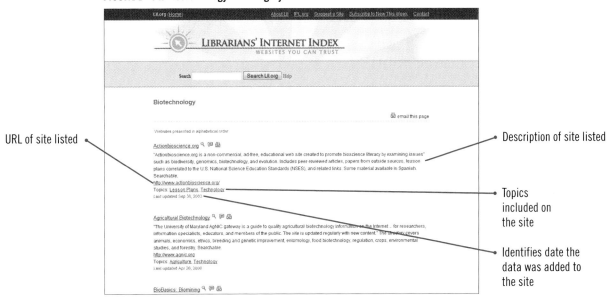

FIGURE D-15: INFOMINE guide information for Biotechnology links

You can choose to include sites selected by a Web robot

Description of site

Click to see more information about the site and this review

Higher score means a better match to search expression

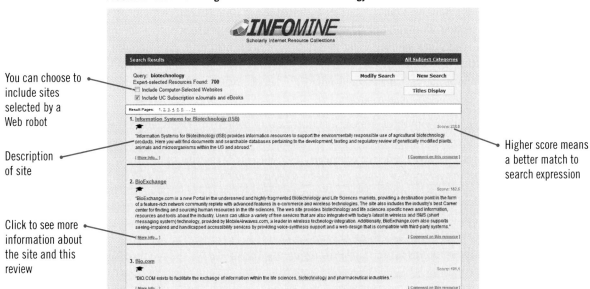

Courtesy of ©1994-2009 INFOMINE, The Regents of the University of California. System developed and supported by the Library of the University of California, Riverside, IMLS and FIPSE.

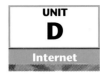

Understanding Advanced Searching Techniques

To get reliable results from a search engine or a metasearch engine, you must select your keywords carefully. When the objective of your search is straightforward, one or two words often will work well. More complex search questions require more complex queries to broaden or narrow your search expression. Recall that you can restrict the search to pages that contain a specific phrase by enclosing your search expression in quotation marks. You can also use various additional techniques to perform advanced searches that will return results pages more relevant to your search question. Some of the questions Ranjit and Nancy ask require you to find specific information. You decide to learn about techniques for formulating complex queries to reduce the number of irrelevant hits in your search results.

The following terms are associated with advanced Web searching:

- **Advanced Search Pages in Search Engines**

  Most search engines use an Advanced Search page to provide users with a step-by-step process for conducting an advanced search. You use menus, option buttons, and text boxes to make selections that identify your search criteria. Figure D-16 shows the Advanced Search page on the Google Web site.

- **Search Filters**

  A **search filter** eliminates Web pages from a search. You can access search filter options for a search engine on its Advanced Search page. You can use the filter to specify a language, date, domain, host, or page component (such as a URL, link, image tag, or title tag). For example, you could search for a term, such as *exports*, in Web page titles and ignore Web pages in which the term appears in other parts of the Web page. You can also use the keywords to filter your results by typing the keywords in a text box that indicates that the results pages will contain *all* of the keywords or in a text box that indicates that the results pages will contain *any* of the keywords. For example, if you wanted to find pages about holiday cards, you would type the keywords *holiday cards* in the text box that restricts the search to all of the keywords; but if you wanted to find information about the holidays and cards but not necessarily "holiday cards," you would type the keywords *holiday cards* in the text box that opens up the search to include Web pages that contain only the keyword "holiday" or only the keyword "cards."

- **Boolean Operators**

  If you want, you can conduct an advanced search from the start page in a search engine by using Boolean operators. **Boolean operators**, also called **logical operators**, specify the logical relationship between the elements they join, just as the plus sign specifies the mathematical relationship between the two elements it joins. Most search engines recognize at least three basic Boolean operators: AND, OR, and NOT. You can use these operators in many search engines by simply including them in the search expression.

- **Precedence Operators**

  When you join three or more search terms with Boolean operators, you can easily become confused by the expression's complexity. To reduce the confusion, you can use precedence operators along with the Boolean operators. A **precedence operator**, also called an **inclusion operator** or a **grouping operator**, clarifies the grouping within a complex expression and is usually indicated by parentheses. Table D-1 shows several ways to use Boolean operators and precedence operators in more complex search expressions that contain the words *exports*, *France*, and *Japan*.

- **Location Operators**

  A **location operator**, or **proximity operator**, lets you search for terms that appear close to each other in the text of a Web page. The most common location operator offered in search engines is the NEAR operator. For example, if you are interested in French exports, you might want to find only Web pages in which the terms *exports* and *France* are close to each other, so to perform this search you would type *exports NEAR France*.

FIGURE D-16: Google Advanced Search page

TABLE D-1: Use of Boolean and precedence operators in search expressions

search expression	search returns Web pages that include	use to find information about
exports AND France AND Japan	All of the three search terms	Exports from France to Japan or from Japan to France
exports OR France OR Japan	Any of the three search terms	Exports from anywhere, including France and Japan, and all kinds of information about France and Japan
exports AND France NOT Japan	Exports and France, but not Japan	Exports to and from France to anywhere else, except exports shipped to and from Japan
exports AND (France OR Japan)	Exports and either France or Japan	Exports from or to either France or Japan
exports AND (France NOT Japan)	Exports and France, but not if the Web page also includes Japan	Exports to and from France, except exports to and from Japan

Understanding search engine assumptions

When you enter a single word into a search engine, it searches for matches to that word. When you enter a search expression that includes more than one word, the search engine makes assumptions about the words that you enter. Most search engines assume that you want to match all of the keywords in your search expression (as if you had used the AND operator); however, a few search engines assume that you want to match any of the keywords (as if you had used the OR operator). These differing assumptions can make

dramatic differences in the number and quality of hits returned. You can always override the assumptions the search engine makes by using the advanced search page or Boolean operators. The best way to determine how a specific search engine interprets search expressions is to read the Help pages on the search engine Web site. Read these Help pages regularly because search engines change the way they interpret search expressions from time to time.

Conducting a Search Using the Advanced Search Page

The Advanced Search page in a search engine provides users with a step-by-step process for conducting an advanced search. You use menus, option buttons, and text boxes to make selections that identify your search criteria. ▓▓▓▓ Nancy is writing an article about Finland and would like to interview a professor she once met who taught graduate business students there. She does not remember the professor's name or the name of the university at which the professor teaches, but she does remember that the professor was part of the School of Economics at a university in Finland. She asks if you can search the Web to find the names of some Finnish universities that have a School of Economics. You decide to use the Advanced Search page of a search engine to conduct your search.

STEPS

1. **Go to the Online Companion page for Unit D, then click one of the links under Lesson 8**
   The home page of the search engine you chose opens.

2. **Click the Advanced Search or Advanced link on the Web page**
   If you do not see a link to an Advanced Search page, look for an "Options" link, or try another search engine. First, you want to restrict the search to Web pages in English since you do not speak Finnish.

3. **Look for the section that restricts the search to Web pages in a specific language, then select the option to restrict the search to only Web pages written in English**
   Next, you want to restrict your search to the domain .fi because schools in Finland use that domain.

4. **Look for the section that restricts the search to a specific domain, then select the appropriate option or type in the appropriate text box to restrict the search to Web pages in the Finland country domain (.fi)**
   If the search engine you chose does not allow you to restrict the search to a domain, skip Step 4.

5. **In the section that provides options for identifying whether you want the search engine to search for all or any of the keywords you specify, look for options such as "Any of the words" or "All of the words," select the option for All of the words, then type Finland in the appropriate text box**

6. **Look for an option that restricts the search engine to searching for an exact phrase, then type School of Economics in the appropriate text box**
   Figure D-17 shows the completed Advanced Search page in Google.

7. **Click the appropriate button to start the search**
   The search results page opens. Figure D-18 shows the search results in Yahoo!.

FIGURE D-17: Completed advanced search page in Google

Search expression appears here automatically as you fill in the boxes on the page

Results pages must include this term

Results pages must include this exact phrase

Click to restrict your search to specific topics

Some search engines will include "site:.fi" as part of the created search expression

Results pages must be in English

Results pages are restricted to the .fi top-level domain

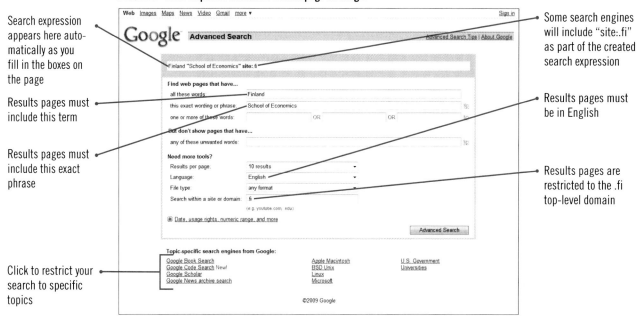

FIGURE D-18: Results page in Yahoo! after an advanced search

Search expression created automatically after using the advanced search page

Search results

Number of hits

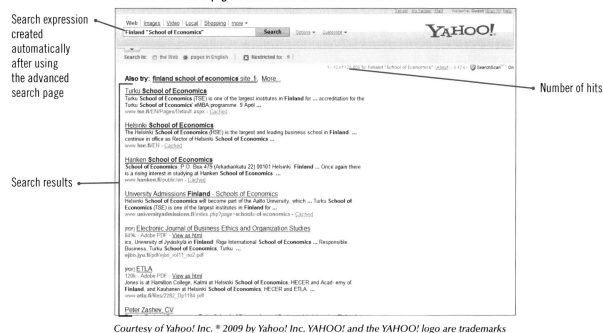

Courtesy of Yahoo! Inc. ® 2009 by Yahoo! Inc. YAHOO! and the YAHOO! logo are trademarks of Yahoo! Inc.

Using search engines with clustering features

One problem with using search engines is that they often generate thousands (or even millions) of hits. Scrolling through hundreds of results pages looking for useful links is not very efficient. Some search engines use an advanced technology to group search results into clusters. The clustering of results provides a filtering effect. The filtering is done automatically by the search engine after it runs the search. Figure D-19 shows the search results for weather patterns in the past six months in Southeast Asia in Clusty, a search engine that clusters results.

FIGURE D-19: Search results page in Clusty clustered search

Search results collected into clusters of links

Conducting a Search Using Boolean Operators

Sometimes the Advanced Search page does not offer you enough options to structure your search expression the way that you want. In that case, you can try searching using Boolean operators. Ranjit is writing about fast-food franchises in various developing countries around the world. He would like to feature this industry's experience in Indonesia in an upcoming story and asks you for help. You recognize this request as an exploratory question and decide to use Boolean operators in a search engine to conduct a complex search for Web pages that Ranjit can use for his research.

STEPS

1. **Go to the Online Companion page for Unit D, then click one of the links under Lesson 9**

   The home page of the search engine you chose opens.

2. **Type "fast food" franchises Indonesia OR Thailand in the search expression text box**

   This query instructs the search engine to look for Web pages containing the following characteristics: the exact phrase "fast food"; the word "franchises"; and either the word "Indonesia" or the word "Thailand." You do not need to type the Boolean operator "AND" because all of the search engines listed under Lesson 9 use all the keywords in the search expression by default. Figure D-20 shows the search expression in the Bing search engine.

3. **Click the appropriate button to start the search**

   The search results appear in the window.

4. **Note the number of hits at the top of the list of links, then examine some of the descriptions of the first 10 results**

   You may need to go to several results pages to find the information you are looking for.

5. **Exit your Web browser**

FIGURE D-20: Search expression with Boolean operators in Bing

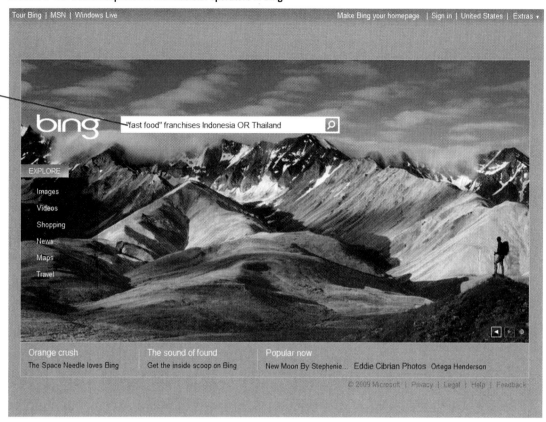

Search expression

Searching the Deep Web

One weakness of most current search engines and Web directories is that they only search static Web pages. A **static Web page** is an HTML file that exists on a Web server computer. The robots used by search engines to build their databases can find and examine these files. An increasing number of Web sites do not store information as HTML files. Instead, they store information in a database, and when a user submits a query, the Web server searches the database and generates a Web page on the fly that includes information from the database. These generated Web pages are called **dynamic Web pages**. For example, if you visit Amazon.com and search for books about birds, the Amazon.com Web server queries a database that contains information about books and generates a dynamic Web page that includes that information. This Web page is not stored permanently on the Web server and cannot be found or examined by search engine robots. Much of this information can only be accessed by users that have a login and password. In 2001, Michael Bergman of BrightPlanet published a paper that explored the difficulties that search engines face when trying to include this information in their search databases. He called this information the **deep Web**; other researchers use the terms **hidden Web** and **invisible Web**. Researchers working at the University of Utah have created an experimental Web site that allows visitors to search the deep Web. The home page of this site, called DeepPeep, is shown in Figure D-21.

FIGURE D-21: DeepPeep home page

Internet

Practice

For current SAM information including versions and content details, visit SAM Central (http://samcentral.course. com). If you have a SAM user profile, you may have access to hands-on instruction, practice, and assessment of the skills covered in this unit. Since we support various versions of SAM throughout the life of this text, you will want to check with your instructor for instructions and the correct URL/Web site to access those assignments.

▼ **CONCEPTS REVIEW**

Describe the function of each element in the Google Web page shown in Figure D-22.

FIGURE D-22

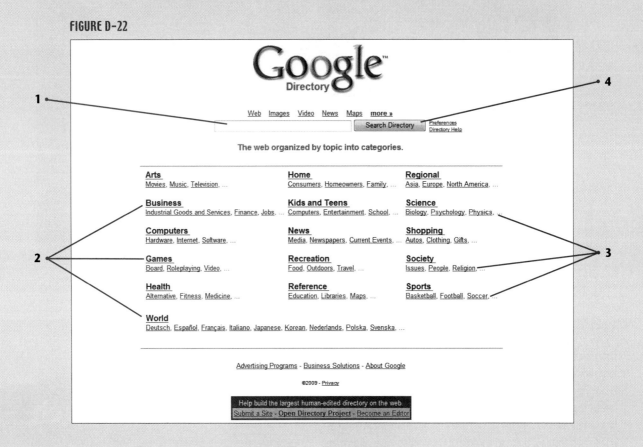

Match each term with the statement that best describes it.

5. **Search engine**
6. **Web robot**
7. **Subject guide**
8. **Boolean operator**
9. **Metasearch engine**
10. **Boolean expression**
11. **Hit**

a. Describes the relationship between words in a search expression
b. A Web site that finds other Web pages containing the word or phrase you specify
c. Japan AND (food OR sushi)
d. Often called a spider
e. A search engine that organizes references into categories and subcategories
f. A Web page that is indexed in the search engine's database and contains text that matches the search expression
g. Provides search results from several search engines

Select the best answer from the list of choices.

12. **What is the term that describes a Web page found by a search engine that matches your search expression?**
    a. Bot
    c. Results pages
    b. Query
    d. Hit

13. **Which of the following is a list of links to Web pages organized into hierarchical categories?**
    a. Search engine
    c. Metasearch engine
    b. Web bibliography
    d. Advanced search page

14. **Mamma.com is an example of a** _____
    a. Web spider.
    c. search engine.
    b. Boolean operator.
    d. metasearch engine.

15. **Which of the following allows you to search for terms that appear close to each other in the text of a Web page?**
    a. Location operator
    c. Search filter
    b. Search operator
    d. Precedence operator

16. **Which of the following Boolean expressions will search for Web pages that contain the words "ranking" or "rating" as well as the word "college"?**
    a. College OR ranking OR rating
    c. College AND ranking NOT rating
    b. College AND ranking AND rating
    d. College AND ranking OR rating

▼ SKILLS REVIEW

1. **Use a search engine.**
   a. Go to the Online Companion page for Unit D, then click one of the search engine links under Skills Review 1.
   b. Use capital Bulgaria as a search expression.
   c. Perform the search.
   d. Examine the search results to find the capital of Bulgaria.
   e. Record the number of hits. (*Hint*: This is usually noted at the top of the search results page.)
   f. Use a different search engine to search for the same information.
   g. Record the number of hits on this page.
   h. Note which of the two search engines found more hits.
   i. Briefly explain which search engine provided the information you were searching for closer to the top of the search results.

2. **Use a Web directory.**
   a. Go to the Online Companion page for Unit D, then click one of the directory links under Skills Review 2.
   b. Follow the category and subcategory links that you think will lead you to lists of museums and art galleries.
   c. Note which Web directory you used and the category path to the page that lists categories for museums and art galleries.
      (*Hint*: You might find that museums and art galleries are listed in different subcategories.)

3. **Use a metasearch engine.**
   a. Go to the Online Companion page for Unit D, then click one of the metasearch engine links under Skills Review 3.
   b. Use Olympics 2008 gymnastics gold men as a search expression, then perform the search.
   c. Scroll through the results and look at the first result returned from five search engines shown on the results page.
   d. Read the descriptions of the links returned. You are looking for the name of the man who won the all-around gymnastics gold medal at the 2008 Summer Olympics.
   e. Follow the links to find the winner's name, keeping a list of the links you follow.
   f. When you find the gold-medal winner, record his name. Did you go down any wrong paths? Were you surprised at any of the hits that resulted from your search expression?

4. Use a subject guide.

    a. Go to the Online Companion page for Unit D, then click one of the subject guide links under Skills Review 4.

    b. Starting with a link that is likely to contain links to information about health and fitness, follow the appropriate links to find a list of links that contain general information about fitness.

    c. Record the URL of two of the sites you find.

5. Conduct a search using the Advanced Search page.

    a. Go to the Online Companion page for Unit D, then click one of the search engine links under Skills Review 5.

    b. Go to the Advanced Search page.

    c. Specify the last 3 months as the search time frame.

    d. Specify Oceania as the region.

    e. Enter marsupials as a term that must be included and numbats as a term that must not be included.

    f. Perform the search.

    g. Record how many hits your search turned up (even if it is zero).

6. Conduct a search using Boolean operators.

    a. Go to the Online Companion page for Unit D, then click one of the search engine links under Skills Review 6.

    b. Use the following Boolean expression to search for information about Scotland, Edinburgh or Glasgow, bagpipes, and folk groups: Scotland AND (Edinburgh OR Glasgow) AND bagpipes AND folk groups. (*Hint*: Although you do not need to use the AND operator in many search engines, it is fine to do so even if the search engine includes all of the search terms by default.)

    c. Refine the search further by specifying to exclude pages with the word "accommodations." Use the following Boolean expression: Scotland AND (Edinburgh OR Glasgow) AND bagpipes AND folk groups NOT accommodations.

    d. Find a Web page listing Scottish folk groups and folk bands and note the URL.

    e. Exit your browser.

▼ INDEPENDENT CHALLENGE 1

A friend is putting together a Web site on rural living. She wants you to help her find additional Web sites on rural living so she can create a page of links to these Web sites as a resource to her visitors. You use Web search tools to find Web sites on this topic and select a small number of links that seem particularly useful.

    a. Go to the Online Companion page for Unit D. The links under Independent Challenges are for search engines, directories, and metasearch engines. Use these links as a starting point for your search.

    b. Choose at least one search tool from each category and conduct a search using the keywords rural and living.

    c. Extend or narrow your search using each tool until you find five Web sites that you believe are comprehensive guides or directories that your friend should link to on her Web site.

    d. For each Web site, record the URL and note why you believe the Web site would be useful to someone looking for information and resources on rural life. Identify each Web site as a guide, directory, or other resource. (*Hint*: You can click in the Address bar or Location bar to select the URL, right-click the selected URL, then click Copy on the shortcut menu to copy the selected text to the Clipboard. You can then paste the copied text into a word-processing or other document.)

▼ INDEPENDENT CHALLENGE 2

You are a manager at Key Consulting Group, a firm of geological and engineering consultants who specialize in earthquake-damage assessment. When an earthquake strikes, Key Consulting Group sends a team of geologists and structural engineers to the quake's site to examine the damage to buildings and determine what kinds of reconstruction will be needed. In some cases, the buildings must be demolished. Because an earthquake can occur without warning in many parts of the world, Key Consulting Group needs quick access to information about local conditions in various parts of the world, including the temperature, rainfall, and currency exchange rates. It is early July when you receive a call that an earthquake has just occurred in Japan. You decide to use the Web to obtain information about local midsummer conditions there.

a. Use a search tool to search for information on weather conditions in Japan in July and current exchange rates.

b. Record the daily temperature range, average annual rainfall, and current exchange rate for your currency to Japanese currency.

▼ INDEPENDENT CHALLENGE 3

You work as a marketing manager for Lightning Electrical Generators, Inc., a firm that has built generators for more than 50 years. The generator business is not as profitable as it once was, and John Delaney, the firm's president, asked you to investigate new markets for the company. John mentioned the fuel cell business, and explained that a fuel cell creates energy from gasoline through a chemical reaction, rather than burning it like a car does. John wants you to study the market for fuel cells in the United States. He wants to know which firms currently make and sell these products, and he wants to get some idea about the power ratings and prices for individual units.

a. Use a search tool to search for information about fuel cells. Design your searches to find the manufacturers' names and information about the products they offer.

Advanced Challenge Exercise

■ Narrow your search to find Web pages that contain the exact phrase "negative impact on the environment."

■ Narrow your search further by excluding pages that contain the term *fossil*.

■ Narrow the search further by excluding Web pages whose domain name is .edu.

b. Prepare a short report that describes the information you have gathered, including the manufacturer's name, model number, product features, and suggested price for at least three fuel cells.

▼ REAL LIFE INDEPENDENT CHALLENGE

You can find information about almost anything on the Web. To put the Web to the test, find the answer to the questions listed in this Independent Challenge.

a. Go to the Online Companion page for Unit D, then click one of the links under Independent Challenges.

b. Ask questions and perform searches to find the following pieces of information:

• The current temperature in Varberg, Sweden

• A picture of the flag of the state of Washington

• The telephone area code for New Orleans, Louisiana

• The number of miles in 30 kilometers

• The capital of British Columbia in Canada (*Hint*: Include the word "city" in your question.)

Advanced Challenge Exercise

■ Use Boolean logic to search for a page in which the terms *republican* and *democrat* are near the term *libertarian*.

■ Find a Web directory devoted to politics.

■ Find a subject guide devoted to political science.

c. When you have found the answer to a question, record the search expression you used, the name of the search engine you used that led you to the Web site that contained the answer, the URL of the Web site that contained the answer, and the answer to the question.

Internet

▼ VISUAL WORKSHOP

Go to the Online Companion page for Unit D, then click the Google link under Visual Workshop. Set up the Google Advanced Search page so that it appears similar to the search page shown in Figure D-23. After you have set up the search page to search for Web pages related to coffee production in Costa Rica or Nicaragua, run the search, and record the number of hits you receive. Then rewrite the search expression using Boolean operators.

FIGURE D-23

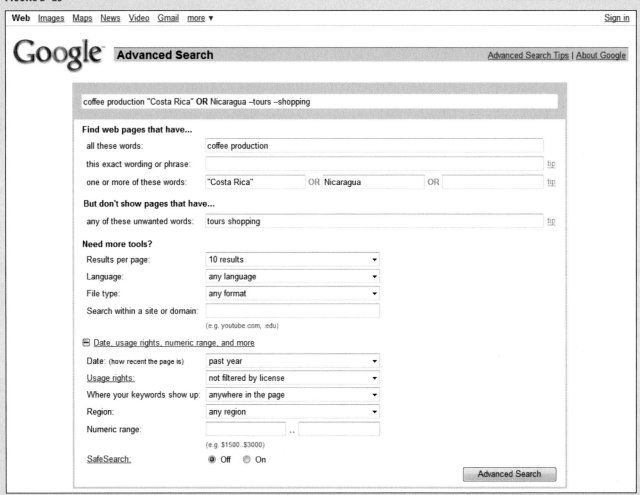

Getting Information from the Web

For both businesses and individuals, the Web can be a valuable source of up-to-date information. You can get the latest news, print a map of your neighborhood, find a local business, and even reconnect with long-lost friends. You can access much of this information from the home pages of many search engines and directories. For example, the Yahoo! directory's home page includes a collection of hyperlinks to general news stories, sports scores, stock market reports, and weather. In this unit, however, you will learn how to use specialized search engines and Web sites to search the Web for current information. You will also learn how to evaluate Web pages and how to cite Web resources. You have just been hired by Cosby Promotions, a public relations firm. You are responsible for helping staff members stay current on news items and for providing up-to-date travel information to staff and clients.

OBJECTIVES

Get the news

Obtain weather reports

Obtain maps and city guides

Find businesses and people

Find online reference tools

Evaluate Web resources

Evaluate user-generated content

Understand copyright and cite
   Web resources

Getting the News

You can easily find current news stories on the Web by using a news search engine. A **news search engine** searches only online news sites. All the major U.S. broadcasters, including ABC, CBS, CNN, Fox, MSNBC, and National Public Radio (NPR), maintain Web sites that carry news features. Broadcasters in other countries, such as the BBC, also provide news reports on their Web pages. Major newspapers, such as *The New York Times*, *The Washington Post*, and *The Times* in London, offer Web sites that include current news and many other features from their print editions. News search engines also search the Web sites of wire services. A **wire service** (also called press agency or a news service) is an organization that gathers and distributes news to newspapers, magazines, broadcasters, and other organizations that pay a fee to the wire service. Although there are hundreds of wire services in the world, most news comes from the four largest wire services: United Press International (UPI) and the Associated Press (AP) in the United States, Thomson Reuters in Great Britain, and Agence France-Presse in France. Some new search engines also search **blogs**, Web sites that contain commentary on current events written by individuals. Marti Cosby, the president of Cosby Promotions, wants you to find recent news stories about NASA because a technical company heavily involved with the space program might become a client of Cosby Promotions. You decide to use a news search engine to look for recent news articles that mention NASA.

STEPS

1. **Go to the Online Companion page for Unit E, then click one of the links to a news search engine under Lesson 1**

    Some of the news search engines listed are Web sites devoted strictly to searching news sites; others are general search engines that have a page devoted to searching news sites.

TROUBLE
If the results pages list ordinary Web sites instead of news sites, click the Back button in your browser, then repeat the search, making sure you click the Search News button (or something similar).

2. **Type NASA in the search expression text box, then click the appropriate button to start the search**

    The search results page returned by the news search engine you chose lists articles related to NASA. See Figure E-2 for the results page for this search in the Yahoo! news search engine. Note that on the results pages of some news search engines, you can click a link to sort the results by date instead of by relevance.

3. **Explore two links that you believe will provide interesting information about NASA**

    When you click one of the links, a story opens from the publication's Web site, similar to the one shown in Figure E-3.

Understanding RSS

Really Simple Syndication (RSS) is a file format that makes it possible to share updates, such as headlines, weather updates, and other Web site content, via a **feed**, which is simply a file containing summaries of stories and news from a Web site. Most RSS feeds must be read through a program called an **aggregator** that lets you receive feed content. Internet Explorer and Firefox, and some email programs, have a built-in aggregator. For Internet Explorer users, Web sites can also provide an RSS update on a section of a page via a **Web slice**. You can use an RSS search engine to search the Web for feeds relevant to your search expression; to find sites that offer Web slices, you can look on the Internet Explorer 8 Add-ons Gallery Web page at www.ieaddons.com, and then click Web Slices. Figure E-1 shows the page listing feeds available from Yahoo! News. To subscribe to a feed, click the Feeds button on the Command bar in Internet Explorer or in the Location bar in Firefox. To subscribe to a Web slice, click the Add Web Slices button on the Command bar in Internet Explorer.

FIGURE E-1: Subscribing to Yahoo! News

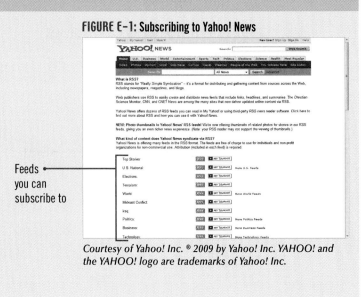

Feeds you can subscribe to

Courtesy of Yahoo! Inc. ® 2009 by Yahoo! Inc. YAHOO! and the YAHOO! logo are trademarks of Yahoo! Inc.

FIGURE E-2: Yahoo! news search results for NASA

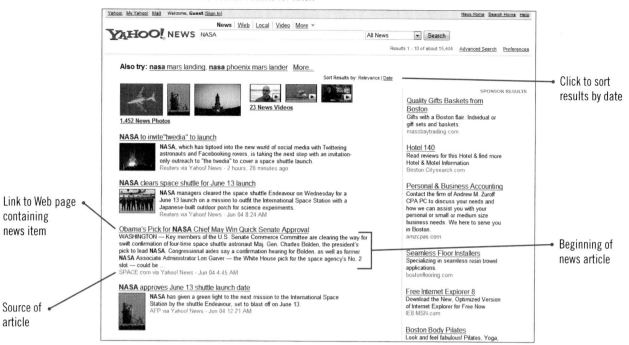

Click to sort results by date

Link to Web page containing news item

Beginning of news article

Source of article

Courtesy of Yahoo! Inc. ® 2009 by Yahoo! Inc. YAHOO! and the YAHOO! logo are trademarks of Yahoo! Inc.

FIGURE E-3: NASA-related news story on the Space.com News page

Searching the archives on a news Web site

You can search the archives of most online news sources. Look for a search text box on the home page of the news Web site. Usually the site will return a list of links to relevant articles. Most online news sources allow you to view recent articles without registering or paying, but many require that you register or pay a fee for access to older articles. This is often indicated in the list of results.

Obtaining Weather Reports

You can obtain up-to-the-minute weather reports in destinations all over the world. This information is particularly useful for travelers. You can use the Web to check the weather report to find current local weather conditions and forecasts. ▓▓▓ Marti is planning two trips in the near future. She is going to Nashville later in the week to meet with some new country music artists whom she hopes to sign as clients for the agency. Next week, she is going to Europe where she will visit clients in Venice. She wants you to check the local weather conditions in both cities.

STEPS

1. **Go to the Online Companion page for** Unit E, **then click one of the links to a weather service under Lesson 2**

TROUBLE
If a page appears telling you that no locations matched your search, click the Back button on the browser toolbar, then try typing simply "Nashville."

2. **Type** Nashville, TN **in the text box labeled "Forecast," "City, State," "Local Weather," or something similar, then click the button next to that text box or press** [Enter] **to start your search**

   Depending on the Web site you chose, the current forecast for Nashville, TN, or a list of cities appears.

3. **If a list of cities appears, click the** Nashville, TN **or the** Nashville, Tennessee **link**

   A Web page showing current weather conditions in Nashville appears. Figure E-4 shows this information on the Weather.com Web site. Now you need to find the local weather conditions in Venice, Italy.

QUICK TIP
Weather-forecasting sites often report slightly different (and sometimes completely different) forecasts for the same time period in the same area. To get the most complete information, check two or three sites and compare the forecasts.

4. **Return to the Online Companion page for** Unit E, **then click a link to a different weather service under Lesson 2**

   Choose a different weather service than the one you chose in Step 1.

5. **Type** Venice **in the text box labeled "Forecast," "City, State," or something similar, then click the button next to that text box or press** [Enter]

   Depending on the Web site you chose, you may see a page showing the current weather conditions in Venice, Italy; a page showing the current weather conditions in a U.S. city named Venice; or a page listing links to weather conditions for a number of cities named Venice.

6. **Click** Venice, Italy **in the list of cities, or if the page that opens shows only links to cities named Venice in the United States, click a link on the home page for** World Forecasts **or** World Weather **if necessary, type** Venice, Italy **in a text box labeled "City, Country" or something similar, then click the appropriate button or press** [Enter] **to start the search**

QUICK TIP
In many search engines, you can type *weather* followed by the name of a city as the search expression, and the first result will be the current forecast for that city.

7. **If the page that opens shows a list of links to weather conditions for a number of cities named Venice, click the** Venice, Italy **link**

   Compare your screen to Figure E-5, which shows the weather for Venice, Italy on AccuWeather.com.

Searching for Web sites that have been modified recently

Sometimes you might want to find information about a topic on sites that have been recently modified because you want only the latest and most up-to-date information. Many search engines allow you to choose a date range when you enter a search expression. Some search engines let you choose preset time range options, such as "in the last week" or "in the last 3 months," to limit your search to sites that were last modified within the selected time period. Other search engines let you limit searches to dates before or after a specific date. And some search engines provide a way to search for sites within a specified date range; for example, you could limit a search to sites modified between April 24, 2011 and November 11, 2011.

FIGURE E-4: Weather.com results for Nashville, TN

Type city here to get forecast

Click for extended forecasts

FIGURE E-5: AccuWeather results for Venice, Italy

Type city here to get forecast

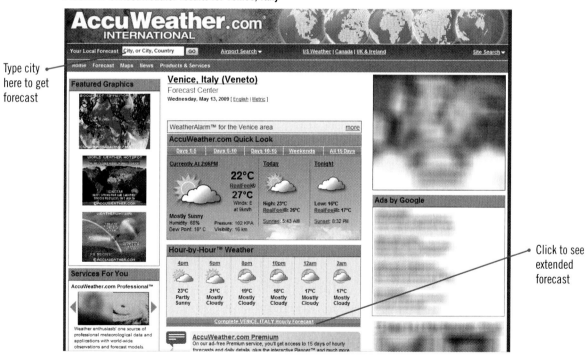

Click to see extended forecast

Obtaining Maps and City Guides

The Web includes a number of Web sites that provide maps and driving directions. Some sites allow you to email the map image or download it to your computer or a handheld device such as a personal digital assistant (PDA) or a mobile phone. These sites usually include links to terms and conditions that govern your use of any maps you download, print, or email. Be sure to review those terms and conditions for your chosen site. You can also use the Web to find a wealth of travel information, such as hotel and restaurant listings and sightseeing guides. While Marti is in Nashville, she wants to stop at Ryman Auditorium, the original home of the Grand Ole Opry. Marti gives you the address, 116 Fifth Avenue North, and asks you to find a map of Nashville on the Web that shows the location of Ryman Auditorium. She also asks you to look for additional information about Ryman Auditorium.

STEPS

1. **Go to the Online Companion page for Unit E, then click one of the links under Map Sites in Lesson 3**

   The home page of the site you chose appears.

> **TROUBLE**
> On an international map site, click United States in the country list before typing the address.

2. **Type 116 Fifth Avenue North in the text box labeled Address or something similar, then type Nashville (the city) and TN (the state) in the appropriate text boxes, or type 116 Fifth Avenue North, Nashville, TN in the Search box**

   The completed page on the Google Maps site is shown in Figure E-6.

> **TROUBLE**
> If a page opens telling you that the address could not be found, click the Back button, then change the address to "116 5th Avenue North".

3. **Click the appropriate button to start the search, usually Get Map, Go, or Find**

   The map appears for the address you entered. If you used Bing Maps, you will see a map similar to the one shown in Figure E-7. The exact location of the address you searched for—Ryman Auditorium—is marked on the map. On some sites it is marked with a red star, circle, or other indicator, and on other sites with a text box containing the address. Most maps include navigation tools that you can use to zoom in or out on the map, a link you can click to view a printable version of the map, and a link you can click to obtain directions to the address. Now you will use a city guide to obtain additional information about Ryman Auditorium.

4. **Return to the Online Companion page for Unit E, then click one of the links under City Guides in Lesson 3**

> **QUICK TIP**
> In some search engines, you can type a zip code as the search expression, and the first result will be a map of the city for that zip code.

5. **Type Nashville, TN in a search text box, then click the appropriate button to start your search**

6. **Click the Attractions or Things to Do link or type Ryman Auditorium in a search text box**

   More detailed information about Ryman Auditorium appears.

Using satellite view

Some map sites offer a satellite view of a location—the location shown in pictures taken from a satellite. To see the satellite view, click the Satellite link or button on the map. On most sites that offer satellite view, you can see the street names overlaid on the satellite image if you want. To use this feature, click the Labels link button or check box. Bing Maps also offers a bird's eye view of some locations. If this button is available on a map, you can click it to see a lower angle, higher resolution satellite view of the area.

FIGURE E-6: Address entered in Google Maps

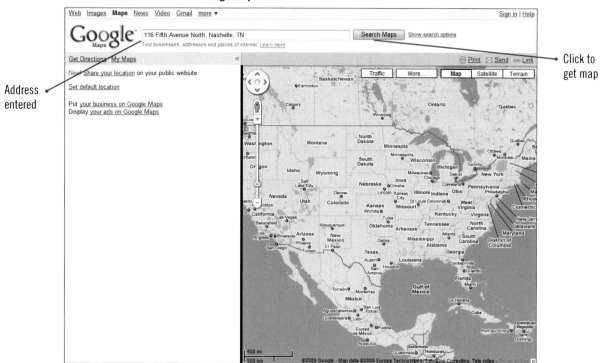

Address entered

Click to get map

FIGURE E-7: Map from Bing Maps showing the location of Ryman Auditorium

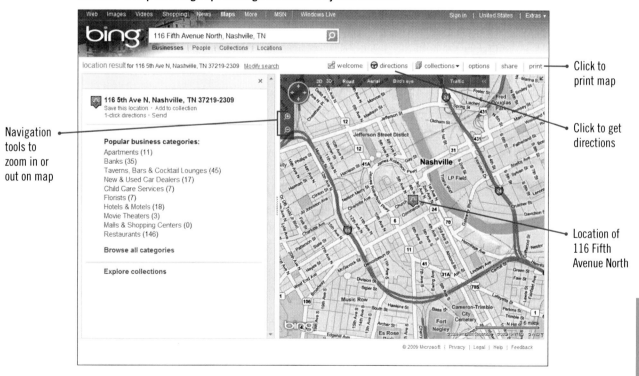

Navigation tools to zoom in or out on map

Click to print map

Click to get directions

Location of 116 Fifth Avenue North

Internet

Finding Businesses and People

Yellow page directories are search engines that specialize in finding businesses; the businesses are grouped by type and location as in the yellow pages phone book. **White page directories** are search engines that enable you to search for addresses and telephone numbers for individuals as you would in a white pages phone book. In fact, this information is usually based on the printed telephone directory. Most sites that offer these types of directories offer both yellow and white pages directories. In addition, you can search for information about a person by simply typing the person's name into the search expression text box in a search engine. Marti needs to develop reciprocal relationships with public relations firms in Nashville. She wants to contact a few of them on her trip, so she asks you to use a yellow pages directory to find public relations firms in Nashville. She also asks you to become more familiar with methods of searching for people on the Web.

STEPS

1. **Go to the Online Companion page for Unit E, then click one of the links under Yellow and White Pages Directories in Lesson 4**

   All of these links are to sites that offer both yellow and white pages searches.

   TROUBLE
   If you chose a site whose home page asks you to choose a country, click the United States link, then perform Step 2.

2. **Click the Yellow Pages or Business link, if necessary**

   The page that contains search text boxes for the yellow pages directory on the site you chose opens.

3. **Click the Category option button or Category link, if necessary, then type public relations in the Category, Business Type, or Keyword text box**

4. **Type Nashville, TN in the appropriate text box or boxes, then click Search (or something similar)**

   A results page opens. This page might display a listing of results or additional categories that you can click to filter the results further. Figure E-8 shows the results pages for SuperPages with a list of categories on the left.

   TROUBLE
   If you chose a site whose home page asks you to choose a country, click the link for your country. If you choose a site that assumes you are searching only the U.S. or the U.S. and Canada and you need to search another country, click the International or World Directories link, click the link for your country, then perform Step 7.

5. **If a list of categories appears on the results page, click Public Relations Counselors or Communications & Public Relations Consultants or something similar**

   The listings include a name, address, telephone number, and link to a map and driving directions. Most yellow pages directories also provide links to the Web sites of firms (if the firm has one).

6. **Return to the Online Companion page for Unit E, then click one of the links under Yellow and White Pages Directories in Lesson 4**

7. **Click the White Pages or People Pages link, if necessary, then type your first and last names, address, city, and state or province in the appropriate text boxes**

   Figure E-9 shows the People Search section on WhitePages.com.

8. **Click Search (or something similar)**

   Look for your name in the results pages.

9. **Return to the Online Companion page for Unit E, then click one of the links under Search Engines in Lesson 4**

   QUICK TIP
   Due to the popularity of the Google search engine, searching for information about someone by using a search engine is often referred to as "Googling" the person.

10. **Type your name in the search expression text box of the search engine you chose, then click the appropriate button to start the search**

    A search on your name might result in many hits or no hits at all.

FIGURE E-8: Results page for SuperPages search

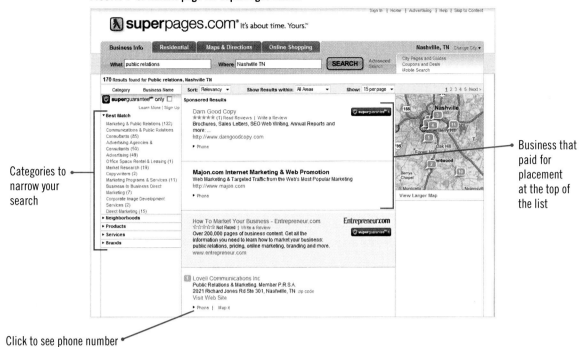

Categories to narrow your search

Business that paid for placement at the top of the list

Click to see phone number

FIGURE E-9: People Search section on WhitePages.com

Type your information here

Click to start search

Copyright ® 1996–2009 WhitePages.com, Inc.

Privacy concerns

Many people expressed concerns about privacy violations when white pages information became easily accessible on the Web. (In fact, in the Google search engine, you can type a phone number in the search text box and get the white pages listing and a link to a map to the person's address.) Some Web sites make unpublished and unlisted telephone numbers available for public use. In response to these privacy concerns, many white pages sites now offer individuals ways to remove their listings. If you want to remove your listing from a white pages site, check out the Web site's Help or FAQs (Frequently Asked Questions) links. Of course, many companies allow anyone who pays for their services to access more information about individuals than most people ever imagined would be available to the paying public. Even if you do not purchase goods or services online, credit card companies store consumer information in computers that are connected to the Internet. Also, businesses, whether online or in the mall, are using more sophisticated technology to track and record what consumers buy and sell. Consumers should be vigilant about guarding their personal information.

Finding Online Reference Tools

The Web is full of pages that contain many useful items of information; these pages form an online library of sorts. Some Web sites collect links to many references in one place. For example, the LibrarySpot and Internet Public Library Web sites are collections of hyperlinks to reference materials, electronic texts, and other library Web sites. Another useful resource is the U.S. Library of Congress Web site, which includes links to a huge array of research resources, ranging from the Thomas Legislative Information site to the Library of Congress archives. In addition, the Web contains many text resources, including dictionaries, thesauri, encyclopedias, glossaries, grammar checkers, rhyming dictionaries, and language-translation pages. ▄▄▄ In preparation for her trip to Venice, Marti asks you to find some information for her. First, she wants to know how Venice is connected to Italy's mainland. She also wants you to find some general information about the culture and history of Italy. Finally, she would like to know how to say "I don't speak Italian" in Italian. You decide to use some of the Web's library and text resources to find this information.

STEPS

TROUBLE
If there is more than one Encyclopedias link, click the one for general information.

1. **Go to the Online Companion page for Unit E, then click one of the links under Internet Libraries in Lesson 5**

   The home page of the Web site you chose opens.

2. **Click the References link (or something similar), if necessary, then click the Encyclopedias link**

   The Encyclopedias page opens.

3. **Click one of the links to a general encyclopedia**

   The home page for the encyclopedia you chose opens.

QUICK TIP
Some sites offer information for free as long as you register with them and provide your name, address, phone number, and email address. This might result in you receiving much more junk email than you had before. Check the privacy policy on the Web site before you register to make sure that they do not sell your information to other Web sites.

4. **If there is an option to search the encyclopedia you chose or another source, click the option to search the encyclopedia, type Venice in the search expression text box, then click the appropriate button to start the search**

   A list of articles appears. Some will be labeled as available only to paid subscribers or members of the site.

5. **Click an article that is not labeled as a subscriber or member article and that contains general information about Venice**

   The article opens. Somewhere in the article, it should state that Venice is connected to Italy's mainland by a railroad and highway bridge.

6. **Return to the Online Companion page for Unit E, then click the U.S. Library of Congress link under Lesson 5**

   The home page of the U.S. Library of Congress Web site opens. See Figure E-10.

TROUBLE
If you don't see the links specified in Step 7, the Web site was probably redesigned since this book was printed. Look for similar links, or find the Web site's search text box, then type Italy in it to try to find the relevant page.

7. **Click the Research Centers link, click the European link, look for and click a link to a page about European countries, then click the Italian Collections link**

   A page containing information describing the collections of books and documents concerning Italy that are available at the Library of Congress opens. You note the URL for Marti.

8. **Return to the Online Companion page for Unit E, then click one of the links under Translation Tools in Lesson 5**

   The home page of the Translation site you chose opens.

9. **Click English to Italian in the list box or click English as the source language and Italian as the target language, then type I don't speak Italian in the appropriate text box**

10. **Click Translate (or something similar), if necessary**

    Figure E-11 shows the phrase translated on the SYSTRANet site. The phrase "I don't speak Italian" is "Non parlo italiano" in Italian.

FIGURE E-10: U.S. Library of Congress Web site home page

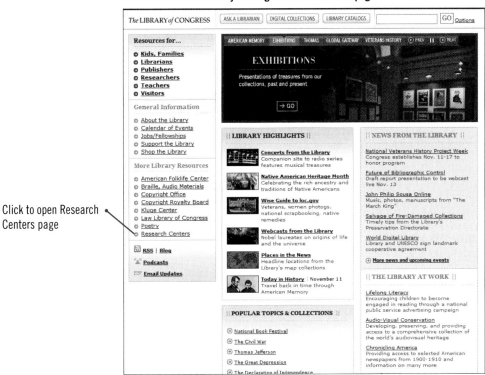

Click to open Research Centers page

FIGURE E-11: Phrase translated in SYSTRANet translation Web site

Click to select source language

Click to select target language

Phrase to translate

Translation appears here

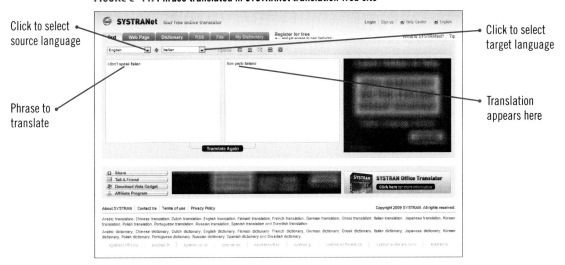

Archiving the Web

The Web itself has become the subject of archivists' attention. The Internet Archive's Wayback Machine (*www.archive.org*) provides researchers a series of snapshots of Web pages as they were at various points in the history of the Web. The name "Wayback Machine" is from an old cartoon in which the characters used the Wayback Machine to journey to a historical event. The archive has over a petabyte (a **petabyte** is approximately 1,000,000,000,000,000, or 10^{15}, bytes) of data stored and is growing at the rate of 20 terabytes (one **terabyte** is approximately 1,000,000,000,000, or 10^{12}, bytes) per month. To use the Wayback Machine, you type a URL, and then select a date from a list that opens. The archived version of the Web page you selected opens in your browser.

Evaluating Web Resources

When using the Web for important research, there can be significant risks of obtaining and relying on inaccurate or unreliable information. As a result, it is important to evaluate and verify the information you view. ▰▰▰▰ You are asked to conduct research for the Cosby Promotions client, Tax Reform for Americans Now, a nonprofit group promoting a change in the federal tax system. You found a Web page created by a professor at San José State University which lists summaries and links to reports and Web sites related to tax reform. Figure E-12 shows the top and bottom portions of this Web page. Before you pass along your findings, you need to evaluate the quality of the Web site you found.

DETAILS

To evaluate a Web site, consider the following:

- **Author Identity**

  Research published in scientific journals, literary journals, books, and research monographs is subjected to peer review or edited by experts in the appropriate subject area. Information on the Web is seldom subjected to that type of review and editing process. The Web page shown in Figure E-12 has links at the top and bottom that bring you to a page listing the qualifications of the person who created the page.

  - **Author identity**

    A Web page that presents empirical research results, theories, or other information that is the result of a research process should identify the author and provide the author's background and credentials.

  - **Author affiliations**

    Information about the author's affiliations will help you determine the level of independence and objectivity that the author can bring to bear on the research questions or topics.

  - **Author qualifications**

    The author's qualifications should pertain to the material that appears on the Web site. For example, does the author have an advanced degree in the field about which he or she is writing?

  - **Author contact information**

    The Web site should provide author contact information so that you can contact the author or consult information directories to verify the contact information.

  - **Domain identifier**

    Examine the domain identifier in the URL. If the site claims affiliation with an educational or research institution, the domain should be .edu for educational institution. A nonprofit organization would most likely have the .org domain, and a government unit or agency would have the .gov domain.

- **Content**

  Read the content critically and evaluate if the included topics are relevant to the Web site. Assess the depth of treatment the author gives to the subject.

- **Form and Appearance**

  Look at the design critically; Web page design elements that suggest low quality include loud colors that distract the user, graphics that serve no purpose, flashing text, grammatical and spelling errors, and poor organization. A Web site that is a legitimate source of accurate information presents information in a professional format that helps convey its validity.

- **Objectivity**

  Evaluate how the Web site presents its information. Factual information should not be presented with emotional language designed to sway your opinion.

- **Currency**

  If the Web page has a clearly stated publication or revision date, you can determine the timeliness of the content. Older Web pages might contain outdated information.

Clear description of the Web page

Link to information about the Web page creator

Tax Reform Information

The purpose of this web page is to objectively note reports and websites related to tax reform and provide links to further information from members of Congress and others. The focus is on federal tax reform, but there are also links to some state tax reform activities.

Compiled by Professor Annette Nellen

Visit Professor Nellen's Tax Reform Blog - click here

Background Information on Tax Reform

- 21st Century Taxation - Professor Nellen's website with a articles on various tax reform issues
- President Bush's Advisory Panel on Federal Tax Reform (panel's website with final report (11/1/05) and testimony)
  - Annette Nellen - Brief overview to tax reform and Panel's proposals - outline + slides
  - Leonard E. Burman and William G. Gale, "A Preliminary Evaluation of the Tax Reform Panel's Report," Tax Notes 12/5/05
- Treasury Department reports on business competitiveness:
  - *Business Taxation and Global Competitiveness* (7/23/07)
  - Approaches to Improve the Competitiveness of the U.S. Business Tax System for the 21st Century (12/07)
- Legislative proposals (sampling) and hearings of the 110th Congress:
  - A variety of hearing either directly on tax reform or related topics (such as health care reform or small business reform) were held in the 110th Congress. Some of the hearings in the Senate Finance Committee were labeled as being in anticipation of tax reform. So it looks like the topic will get more attention in 2009. Part of the reason for the interest is the expiring 2001 and 2003 tax cuts, AMT problems, the tax gap and international competitiveness.
    Click here for a list with links to key tax reform related hearings of the **111th Congress**
    Click here for a list with links to key tax reform related hearings of the 110th Congress.
  - Congressional Research Service report on *Tax Reform: An Overview of Proposals in the 110th Congress* (1/08)
  - H.R. 1040 - Freedom Flat Tax
  - H.R. 25 - Fair Tax Act (national sales tax)
  - H.R. 3818 - the Taxpayer Choice Act of 2007 - repeals the individual AMT and gives taxpayers a choice of filing systems: the current one with its various deductions and credits, or a simplified one with a 2 rate structure and deductions only for personal and dependency exemptions and a standard deduction. Also see information from the Republican Study Committee.
  - H.R. 473 - "To establish a commission to develop legislation designed to reform tax policy and entitlement benefit programs and ensure a sound fiscal future for the United States, and for other purposes." The commission would be called the Securing America's Future Economy (SAFE) Commission.
  - S. 55 - To repeal the individual AMT starting in 2007. While this might not sound like tax reform, it affects a lot of individuals and will likely require some significant changes to cover the ~~effect or repeal.~~

The Jo~~int~~ ~~ee on~~ reported th~~at~~ ~~94, e~~ ~~nd gift ta~~ ~~ited~~ 1% of ~~federal~~ ~~5, 1/14/~~ age 16). ~~Senate~~ ~~at states that in~~ fiscal year 1996, less than 1% of federal revenues were derived from estate and gift taxes.

- Call for Repeal of AMT: In 1997, Senator Kyl introduced S. 73 to repeal the corporate alternative minimum tax (AMT). Senator Kyl points out that the corporate AMT is not really a tax, but instead serves as a prepayment of a corporation's regular income tax. He calls this practice one of businesses being "forced to make interest-free loans to the federal government under the guise of the AMT." He also notes that most of the corporations that pay AMT are relatively small. In addition, Senator Kyl points out that AMT causes corporations to maintain two sets of tax records. Finally, Senator Kyl suggests that repeal of the AMT will "help free up badly needed capital to assist in business expansion and job creation." (Cong. Rec. 1/21/97). In the 106th Congress, S. 54 was introduced to repeal the corporate AMT.

H.R. 1233 (108th Congress) calls for repeal of the AMT.

To obtain copies of the bills listed above:

- Congressional Record/Legislative Proposals

Comment Letters Submitted by Joint Venture's Tax Policy Group For Tax Reform Hearings Held by the House Ways and Means Committee in 1996

- Impact of Tax Reform on State and Local Government
- Impact of Tax Reform on International Competitiveness
- Impact of Fundamental Tax Reform on Domestic Manufacturing

More about ...

- Information from the Joint Tax Committee of Congress.
- Information from the Joint Economic Committee of Congress.

Link to information about the Web page creator

Date the page was last updated

This page last revised on May 19, 2009.

Any views and opinions expressed in this page are strictly those of Professor Annette Nellen. The contents of this page have not been reviewed or approved by San José State University.

Evaluating User-Generated Content

User-generated content is content on Web sites created by the user. **Web 2.0** is a term coined during a brainstorming session between Tim O'Reilly and Dale Dougherty of O'Reilly Media and representatives of MediaLive International to describe user-generated content. During the session, they were characterizing the change in the way people use and access the Web and the change in the technology used on the Web itself. They described Web 2.0 users as people who not only interact with content, but who also use applications to create it. Using Web sites that consist primarily of user-generated content as a primary resource for formal research is generally not good practice, although these sites can be good places to discover new ideas and opinions. A colleague suggested you use Wikipedia as a resource for some of your research for the Cosby Promotions client, Green for Our Children. Wikipedia is a user-generated site, so you decide to research that site, and user-generated sites in general, before you use them as primary sources in your work.

DETAILS

Consider the following if you use user-generated sites to gather information:

- **Wiki Sites**

  An example of user-generated content is a wiki site. A **wiki** is a Web site that is designed to allow multiple users to contribute content and edit existing content quickly. (*Wiki* is a Hawaiian word that means "fast.") The information on wiki sites is the result of collaborative work from any interested user. This contrasts with blogs (online journals), which are usually focused on the opinions of the blog owner, who controls the site.

- **Wikipedia**

  Wikipedia is a wiki site that hosts a community-edited set of online encyclopedias in more than a dozen different languages. The concept behind Wikipedia is similar to that behind the Open Directory Project. Instead of hiring experts to review and edit entries, which is what print encyclopedias do, Wikipedia relies on contributions from anyone for its entries. Those entries then can be edited by anyone else who reads them and thinks they should be changed in some way. The idea is that with enough people reading, editing, and re-editing the entries, the information on the site will evolve to a higher degree of accuracy. The home page of Wikipedia is shown in Figure E-13 and the About page for the Web site is shown in Figure E-14.

- **Authorship of a Wiki Site**

  Because of the open nature of wiki sites, the information stored on them is only as good as the contributors, and consequently, some of the information on these site can be potentially inaccurate, incomplete, or biased. On many wiki sites, including Wikipedia, contributors may post and edit articles anonymously, in which case the author is identified only by the IP address of his or her connection to the Internet. Even when the author or editor of an article chooses to be identified, it is often through an account name, and the biographical information included with the account is entered by the account holder. That is, the information can be as limited or incorrect as the account holder chooses.

- **User-Generated Sites as Primary Sources**

  If you are looking for tips on good places to visit on vacation, a user-generated site can be a great resource. For example, Wikitravel is a wiki site that invites travelers to share their experiences in a collaborative world travel guide. However, user-generated sites should not be relied upon as primary sources for serious research. Think about it this way: If you want to travel to Nova Scotia, and someone said "My friends, Sam and Sue, said the Courtyard in Halifax is wonderful," you would probably consider staying there. But if you were writing about the effects of nuclear waste on people, someone saying "Sam and Sue said not to worry about it, there really aren't any negative effects," you might not accept this opinion so readily. Very few teachers or employers accept a research project that references a user-generated site as a primary source.

FIGURE E-13: Wikipedia home page

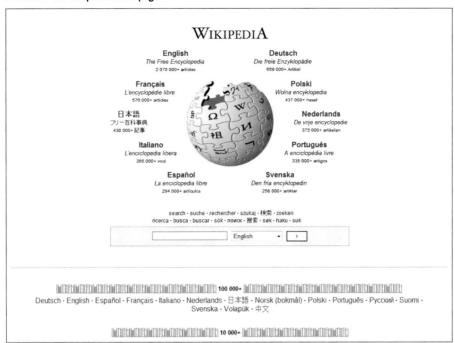

FIGURE E-14: Wikipedia About page

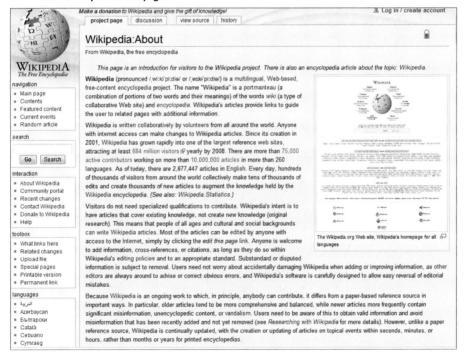

Understanding Copyright and Citing Web Resources

If you use portions of Web page text or an image from a Web page as support for a topic in a research or business document or in a Web page, you must treat it like any other published source and get permission to use it and cite it appropriately. Some files on the Web are in the **public domain**, which means that you can freely copy them without requesting permission from the source. If you cannot find a clear statement of copyright terms or a statement indicating that the files are in the public domain, you should not use them. ░░░░ Marti reminds you to collect information about the sites you visit so you can include a proper reference to your sources in any report you write. You decide to learn more about how to properly cite Web resources.

DETAILS

Things to consider when citing Web resources are described below:

QUICK TIP

In the U.S., works created after 1977 are protected for the life of the author plus 70 years; works copyrighted by corporations or non-profit organizations are protected for 95 years from the date of publication or 120 years from the date of creation, whichever is earlier.

- Copyright

  A **copyright** is a right granted by a government to the author or creator of a literary or artistic work, which is defined as the tangible expression of an idea. This right gives the owner sole and exclusive rights, such as printing, publishing, reproducing, or selling the work. Creations that can be copyrighted include virtually all forms of artistic or intellectual expression, including books, music, artworks, recordings (audio and video), architectural drawings, choreographic works, photographs and motion pictures, product packaging, and computer software. In the United States, the creator of a work does not need to register that work to obtain copyright protection. In other words, a work that does not include the words "copyright", "copyrighted", or the copyright symbol (©), and that was created after 1989 is copyrighted automatically by virtue of the copyright law.

- Copyright and Ideas

  The idea contained in a work is not copyrightable; instead, the particular form of expression of the idea is the work that can be copyrighted. For example, you cannot copyright the idea to write a song about love, but you can copyright the song you write. If an idea cannot be separated from its expression in a work, that work cannot be copyrighted. For example, mathematical calculations cannot be copyrighted. A collection of facts, however, can be copyrighted, but only if the collection has some degree of creativity: it must be arranged, coordinated, or selected in a way that causes the resulting work to rise to the level of an original work.

QUICK TIP

If you are unsure whether your use is indeed fair use, the safest course of action is to contact the copyright owner and ask for permission to use the work.

- Fair Use, Plagiarism, and Stealing

  The **fair use** of a work includes copying it for use in criticism, comment, news reporting, teaching, scholarship, or research. When you make fair use of a work in academics or reporting, you should always provide a citation to the original work. Failure to cite the source of material that you use (whether it is in the public domain or it is protected by copyright) is **plagiarism** and can be a serious violation of your school's academic honesty policy. Using or reproducing a copyrighted work for other uses, such as putting someone else's comic strip on a Web site owned by a business, is not considered fair use, and you must ask the copyright holder for permission to use the work, and in some cases, pay a fee in order to use it. In this case, using the copyrighted work without permission is stealing the copyright holder's work. A useful Web site for learning more about respecting copyrights is the Stanford University Copyright & Fair Use site, shown in Figure E-15.

QUICK TIP

Although there are no clear standards specifying where or how to break long URLs at the end of a print line, most authorities agree that the URL should be broken at a slash that appears in the URL and that a hyphen should not be added at the end of the line that occurs in the middle of the URL.

- Citation Formats

  For academic research, the two most widely followed standards for print citations are those of the American Psychological Association (APA) and the Modern Language Association (MLA). Their formats for Web page citations are similar to each other and both include the following elements: name of the author or Web page creator (if known), date of the article or date the Web page was last updated (if known), title of the Web site or a description of an untitled page, Web site name, name of the site's sponsoring organization (if any), date the page was retrieved, and the URL. Figure E-16 shows examples of Web page citations.

FIGURE E-15: Stanford University Copyright & Fair Use home page

FIGURE E-16: Examples of correct Web page citations

MLA style for a Web page with an author and an updated date
Ethics Updates – Home Page. Hinman, L. M. September 7, 2006. University of San Diego. March 12, 2012. <http://ethics.sandiego.edu>

APA style for an article on a Web site with a title and an author, dated
Loveland, T. (2004, Fall) Technology education standards implementation in Florida. *Journal of Technology Education* (16)1. Retrieved April 19, 2012, from Digital Library and Archives, University Libraries, Virginia Tech Web site: http://scholar.lib.vt.edu/ejournals/JTE/ v16n1/loveland.html

MLA style for Web page with a Web page title, no author, undated
"The Linux Home Page at Linux Online." Linux Online. Linux Online, Inc. May 15, 2012. <http://www.linux.org>

APA style for Web page with a Web page title, no author, undated
United States Postal Service home page. (n.d.). Retrieved June 18, 2012, from http://www.usps.com

Moving and disappearing URLs

A Web page exists only in an HTML document on a Web server computer. If that file's name or location changes or if the Web server is disconnected from the Internet, someone looking up your reference will not be able to locate the page at the URL you listed. When a page does not exist on a Web site, a page displaying an error message appears when the URL for that page is typed into a browser. These error messages are called 404 error messages because 404 is the status code in HTTP that tells a user the requested Web page

was not found. If you get a 404 page, try going to the home page of the Web site by deleting all the text after the domain name in the Address or Location bar and then pressing the Enter key. You can also use a search engine to search for the page you want. CrossRef.org, an independent registration agency, assigns **digital object identifiers (DOIs)** to provide a uniform way to identify scholarly academic journals and similar documents and provide a persistent link to their locations on the Internet.

Practice

For current SAM information including versions and content details, visit SAM Central (http://samcentral.course.com). If you have a SAM user profile, you may have access to hands-on instruction, practice, and assessment of the skills covered in this unit. Since we support various versions of SAM throughout the life of this text, you will want to check with your instructor for instructions and the correct URL/web site to access those assignments.

▼ CONCEPTS REVIEW

Identify the purpose of each Web page shown in Figures E-17 through E-20.

FIGURE E-17

1.

Copyright ® 1996–2009 WhitePages.com, Inc.

FIGURE E-18

2.

FIGURE E-19

3.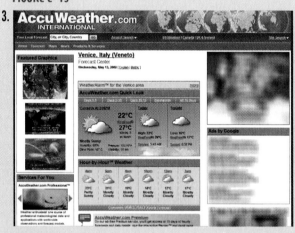

FIGURE E-20

4.

Match each term with the statement that best describes it.

5. **White pages directory**   a. Works that can be freely copied and reproduced

6. **Yellow pages directory**   b. A right granted by a government to an author or creator

7. **News search engine**   c. A directory of business names and addresses

8. **Copyright**   d. A directory of personal information such as address and phone number

9. **Public domain**   e. Searches news stories in multiple publications

Select the best answer from the list of choices.

10. **Which of the following is generally available on a Web site that provides maps?**
    a. Driving directions
    b. Navigation tools to zoom in on the map
    c. Printable map
    d. All of the above

11. **Which of the following is the best way to find out how to say "Good Morning" in another language?**
    a. Use a search engine
    b. Use an online encyclopedia
    c. Use the U.S. Library of Congress Web site
    d. Use an online language translator

12. **Which of the following characteristics might identify a Web page as unreliable?**
    a. Use of the .org domain
    b. References
    c. Author's email address
    d. Spelling errors

13. **Which of the following describes using a copyrighted work for use in news reporting or teaching?**
    a. Copyright
    b. Public domain
    c. Fair use
    d. Plagiarism

14. **Which of the following is not one of the elements you should include when you cite a Web resource?**
    a. Web page creator
    b. Web site ranking in a search engine
    c. Date the Web page was accessed
    d. URL of the Web page

▼ SKILLS REVIEW

1. **Get the news.**
   a. Go to the Online Companion page for Unit E, then click one of the links to a news search engine under Skills Review 1.
   b. Search for recent news stories about Russia.
   c. Return to the Unit E page on the Online Companion, then click another link to a news search engine under Skills Review 1.
   d. Search for recent news stories about Russia.
   e. Note whether you found links to different stories in each news search engine.

2. **Obtain weather reports.**
   a. Return to the Unit E page on the Online Companion.
   b. Use two of the weather forecasting sites listed under Skills Review 2 to find and enter the current temperatures for each of the cities listed in Table E-1.

TABLE E-1

	Stockholm, Sweden	Tokyo, Japan	Santiago, Chile	Cairo, Egypt
Weather Site 1 URL				
Weather Site 2 URL				

3. Obtain maps and city guides.

  a. Return to the Unit E page on the Online Companion, then click one of the links under Map Sites in Skills Review 3.

  b. Find a map of Howard University in Washington, DC. The address is 2400 Sixth St. NW.

  c. Return to the Unit E page on the Online Companion, then click one of the links under City Guides in Skills Review 3.

  d. Find and open the city guide to Washington, DC.

  e. Find the date and time of one upcoming event in the city.

4. Find businesses and people.

  a. Return to the Unit E page on the Online Companion, then click one of the links to a yellow pages directory under Skills Review 4.

  b. Conduct a yellow pages search for art in New Orleans, Louisiana.

  c. Select a category that might include art galleries from the list of possible categories.

  d. Return to the Unit E page on the Online Companion page, then click one of the links to a white pages directory under Skills Review 4.

  e. Conduct a white pages search of a family member.

  f. Return to the Unit E page on the Online Companion, then click one of the links to a white pages directory under Search Engines in Skills Review 4.

  g. Conduct a search of a classmate's name.

5. Find online reference tools.

  a. Return to the Unit E page of the Online Companion page, then click the LibrarySpot link under Skills Review 5.

  b. Click the Quotations link, then click one of the links under General Collections.

  c. Search for a quote about education by using the search expression text box or by using links to categories. Write down one quote and the source.

  d. Return to the Unit E page on the Online Companion, then click the US Library of Congress link under Skills Review 5.

  e. Click the Thomas link, then click Go, if necessary, to open a database containing information about Federal legislation.

  f. Click the Congressional Record Latest Daily Digest link, then write down one of the items listed under Measures Reported.

  g. Return to the Unit E page of the Online Companion page, then click one of the links under Translation Tools in Skills Review 5.

  h. Write down the translation of Good morning in Swedish and Portuguese.

6. Evaluate Web resources.

  a. Return to the Unit E page of the Online Companion, then click the About.com link under Skills Review 6.

  b. Click the Browse Our Channels link, if necessary to expand the list of channels, click the Health link, then click the Asthma link.

  c. Click a link that you think will bring you to links to articles that explain the causes of asthma.

  d. Explore two of the Web sites in the list, then evaluate them using Table E-2.

TABLE E-2

	author contact	author affiliation	.edu, .org or .gov domain	reputable references
Web site 1 URL:	Yes/No	Yes/No	Yes/No	Yes/No
Web site 2 URL:	Yes/No	Yes/No	Yes/No	Yes/No

▼ SKILLS REVIEW (CONTINUED)

7. Evaluate user-generated content.

   a. Return to the Unit E page of the Online Companion, then click one of the wiki index sites listed under Skills Review 7. Each of these sites displays a list of wiki sites on the Web. Use these as a starting point for this exercise.

   b. Explore several wiki sites. Find an example of one that contains information on a topic about which you have some knowledge. Evaluate the content on the site. Is the information presented correct? Is there anything to indicate the author's identity or qualifications?

   c. In a new tab, find an example of a wiki site that offers opinions, similar to Wikitravel. Would you refer to the site you found if you were searching for information about the site's topic?

8. Understand copyrights and cite Web resources.

   a. Return to the Unit E page of the Online Companion, then click the **MLA link** under Skills Review 8. Use the MLA format to write a citation for the Web site you found in Step 7b. (*Hint*: If the link does not bring you to the correct page, look for a link to the FAQ (frequently asked questions) page and scan the questions for the one that would provide the answer, or use the Search box on the page.)

   b. Return to the Unit E page of the Online Companion, then click the **APA link** under Skills Review 8. Use the APA format to write a citation for the Web site you found in Step 7c.

▼ INDEPENDENT CHALLENGE 1

You are a sales representative for Portland Concrete Mixers, a company that makes replacement parts for concrete mixing equipment. You have been transferred to the Olympia area in Washington and want to plan your first sales trip there. Because you plan to drive to Olympia, you need information about the best route as well as a map of the city. You hope to generate some new customers and, therefore, need to identify sales-lead prospects in the Olympia area. Companies that manufacture ready-mixed concrete are good prospects for you.

   a. Go to the Online Companion page for Unit E, then click one of the links under Map Sites in the Independent Challenge 1 section.

Advanced Challenge Exercise

   - Click the link for driving directions on the home page of the site you chose.
   - Type **Portland, OR** as your starting address, then type **Olympia, WA** as your destination address.
   - Click **Get Directions** (or something similar).
   - Zoom in on the map to obtain a more detailed map of the route from Portland to Olympia.
   - Print the map.

   b. Return to the Unit E page of the Online Companion, then click one of the links under Yellow Pages Directories in the Independent Challenge 1 section.

   c. Search for businesses connected to ready-mixed concrete in Olympia, WA.

   d. Select three companies that you think would be good prospects.

   e. Outline your travel plans and list the names and addresses of the three companies you have identified.

▼ INDEPENDENT CHALLENGE 2

You are the owner of a popular nightclub, Ragtime Tonight, which is located near a convention center. An increasing number of your patrons are travelers who make airline, hotel, and car-rental reservations using the Web, and you want to create a Web site that reaches them. While designing the Web site, you decide that you would like to add some ragtime audio clips that play when the Web site is opened using a Web browser. However, you need to know more about allowable usage, copyright restrictions, and licensing before proceeding.

   a. Go to the Online Companion page for Unit E, then click several of the links under Independent Challenge 2 to learn about allowable use and limitations of copyrighted work.

   b. Write a summary of the information you find. Describe what you can do, what you cannot do, and ideas for how you might legally include ragtime music on your Web site at the lowest cost.

▼ INDEPENDENT CHALLENGE 3

You are conducting research on politics in Mexico. Currently, you are studying the history of land ownership in this country. In your report, you want to tie this history together with relevant recent events.

a. Go to the Online Companion page for Unit E, then click several of the links to a news search engine under Independent Challenge 3.

b. Search for recent news articles mentioning land ownership issues in Mexico.

c. Read and summarize the two articles.

Advanced Challenge Exercise

- Find a news search engine that has an advanced search feature.
- Use the advanced search feature to search for articles older than 30 days.
- Read some of the older articles. Note if there have been any developments in the issues since then.

d. Use your favorite search engine and search for two Web sites that contain information about the history of land ownership in Mexico.

e. Evaluate each of the two Web sites you found. Write a brief explanation describing why the sites can be considered reliable or questionable.

▼ REAL LIFE INDEPENDENT CHALLENGE

The resources on the Web can be very useful when you are planning a trip. For a trip you are either planning or one that you would like to plan, use the Web to find maps, hotel and restaurant listings, and sightseeing suggestions.

   a. Decide on a city to visit.

   b. Go to the Online Companion page for Unit E, then click one of the links under City Guides in the Real Life Independent Challenge section and search for information about the city you plan to visit.

   c. Note the names of two restaurants in the city you plan to visit.

   d. Note the name of a hotel in the city where you plan to make reservations.

   e. Find an upcoming event in the city you plan to visit.

   f. Print the first page of the Web page describing the upcoming event. Be sure to include the URL in the header or footer information.

   g. Return to the Unit E page of the Online Companion, then click one of the links under Weather Sites in the Real Life Independent Challenge section and find the current temperature in the city you plan to visit.

   h. Summarize the information you have found about the city you plan to visit. Include the names and addresses of the two restaurants, the URL for the Web page with information about the hotel, a description of the upcoming event, and a brief description of the current weather conditions.

▼ VISUAL WORKSHOP

Go to the Online Companion page for Unit E, then click the Bing Maps link under Visual Workshop. Find the map illustrated in Figure E-21. The address entered is 20 Channel Center St., Boston, MA. When you have found the map, print a copy.

FIGURE E-21

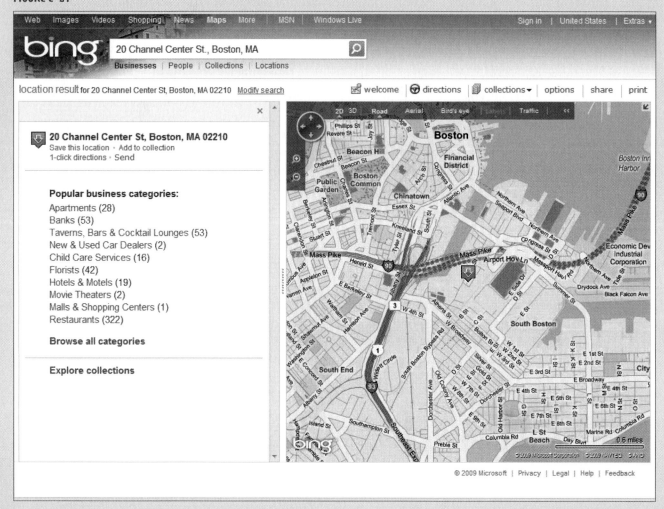

Communicating on the Web

You can enrich your Internet experiences by utilizing Web 2.0 technologies such as virtual communities, blogs, and podcasts, as well as other types of online communication tools such as mailing lists, newsgroups, instant messaging, and social bookmarking sites. These tools all take advantage of user-generated content and enable you to easily exchange ideas and information with other people interested in common topics or issues. Some of these communication methods use **push technology** to send content to users who request it. Some examples of push technology are chat, instant messaging, online social networks, and blogs. Other communication methods are referred to as **pull technology** because subscribers "pull" content to their computers when they want it. Pull technology includes mailing lists, newsgroups, newsfeeds, and podcasts. Some communication methods are both push and pull, depending on who is using them—for example, the person who writes a blog is pushing content to other users who then pull it to their computers so they can read it. DeMaine Art Glass is a small art glass company located in Nebraska. From its combined showroom and studio, DeMaine Art Glass sells stained glass, glass supplies, and books to the public. Your job is to investigate how the manager, Mike DeMaine, can use some Internet communication tools to learn about new industry techniques and trends, as well as to make contact with colleagues in the industry and potential customers.

OBJECTIVES

Understand group communication

Understand chat

Use instant messaging

Learn about virtual communities

Locate and read blogs

Learn about podcasting

Use a social bookmarking site

Protect your identity and
   reputation online

Understanding Group Communication

The Internet stores information on a wide variety of topics. One way to access this information is to use group communication tools. A **mailing list** is a list of names and email addresses for a group of people, sometimes called a **discussion group**, who share a common interest in a subject or topic and exchange information by sending messages to everyone on the list at once. A **Web-based discussion forum** is similar to a mailing list, but members put their messages on a Web site. Users can access and read these messages at their convenience. A **newsgroup** is a system in which messages are stored on Internet servers, sorted by topic. A **thread** is a series of messages on a particular issue in a mailing list, discussion forum, or newsgroup. A **post** is a message sent to a mailing list, discussion forum, or newsgroup, and the act of sending a post is called **posting**. **Lurking** is the practice of reading messages but not contributing to the discussion. ▄▄▄▄▄ Mike started a mailing list for art glass collectors, and he wants you want to find out if other mailing lists, discussion forums, or newsgroups exist for art glass. You start your research by learning more about group communication tools.

DETAILS

Group communication tools are described below:

QUICK TIP

An **announcement list** is a mailing list that is similar to a newsletter in that it sends messages to subscribers, but does not allow subscribers to post to the list.

- #### Using a Mailing List
  To send messages to and receive messages from a mailing list, sometimes called an **email list**, users need to **join**, or **subscribe** to, the list. To post a message to the list, a member sends the message to the **list address**, or the **list name**. The **administrative address** is the email address to which you send **commands**, which are requests to the list server to take a prescribed action. To find a mailing list that interests you, you can use a search engine. You can also find collections of mailing lists at Web sites such as Topica or L-Soft.

- #### Using a Web-based Discussion Forum
  To post messages to a Web-based discussion forum, users need to become a member of the forum first. After filling out a registration form on the Web site, including choosing a user name and a password, users can then post in any thread. Some discussion forums allow people to lurk without becoming a member; others require membership in order to read posted messages. Some Web sites that host discussion forums are Delphi Forums and Yahoo! Groups.

QUICK TIP

Google Groups directory is a Web site that provides tools for accessing and creating Usenet newsgroups and does not delete old newsgroup articles; Google Groups stores more than 800 million newsgroup articles dating from 1981 in its database.

- #### Using a Newsgroup
  Newsgroups are part of the **Usenet** database. A server that stores a Usenet newsgroup is called a **news server**. Usenet is a **distributed database**, which is a database stored in multiple physical locations, with portions of the database replicated in the different locations. A newsgroup's name consists of the top-level hierarchy followed by subcategories, separated from the top-level hierarchy name and each other by a period that further refines the classification. For example, a newsgroup that includes discussions of organic chemistry issues is named *sci.chem.organic*. The original Usenet News Service included the eight main top-level categories that appear in Table F-1. To access the messages in a newsgroup, you need to use a **newsreader**, a program designed to communicate with news server computers. Most mail client software programs, such as Windows Live Mail, have a built-in newsreader. In addition, some Web sites allow you to read newsgroup messages using a browser.

QUICK TIP

A **Frequently Asked Questions (FAQ)** document contains the answers to common questions that users ask about a mailing list and its subject; Web sites often have FAQs also.

- #### Classification of Group Communication Tools
  Posts sent to a **moderated mailing list**, **discussion forum**, or **newsgroup** are read and evaluated by a **list moderator** before they are sent to members of the mailing list. The list moderator is responsible for discarding any messages that are inappropriate for or irrelevant to the list's members. All members of an **unmoderated mailing list**, **discussion forum**, or **newsgroup** automatically receive all messages, regardless of content. Most group communications are **open**; that is, the group automatically accepts all members; a **closed list**, **forum**, or **newsgroup** is one in which membership is *not* automatic. In a closed list, forum, or group, the **list administrator**, a person assigned to oversee the list, forum, or group, can either reject or accept your request to become a member. Figure F-1 shows the Web page describing Mike's unmoderated, open mailing list.

FIGURE F-1: Description of an unmoderated, open mailing list

Identifies list as unmoderated

Identifies list as open

Shows how active the list is

Name of mailing list

Description of mailing list

Click to subscribe to this list

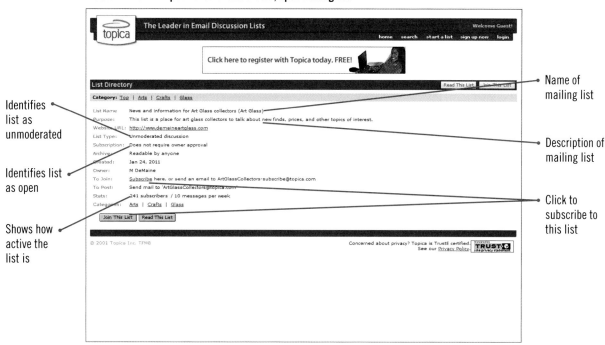

TABLE F-1: Original Usenet News Service top-level categories

category	includes topics related to
comp	Computers
rec	Recreation and entertainment
sci	Science
soc	Social issues and socializing
news	Operation and administration of Usenet
talk	Conversations, debates, and arguments
misc	Miscellaneous topics that do not fall within other categories
alt	Alternative and controversial topics

Warnings about mailing lists

Mailing lists are valuable tools for receiving current and useful information. However, if you subscribe to a mailing list, you need to check your email regularly. Depending on a mailing list's activity, you might receive many messages every day. In fact, some mailing lists can generate hundreds of messages each week. By checking your email frequently, you can respond to, file, or delete messages in a timely fashion. Also, because the list server forwards the email message that you post to every person subscribed to the mailing list, you expose yourself to potential privacy problems because the message you send contains your name and email address. In addition, if you include your signature with your message, you might also be providing your mailing address and phone number to all list members. To protect your privacy, make sure you do not include a signature or any personal information in email messages you post to the mailing list and use a free email account address for your subscriptions (such as Windows Live Hotmail, Gmail, or Yahoo! Mail). Finally, if your email program and ISP allow you to send auto-replies (an automatic email message that gets sent as a reply to every message you receive) when you are away—for example, on vacation—remember to suspend your mailing list subscriptions so that you do not send your auto-reply message to every member of the mailing list every time one of them posts a message. If this happens, you will probably be unsubscribed from the list by the list owner and you may not be allowed to resubscribe.

Understanding Chat

Chat is instantaneous (or **real-time**) communication on the Internet or on the Web. Some chat software lets you give control of your computer to another user so that a person can use your programs or troubleshoot a problem that you are having. You can also use chat to collaborate on a file with another user as you talk to each other. Chats can be continuous, with participants entering and leaving ongoing discussions, or they can be planned to occur at a specific time and for a specific duration of time. Some chats are open to discussion of any topic, whereas other chats are focused on a specific topic or set of participants. Chat participants often omit capitalization and do not worry about proper spelling and grammar, and they frequently use emoticons and the acronyms listed in Table F-2 as shortcuts for common expressions. Chat is an example of push technology. To chat with others, you need to use special software or use an interface available on a Web site. ▟▛▛ Mike has recently heard about chat from some colleagues at an art glass conference. He asked you to investigate whether chat would be a good way for him to communicate in real-time with individuals or groups of people. You begin by reviewing the types of chat.

DETAILS

Following are the types of chat available:

- **Internet Relay Chat**

  Internet Relay Chat (**IRC**) is a communications program that is popular with businesses, which use it for virtual meetings with clients and employees located at different worldwide branch offices. IRC uses a client-server network model: IRC servers are connected through the Internet to form an IRC network, and individual chat participants use IRC clients that connect to the servers in the network. Many IRC networks operate independently of each other; usually you select an IRC server based on its proximity to you. Although the servers in each of these IRC networks are connected to each other as part of the Internet, IRC traffic is segregated by network. Figure F-2 shows this simultaneous interconnection and segregation of IRC network traffic.

- **Web Chat Sites**

  Web chat sites offer the same capabilities as IRC chat networks; however, a Web chat site is often easier to use and does not require users to download and install any special software. In a Web-based chat, some users lurk and others have multiple conversations going at the same time. Although Web sites that provide chat rooms usually have rules of appropriate conduct, you might encounter conversations taking place that are offensive to you. Rules for each site vary, but in general, most Web-based chat sites prohibit **spamming**, the use of automated programs to send messages to multiple chat rooms simultaneously, profane and vulgar language, and threats to individuals (called **flaming**). Some Web sites have a link that lets you identify participants who are not following the agreed-upon rules for the chat room. When a participant is reported, a chat site has the option of prohibiting the offending participant from entering any chat rooms at that site again. Many Web-based discussion forums have chat rooms available as part of the forum, such as Facebook and Delphi Forums, and there are sites devoted exclusively to chat, such as the ICQ Chat Web site and Chatting.com.

- **Instant Messaging**

  With **instant messaging** (**IM**), users chat in real time over the Internet. Instant messages usually occur between two people who know each other, but can occur between a group of people. To chat using IM, both users must have the same IM software or IM software that lets users with different instant messaging software talk to each other. Popular IM programs are ICQ, AIM, Windows Live Messenger, and Yahoo! Messenger.

- **Public and Private Chats**

  A **private chat** occurs between individuals who know each other and are invited to participate in the chat. A **public chat** occurs in a public area, sometimes called a **chat room**, in which anyone who is registered with the chat service can come and go.

FIGURE F-2: Independent IRC networks on the Internet

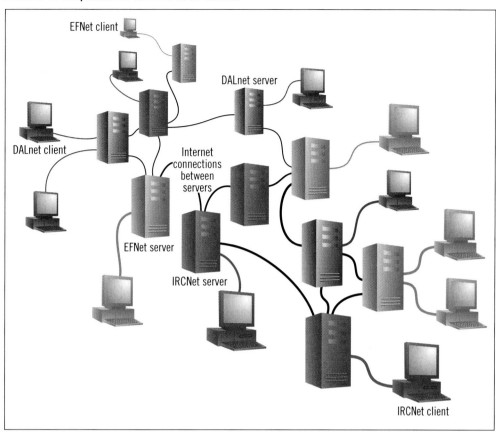

TABLE F-2: Commonly used chat acronyms

acronym	meaning	acronym	meaning
afk	Away from keyboard	irl	In real life (contrasted with one's online existence)
atm	At the moment	jk	Just kidding
bbl	Be back later	lol	Laughing out loud
brb	Be right back	np	No problem
btw	By the way	oic	Oh, I see
cul8r	See you later	rotfl	Rolling on the floor laughing
c-ya	See you	eg	Evil grin
ttfn	Ta-ta (goodbye) for now	wb	Welcome back
imho	In my humble opinion	imnsho	In my not so humble opinion

Protecting your privacy in chat rooms

Most Web chat sites ask you to identify yourself on a registration page before admitting you to the Web chat pages. You should consider carefully whether to provide detailed personal information when you register because most current laws do not require a Web site administrator to maintain the confidentiality of your information. If one Web chat site requires information that you do not want to disclose, simply look for another site with a less intrusive registration page. In addition, although Web sites that provide chat rooms have rules of appropriate conduct, you might encounter conversations taking place that are offensive to you. Fortunately, there are many different Web-based chat rooms available on the Internet, so if your first attempt does not provide a satisfactory experience, simply exit from that chat room and try another one.

Using Instant Messaging

In order for two people to exchange instant messages, both people must be using the same instant messaging software and be logged in to their instant messaging service. **ICQ** (pronounced "I seek you") is one of the most popular instant messaging software programs available, with over 220 million worldwide users. **AOL Instant Messenger** (**AIM**) was created a few years after the introduction of ICQ. AOL originally created AIM to allow its members to chat with each other, but AOL subsequently made AIM available to anyone (even those people without AOL accounts) for use on the Web. Microsoft developed **Windows Live Messenger**, which you can download from Microsoft's Web site. Because both users must be online for an instant message session to occur, IM software alerts you when your friends are online, as long as you are signed into the service. If someone sends you a message, a Conversation or Instant Message window opens and its corresponding button on the taskbar blinks. ▰▰▰ You think instant messaging will be useful for Mike to stay in touch with his colleagues, so you investigate various IM software.

STEPS

QUICK TIP

Some IM software, such as Trillian by Cerulean, allows people with different instant messaging software to talk to each other.

1. **Go to the Online Companion page for** Unit F, **then click the** AOL Instant Messenger link **or the** Yahoo! Messenger link **under Lesson 3**

   The AOL Instant Messenger (AIM) home page appears in your browser window. See Figure F-3.

2. **Click the** FAQ **or the** More info link

   A page with the FAQs for the site or a page containing more information about the instant messaging program you selected opens.

3. **Return to the Online Companion page for** Unit F, **then click the** Windows Live Messenger link

   The page from which you can download Windows Live Messenger appears in your browser window.

4. **Follow some of the links on the page to learn more about Windows Live Messenger**

   Windows Live Messenger was included with the Windows Vista operating system, but if you have the Windows 7 operating system, you need to download it from Microsoft's Web site. See the Clues box on the next page for more information.

DETAILS

Following are details about using Windows Live Messenger:

QUICK TIP

Some IM programs refer to contacts as buddies.

QUICK TIP

To stop Messenger from starting automatically when you start Windows, sign in to Messenger, click the Show menu button, point to Tools, click Options, click Sign In in the list on the left of the Options dialog box that opens, then deselect the Automatically run Windows Live Messenger when I log on to Windows check box.

- If Windows Live Messenger is installed, you can click the Add a contact or group button to the right of the Search contacts text box, click Add a contact to open a dialog box, type the instant messaging address of a friend in the Instant messaging address text box, click Next, add a message if you want, and then click Send invitation.

- To start an instant messaging session with someone using Windows Live Messenger, double-click the person's name in the list of Available contacts in the Windows Live Messenger window to open a Conversation window with your contact's name and instant messaging address in the title bar.

- To send a message, type your message in the bottom part of the window, then press [Enter]. Your message appears in a balloon in the lower-right corner of your contact's computer screen. The person who receives the instant message can click the balloon to open a conversation window with the message that was sent appearing under the sender's name.

- When your contact replies, his or her message appears in the conversation window on both users' computer screens under his or her name. Figure F-4 shows a sample instant messaging session.

- To end the instant messaging session, click the Close button in the Conversation window. To sign out of Windows Live Messenger (if you don't want others to know you are online), click the Show menu button on the toolbar to the right of the Search contacts text box in the Windows Live Messenger window, point to File, and then click Sign out.

FIGURE F-3: AIM home page

More Info link

FIGURE F-4: Conversation window with an instant messaging session in Windows Live Messenger

Show menu button

Add a contact or group button

Double-click an available contact to open a Conversation window

Name and email address of person with whom you are having a conversation

Message from the person who clicked Send first appears first in the window

Your classmate's message appears under his or her name

Type your message here

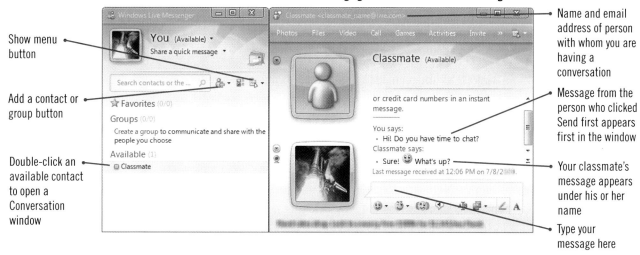

Downloading and installing Windows Live Messenger from Microsoft

If Windows Live Messenger is not already installed on your computer, you can download it from Microsoft's Web site. Go to *www.microsoft.com*, type **messenger** in the search box on the home page, and then press [Enter] or click the Search button to search Microsoft's Web site. In the list of results, look for a link to Messenger, Windows Live, or Windows Live Essentials. Once you find the page with the Messenger download, click the Download link. In the dialog box that opens, click Run to install the software directly from Microsoft's Web site. Depending on which download page you visit, you might see a different list of programs that will be included in your download. These programs, including Mail, Photo Gallery, and Movie Maker, make up Windows Live Essentials. You can choose which of these programs to include in your download. In order to use Windows Live Messenger, you need a Windows Live ID. If you don't have one, start Messenger, click the Sign up link, and then follow the instructions.

Learning About Virtual Communities

The Web is home to many **virtual communities**, also known as **online social groups**, which are places on the Internet where a user can post a **profile** of him or herself—a brief description of the user's personality, likes and dislikes, and a picture, among other information—and then post a blog or share information. Many of these sites allow people to post comments on other people's profile pages. Online social groups are useful tools for people who want to make new friends, establish acquaintances before moving to a new location, discuss politics, obtain advice, or make any number of other types of connections. Online social groups are another example of push technology. Most, if not all, social networking sites rely heavily on advertising to generate the revenue they need to operate. Some sites also charge members a monthly membership fee. Other sites charge for access to specific site features. You think a virtual community would help Mike stay in touch with his colleagues in the industry. You learn more about virtual communities.

DETAILS

The following are different types of virtual communities:

QUICK TIP

Many virtual community sites provide a directory that lists members' locations, interests, and qualities so that one member of the community can contact any other member, but the recipient is not required to respond.

- **General Virtual Communities**

  One of the first online communities was craigslist, an information resource for San Francisco area residents that was created in 1995 by Craig Newmark. That community has grown to include communities for most major cities in the United States and in several other countries. Another community is Friendster. Figure F-5 shows the Friendster login page. Members of Friendster post profiles with information about themselves and upload their photos.

- **Targeted Community Networks**

  A targeted virtual community is designed to attract people who have specific interests. For example, MySpace is a virtual community targeted at a young audience of music fans. Members can post and download digital music files, play games, create blogs, and send instant messages to each other. MySpace can charge more for the advertising it sells because it can identify characteristics of its members for its advertisers. Facebook, another virtual community originally targeted to college students, now has a much broader audience, although its main demographic remains young adults.

- **Business Networks**

  Some sites, including LinkedIn, Ryze, and tribe.net, focus on business networking. People use these sites to look for a new job, find potential business partners, hire someone, and conduct other activities related to business. Members of virtual communities devoted to business connections are looking for solutions to their business problems, whether it is a company looking for an employee with specific talents, a business hoping to place its product in a retail store, or an organization looking for a consultant who can provide training on a specific topic. Recently, Facebook has become a communication tool for corporations. For example, Cinemark Theaters, Marble Slab Creamery, and Pepsi use Facebook pages to promote their products and bring users together for marketing and research opportunities through sweepstakes and other promotions. Figure F-6 shows the Facebook page for Course Technology, the publisher of this textbook.

QUICK TIP

It is possible for fans and supporters to create entire Web sites about someone without their knowledge or consent, so look for information on a site identifying who created the Web site.

- **Political Networks**

  Many political organizations used the Internet in a variety of ways to rally supporters, raise funds, and get their messages out to voters. For example, Facebook has become a communication tool for political candidates. In the 2008 presidential elections, several of the candidates successfully used their virtual communities to raise millions of dollars for their campaigns. These sites allowed people to discuss issues, plan strategies, and arrange in-person meetings called **meetups**. Meetup.com is a Web site that specializes in arranging meetups.

FIGURE F-5: Friendster Log In page

FIGURE F-6: Course Technology's Facebook page

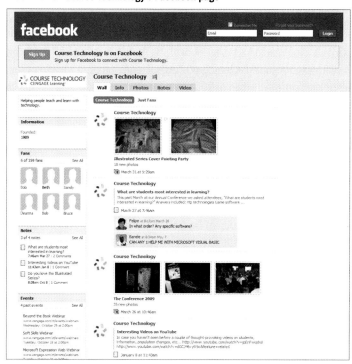

Video-sharing sites

With the explosion of online social networks, the Internet was ready for its next frontier. At dinner one night, three friends were commiserating on the lack of support for sharing videos on the Web. At the time, photo sharing was relatively easy, but Steve Chen, Chad Hurley, and Jawed Karim noted that there were no similar sites for sharing videos. They hatched a plan and in 2005, they launched the video-sharing site YouTube. In 2006, Google bought the site for $1.65 billion and by 2007, YouTube's community was viewing over 100 million videos each day. When YouTube started, it was immediately picked up by people already participating in well-established online social networks. Word-of-mouth traveled quickly, and users quickly began uploading and sharing content on YouTube. YouTube did not really need to advertise itself—its innovative approach became a social network of its own, and the people using it were quick and eager to spread the word. In addition to videos uploaded by people, YouTube has strategic partnerships with many major networks and music labels to broadcast their content. YouTube also relies heavily on display ad placement, brand channels (advertising focused on a specific brand), and contests to generate revenue. As the popularity of YouTube grew, some established Web sites, including Yahoo!, added online video sharing services to their sites, and many new sites exclusively devoted to video sharing appeared, such as Dailymotion, Veoh, and Metacafe.

Locating and Reading Blogs

Web logs, or **blogs**, are online journals. Blogs were catapulted into the mainstream media when political candidates for president in the 2004 United States presidential election used them as a way to organize their supporters and provide a means by which candidates could freely discuss campaign issues in an unfiltered way. Because anyone can write a blog, blogs are now created and viewed by millions of Internet users, providing unlimited and unrestricted information about any topic. Some are from well-known news organizations such as *The New York Times*, CNN, ZDNet, Reuters, and local newspapers in many markets. Other blogs are written by individuals who might not claim any affiliation to an organization. Figure F-7 shows the About Me page of a blog created by an individual. Fortunately, it is easy to find blogs based on their tags, content, and authors. **Tags** are one-word descriptions of the blog content that bloggers use to categorize their blogs. You will learn more about tags later in this unit. Google Blog Search is one resource that categorizes blogs and makes it easy to search for them. ▄▄▄ Mike is considering starting a blog and has asked you to research blog posts about art glass.

STEPS

QUICK TIP

When searching for blogs, you should use the skills you learned in Unit E to evaluate the resources the blog contains and the credentials of its authors.

1. **Go to the Online Companion page for** Unit F, **then click the** Google Blog Search link **under Lesson 5**

2. **If necessary, click in the search text box, type** art glass, **then click the** Search Blogs button
   The Google Blog Search Web page shown in Figure F-8 returned links to over 13 million postings related to the search text, *art glass*. Each blog posting includes a link to the blog's source and to the complete posting, a date or time on which the posting was published, a brief description of the posting, and a link to the site. You can use the feature on the left side of the page to fine-tune your search to a specific time period.

QUICK TIP

Although blogs are a very popular and easy way to disseminate information, it is important to keep in mind that blogs are not subject to the same ethical guidelines of professional reporters, and that the information contained in any blog should always be regarded as personal opinion and not as "hard" news.

3. **Click the** Last 12 hours link
   The search results list is reduced to include only those blogs updated within the last 12 hours.

4. **Click the** Back button **in the browser to return to your search results, then click any result**
   Examine the page that opens in the browser window. If a result is not a blog, click the Back button in the browser, and then click a different link. Look for tags or a list of categories.

5. **Click any tag or category link to see the list of posts that have that tag applied or are filed in the category you clicked**

Understanding microblogs

A **microblog** is a form of blogging that sends short messages— usually 140 characters or fewer—on a very frequent schedule. Whereas a blogger might spend hours updating his blog daily, weekly, or monthly with long posts that include text, photos, and links, a microblogger might update his content hourly or even more frequently using just a few words or a single sentence. Microblog postings are sometimes called **tweets**, and the act of microblogging is sometimes called **tweeting**; both terms are references to the popular microblog Web site, Twitter. Many organizations, including well-known retailers and educational institutions, now use microblogs to communicate with customers, students, and other types of followers. For example, the CNN network blasts news updates to over 1.5 million followers on a regular basis. Some microblogs, such as Yammer, are used by companies and other organizations to provide a private network for employees to use to communicate about work-related businesses by restricting followers to people with valid email addresses.

FIGURE F-7: About me page on an individual's blog

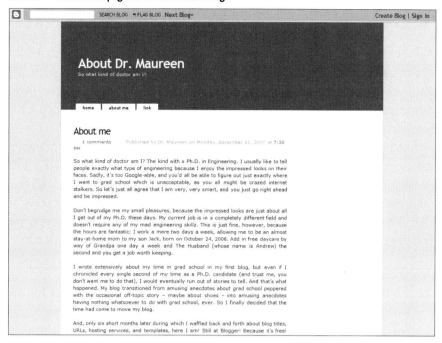

FIGURE F-8: Results of Google Blog search for "art glass"

Use these links to narrow search to a specific timeframe

Click to read full blog entry

Description of blog posting

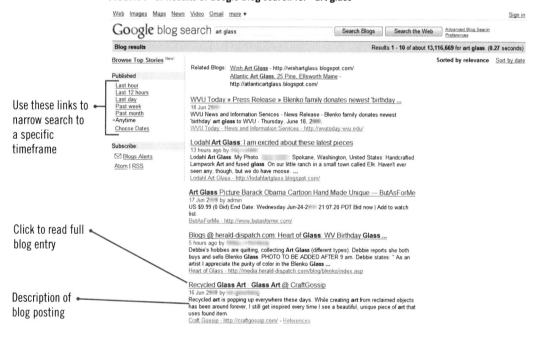

Blogs and public opinion

Blogs are an important way of gathering public opinion. Prior to the 2004 presidential election, CBS News reported a story questioning the legitimacy of President Bush's service in the Texas Air National Guard in the 1970s. The story was based on documents that many people believed to be forged. Bloggers responded to the story immediately—some even while the story was airing on CBS—to question the validity of the documents on which the story was based. In this case, the bloggers kept public pressure on the network to prove the validity of the documents, something that CBS News was ultimately unable to do. Although the bloggers were extremely active in reporting the story, mainstream media outlets, whose reporters are subject to ethical guidelines and therefore more careful to report only verified facts, eventually picked up and reported the stories being circulated in the blogs. Ultimately, CBS News recanted its allegations. It was widely speculated in the media that blogs led the charge for the withdrawal of the story.

Learning about Podcasting

A **podcast** is a subscription audio or video broadcast that is created and stored in a digital format on the Internet. **Podcasting** is the practice of posting an audio or video feed for subscribers to listen to or watch at their convenience on their computers or MP3 players. To subscribe to a podcast and check for and download new podcasts, you need to use **podcatching software**. Two popular versions of podcatching software are Juice and iTunes, both of which are free downloads from the Internet. After you install the podcatching software on your computer or portable media player, you can use the Internet to find podcasts so you can subscribe to them. Figure F-9 shows the Stanford University Educators Corner page, which contains podcasts from the Stanford Technology Ventures Program. Most Web browsers can play content from podcasts as long as the computer has a media player such as Windows Media Player or Apple's QuickTime installed on it. You want to explore the different categories of podcasts to see if you can find sources of information that might interest Mike.

STEPS

1. **Go to the Online Companion page for Unit F, then click one of the links to a Podcast Directory under Lesson 6**

   Figure F-10 shows the Podcast Directory page for LearnOutLoud.com, a site that promotes the use of audio and visual podcasts on hundreds of subjects that are geared toward personal and professional education and development.

2. **Click the links on the site you selected to explore the different categories of podcasts**

   As you review the podcasts, notice the dates of the broadcasts. You will probably notice that the broadcast dates are very recent, some occurring on the day of or within a few days of completing this step. Some sites provide archives of past podcasts that become a source for online research.

   > **TROUBLE**
   > If the file does not play on your computer, close the window that opened, and skip Step 3.

3. **If the site allows you to do so, click the link to play the file, then, if necessary, select a media player**

   If your computer has the necessary media player to play the podcast, it will start in a new window. Listen to the podcast for a few minutes to get a sense of the content it provides, and then close the window playing the podcast. Next, you will search the site for podcasts that might interest Mike.

   > **QUICK TIP**
   > Many instructors record their lectures and make them available as podcasts for students who miss class.

4. **Click in the search text box, type art gallery, then click the Search button**

   The search results in most podcast directories contain a list of each podcast that contains your search text, along with a brief description. The summary gives you a quick review of that podcast's contents. The summary might also contain a section with buttons for playback of the audio file, a timeline, links to the podcast's originating Web site, and the date when the podcast was created. You might see quite a few podcasts listed that have nothing to do with art galleries.

   > **TROUBLE**
   > If the podcast does not play on your computer, close the window that opened, and skip Step 5.

5. **If the site allows you to do so, click the link or button to play a file, then, if necessary, select a media player**

   If your computer has the necessary software, the podcast begins playing. Listen to or watch it for a few moments until you hear the search expression you specified, and then close the window playing the podcast.

FIGURE F-9: Podcasts page for the Stanford Technology Ventures Program

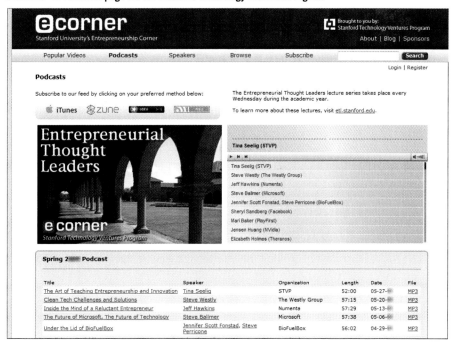

FIGURE F-10: Podcast Directory page for LearnOutLoud.com

Types of podcasts

Podcasting was originally intended to make it easy for people to create and broadcast their own radio shows, but podcasting has evolved to include many other types of broadcasting. Today there are podcasts on many different topics. Podcasts are used by the media to interview politicians and professors on specific subjects, by colleges and universities in distance learning classes, and by movie studios to promote new movie releases. You might find podcasts that contain material that you find controversial, objectionable, or offensive. In these cases, you can simply stop the playback or unsubscribe from the podcast. Because the software that is used to create a podcast is free and easy to download from the Internet, new podcasts are posted on the Internet every day. Some podcasts have different names that further identify the type of content they contain, such as a *Godcast* to denote a religious broadcast, a *vidcast* to identify a video feed, or a *learncast* to identify content that is educational in nature, such as a podcast from a university or other educational institution.

Using a Social Bookmarking Site

When you save a favorite or bookmark in your browser, the favorites and bookmarks are available only when you open your browser on your computer. A **social bookmark** is a favorite or a bookmark saved to a public Web site that you can access from any computer connected to the Internet. You can also share your social bookmarks with other users who visit the bookmarking site. To create social bookmarks, you need to register with a social bookmarking site. As with blogs, users can apply tags to categorize bookmarks. Note that inexperienced users might add tags to Web sites using keywords that are uncommon to other users, or they might misspell the keywords, making their resources difficult to find. ▄▄▄▄ Mike wants to create an account on a social bookmarking site so he can access his favorites and bookmarks when he travels and so he can link to it from his new blog for interested readers. He asks you to investigate a few of these sites.

STEPS

QUICK TIP
You can bookmark and tag Web content other than Web pages, including podcasts.

1. **Go to the Online Companion page for Unit F, then click the delicious link under Lesson 7**
   The home page of delicious opens. See Figure F-11.

2. **On the home page, click the Learn More link (or something similar)**
   A description of the delicious site appears.

3. **Read the page to learn more about social bookmarking, then click the browser's Back button**
   You return to the delicious home page.

TROUBLE
If you cannot find the Explore Tags tab, look for a Help link, then look in Help for information about tags.

4. **Click the Explore Tags tab near the top of the delicious home page, below the Learn More link**
   Bookmarks grouped by popular tags appear on the page. Most social bookmarking sites use a tag cloud to present the tags in a visual way, making more frequently used tags visible to the site's users. In a **tag cloud**, the most popular tags used by people appear in a larger font size, making it possible to see which keywords are being used as tags the most, and as a result, which categories contain the most bookmarks to other sites.

5. **Click the Learn more about tags link**
   A tag cloud showing popular tags appears in the window, along with more information about tags. See Figure F-12.

QUICK TIP
Notice that the URL for the page that opened includes a subfolder with the name of the tag you clicked.

6. **Examine the tags in the tag cloud and click one that you think might be of interest to Mike**
   Notice that each linked site shows the number of people who have tagged the link. Clicking the link to the number of users opens another Web page that shows their user IDs and any comments that they have made about the linked site. It is this community of users that makes a social bookmarking site a "social" activity. Clicking a link to a user opens that user's list of social bookmarks.

FIGURE F-11: Home page for the delicious social bookmarking site

Click to open a page describing the Web site

Click to see bookmarks grouped by tags

Reproduced with permission of Yahoo! Inc. ® 2009 by Yahoo! Inc. YAHOO! and the YAHOO! logo are trademarks of Yahoo! Inc.

FIGURE F-12: Tag cloud for the delicious social bookmarking site

More popular tag

Less popular tag

Reproduced with permission of Yahoo! Inc. ® 2009 by Yahoo! Inc. YAHOO! and the YAHOO! logo are trademarks of Yahoo! Inc.

Mashups

A software program uses an **Application Programming Interface** (**API**) as a means of communication with an operating system or some other program to handle specific tasks such as displaying content on the screen or printing. Programmers can write their own APIs or they can reference APIs that have already been developed for specific operating systems. Instead of keeping data to itself, a company such as eBay or Amazon.com writes an API and makes it available to *any* developer who wants to use it—usually for free. This sharing of data is called **Web services**. As more companies put more APIs on the Internet, developers used them to enhance their own sites by combining content from two or more sites. Amazon.com was the first to make APIs available to other developers, who in turn used them to link to and integrate their content with the Amazon.com Web site. For example, an API called GiftPrompter lets you track gifts that you want to give on a calendar with an interface to Amazon.com to ensure that you get the best selection and prices available on the gifts that you select. When Web content is combined in this way, the new Web site is called a mashup. In a **mashup**, a developer combines the services from two different sites using the APIs from one or both sites to create a completely new site that uses features from one or both sites. Because mashups rely on Web site data that already exists and APIs that are created by other companies, developers with the necessary programming background find mashups to be relatively easy to create and maintain—and profitable given the limited efforts needed to create them. For this reason, mashups are one of the fastest-growing segments of Web sites on the Internet. According to a 2007 study by ProgrammableWeb.com, more than 2,400 mashup Web sites exist and more than three mashups are created each day.

Protecting Your Identity and Reputation Online

Online group communication tools can be powerful ways of keeping in touch with friends and family, making business acquaintances, or making the world seem a little smaller by finding people in it who share your hobbies and interests. However, the very nature of these open networks can result in many problems for users who are not careful about how they use them. The information you post in a chat room, on a blog, or to a social network is public—and it is often archived even after you delete it. It is important to protect your reputation and control the information that you make available to the public. ▰▰▰▰ Since Mike has decided to make use of blogs, online social networks, and chat, he thinks he should consider some of the privacy issues connected to these skills. He asks you to investigate.

DETAILS

If you use group communication tools, consider the following:

- **Identity of Online Friends**

  Remember that a person on the other end of a posting can claim to be anyone. There is a strong likelihood that there are many people in the world who share your same name and maybe even some common life details. When you contact someone as a "friend" through the Internet, you might not be contacting the correct person—you might just be contacting someone with the same name. Likewise, you could be contacting someone who is pretending to be someone else. Use common sense and do not reveal personal details unless you are certain of the identity of the person with whom you are communicating.

- **Identity Theft**

  Because the nature of online social networks requires you to provide real information about yourself—your name, hometown, education, birth date, picture, and other personal information—and because this information you provide, by design, is public, you might be putting yourself at risk for identity theft and other privacy problems. Most sites include tools that let you hide parts of your profile from other users until you give them permission to access your complete profile. Be sure to read the site's privacy policy and change the default security settings as necessary to protect your privacy in a way that makes you feel comfortable and secure when using the site.

- **Impact on Image in the Workplace**

  Many employers check MySpace, Facebook, and other online social networks for information that you have posted about yourself. Applicants with exemplary resumes have been passed over for interviews when their social network page shows them acting in ways that are inappropriate for a corporate culture. Schools are especially careful to monitor online sites—most parents would demand action from school districts if they find that their child's teacher is participating in inappropriate online behavior, even if that behavior is on his or his "own time."

- **Personal Information Publicly Accessible**

  Another issue related to privacy is the use of your online profile by people in positions of authority. In one case, students at North Carolina State University took pictures of themselves in a dorm room while consuming alcohol. One of the students posted pictures of the party on his Facebook page. When a university official found the pictures, they became proof of the violation to the student housing contract and proof of the students' underage drinking. In some cases of similar situations on other college campuses, the students were suspended. At some schools, students regarded this lurking by university officials on online sites as an invasion of privacy. Other schools have updated their codes of conduct to specifically authorize the monitoring of student's online profiles as a legal way of taking action against a student when inappropriate or illegal behavior is proven with information students post on their profiles. You can set blogs and profiles as private, but that is not a guarantee that the information you post will remain private. Figure F-13 shows the page that describes the privacy options you have on the virtual community Web site Facebook.

FIGURE F-13: Page that describes the privacy options available to Facebook members

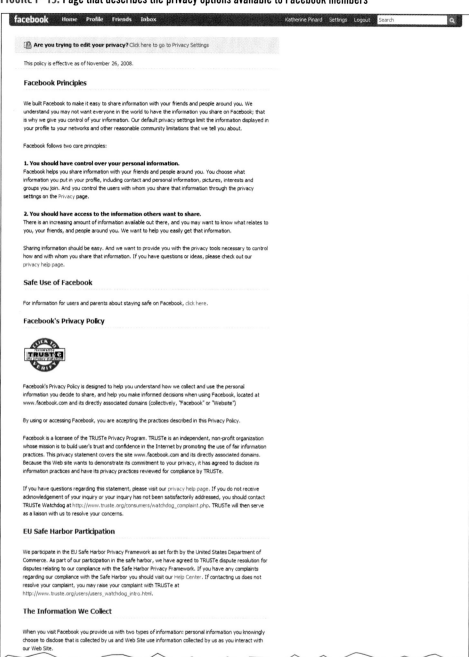

Cyberbullying

Using Internet communication such as email, instant messages, or online social networks to harass, threaten, or intimidate someone is called **cyberbullying**. Cyberbullying is usually associated with children but can involve adults as well. Most online social networks have codes of conduct that establish penalties for this type of behavior, which should be reported immediately. In addition, the site's Help section usually outlines the steps you can take to prevent cyberbullies from contacting you again.

Practice

▼ **CONCEPTS REVIEW**

For current SAM information including versions and content details, visit SAM Central (http://samcentral.course.com). If you have a SAM user profile, you may have access to hands-on instruction, practice, and assessment of the skills covered in this unit. Since we support various versions of SAM throughout the life of this text, you will want to check with your instructor for instructions and the correct URL/Web site to access those assignments.

Identify the communication tool shown in Figures F-14 through F-17.

FIGURE F-14

1.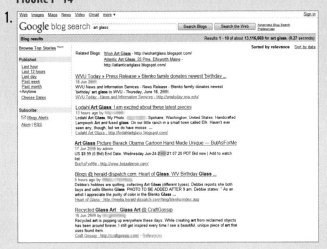

FIGURE F-15

2.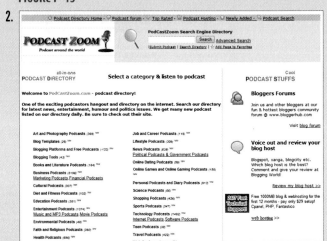

FIGURE F-16

3.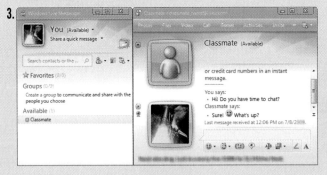

FIGURE F-17

4.

Reproduced with permission of Yahoo! Inc. ® 2009 by Yahoo! Inc. YAHOO! and the YAHOO! logo are trademarks of Yahoo! Inc.

Match each term with the statement that best describes it.

5. **Podcast**
6. **Social bookmark**
7. **List moderator**
8. **Post**
9. **Newsgroup**
10. **IRC**
11. **Virtual community**
12. **Mashup**

a. A place on the Internet where people can gather to discuss issues and share information

b. A favorite or a bookmark saved to a public Web site

c. A Web site created by combining the services from two different sites

d. A real-time communication program

e. Another term for Usenet groups

f. A subscription audio or video broadcast created and stored in a digital format on the Internet

g. A person assigned to oversee one or more mailing lists

h. Sending a message to a mailing list

Select the best answer from the list of choices.

13. **The practice of reading messages but not contributing to the discussion is called:**
    a. moderating.
    b. hanging.
    c. posting.
    d. lurking.

14. **What is the use of automated programs to send messages to multiple chat rooms simultaneously called?**
    a. Spamming
    b. Flaming
    c. Messaging
    d. Texting

15. **In-person meetings arranged via a Web site to allow people to discuss issues and plan strategies are called:**
    a. discussion groups.
    b. ICQs.
    c. meetups.
    d. social groups.

16. **Sending content to users who request it is:**
    a. posting.
    b. flaming.
    c. pushing.
    d. pulling.

17. **A public chat occurs in an area known as a(n):**
    a. instant message window.
    b. chat room.
    c. Internet Relay Chat.
    d. chat session.

18. **In order to read newsgroup messages, you need to use:**
    a. a newsreader.
    b. a news server.
    c. a distributed database.
    d. Usenet.

19. **Which of the following describes using Internet communication to harass, threaten, or intimidate someone?**
    a. Spamming
    b. Lurking
    c. Social networking
    d. Cyberbullying

▼ SKILLS REVIEW

1. Use instant messaging.

   a. Go to the Online Companion page for Unit F, then click the Google Talk link under Skills Review 1.

   b. Click the learn more link, then read about the Google Talk program.

   c. Return to the Unit F page on the Online Companion, then click the Trillian link under Skills Review 1.

   d. Click Learn about Trillian, then read about the features of Trillian.

2. Locate and read blogs.

   a. Return to the Unit F page on the Online Companion, then click one of the Blog Search Engine links under Skills Review 2.

   b. Search for blogs related to landscape design. Open at least three blogs in new tabs.

   c. If any of the blogs you found uses tags, click a tag to find other entries in that blog with that tag applied.

   d. Close all but one open tab.

3. Learn about podcasting.

   a. Return to the Unit F page on the Online Companion, then click one of the links to a podcast directory under Skills Review 3.

   b. Search for a podcast about how to create a podcast.

   c. Listen to a sample podcast from one of the podcasts you found, if possible.

   d. Close your media player, if necessary.

4. Use a social bookmarking site.

   a. Return to the Unit F page on the Online Companion, then click one of the links to a social bookmarking site under Skills Review 4.

   b. Examine the home pages for two of the social bookmarking sites listed. If a demo link is available, click it.

   c. Which social bookmarking site offers the most flexibility? Which is the easiest to use?

   d. Exit your browser.

▼ INDEPENDENT CHALLENGE 1

Big Island Coffee Company (BICC) grows and ships coffee beans to many of the Hawaiian Islands and parts of mainland North America. Manoa Kileahu, BICC's owner, wants to create a marketing campaign that will establish brand-name recognition for BICC. He wants to start by finding out what coffee lovers think is important, so he asks you to find Web sites devoted to coffee lovers. You will use a social bookmarking site so that you can find the best Web sites with this information.

   a. Start your Web browser, go to the Online Companion page for Unit F, then click a link to a social bookmarking site under Independent Challenge 1.

   b. Use the search feature on the site to search for Web sites that appeal to coffee-lovers. Open at least three of these Web sites in new tabs.

   c. If the social bookmarking site you chose provides tags for the displayed sites, click a tag to list sites associated with that tag.

Advanced Challenge Exercise

- Join the social bookmarking site you used in this Independent Challenge.
- Bookmark one of your favorite Web sites on the social bookmarking site.
- If the site you chose uses tags, add appropriate tags to your bookmark.

   d. Exit your browser.

▼ INDEPENDENT CHALLENGE 2

Laura Jensen is president of Rockin' Tees, a small manufacturer of printed t-shirts that specializes in creating designs using images of famous rock bands. Rockin' Tees must either purchase the rights to use band names and likenesses or agree to pay negotiated per-shirt royalties to the bands. Laura needs to estimate the demand for t-shirt designs before she negotiates with the bands' agents and agrees to payment terms. She wants you to check out chat rooms, virtual communities, and blogs related to rock music to find out which rock bands are mentioned frequently.

   a. Start your Web browser, go to the Online Companion page for Unit F, then explore one of the sites listed under Chat Rooms under Independent Challenge 2.

   b. Explore some of the chat rooms available on the site you selected. Would any of them be appropriate places to look for the information Laura wants? Which rock bands are mentioned most frequently in the chats?

   c. Return to the Unit F page on the Online Companion, then explore one of the virtual communities listed under Independent Challenge 2.

   d. Again, search for pages that discuss rock bands.

   e. Return to the Unit F page on the Online Companion, go to one of the blog search sites listed under Independent Challenge 2, and search for blogs about rock music.

   f. Send an email message to your instructor that lists three of the most frequently mentioned bands. Note whether one band is mentioned significantly more than other bands.

   g. Exit your browser and email program.

▼ INDEPENDENT CHALLENGE 3

Dan Rivetti is the director of Triangle Research, a small laboratory that tests metal parts and assemblies using physical and computer models. Usually, Dan knows enough about the general design of the parts and assemblies to be able to develop the testing procedures. Sometimes, however, he wants to conduct background research and contact experts in the field before designing his testing procedures. Dan heard that newsgroups and mailing lists offer such information and the opportunity to post inquiries, but he has also heard that some newsgroups are more reliable than others. Dan asks you to help him evaluate the quality of some newsgroups.

a. Start your Web browser, go to the Online Companion page for Unit F, then click the Google Groups link under Independent Challenge 3.

b. Type sci. in the Search text box, then click Search Groups.

c. Examine and follow some of the links on the results page. Look for two newsgroups in a similar topic area, one moderated and one unmoderated.

d. Examine a sample of messages from each type of newsgroup devoted to the same topic, and decide which group would best serve Dan's needs.

e. Return to the Unit F page on the Online Companion, then click one of the links to a list of mailing lists under Independent Challenge 3. Examine the categories of lists available, and browse or search for a list that might help Dan.

f. Exit your browser.

▼ REAL LIFE INDEPENDENT CHALLENGE

To discuss topics or ideas with people who share an interest in the same topics, consider joining a mailing list, either email or Web-site based.

    a. Start your Web browser, go to the Online Companion page for Unit F, then click one of the links to a mailing list.

    b. Browse through the categories or search for a list that discusses a topic in which you are interested.

    c. Open a new tab, go to the Online Companion page for Unit F, then click one of the links to an online discussion group Web site.

    d. Browse through the categories or search for a list that discusses a topic in which you are interested.

Advanced Challenge Exercise

    ■ Choose a mailing list or a discussion group that interests you. If it is a mailing list, subscribe to the list. If it is an online discussion group, join the group (you might need to register with the site first).

    ■ With many mailing lists and some discussion group Web sites, you need to confirm your registration. Check your email and confirm your registration if you need to.

    ■ Read the messages on the list or in the group for a few days. After you have read several messages, unsubscribe from the list, if you want. For most online discussion groups, it is not necessary to do anything to quit the group.

    e. Exit your browser and email program if necessary.

▼ VISUAL WORKSHOP

Go to the Online Companion page for Unit F, then click the Yahoo Groups link under Visual Workshop. Either conduct a search on this Web site to display a list of groups about origami, or click through the categories to find groups about origami, similar to the list shown in Figure F-18.

FIGURE F-18

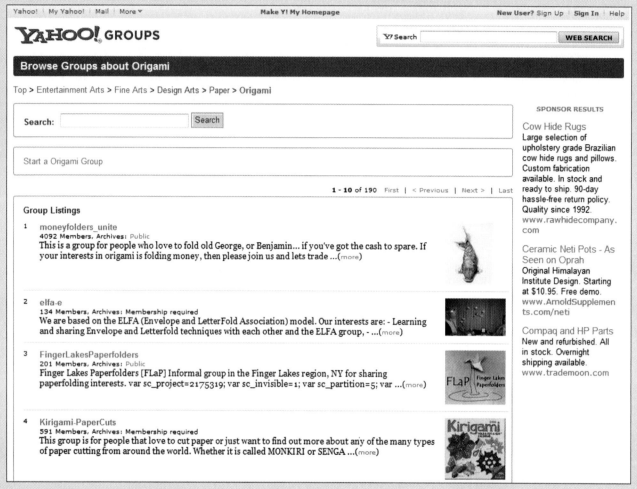

Reproduced with permission of Yahoo! Inc. ® 2009 by Yahoo! Inc. YAHOO! and the YAHOO! logo are trademarks of Yahoo! Inc.

Downloading Programs and Sharing Files

You sometimes need to transfer files between your computer and other computers on the Internet. To **download** a file means to receive the file on your computer from another computer. To **upload** a file means to send it from your computer to another computer. After the transfer is complete, you must know how to install and use the program files that you downloaded. To speed up downloading and uploading, you can compress files to make them smaller.  DigiComm produces and installs digital wireless communications products and technologies worldwide. Nancy Moore, the director of international sales and installations, has asked you, the computer support specialist, to equip staff members with an Internet file transfer program and a program that compresses files.

OBJECTIVES

Investigate freely downloadable
   programs
Download programs and files
Use a download site
Download a program using
   Internet Explorer
Download a program using Firefox
Install a downloaded program
Establish an FTP session
Use FTP to download a file
Open a compressed file
Compress files

Investigating Freely Downloadable Programs

Internet users are often pleasantly surprised to discover that many programs are available for download at no cost. A large selection of programs is available online, from antivirus software to interactive games. ▓▓▓ Before you start downloading programs and files over the Internet, you investigate the types of files and programs that are available.

DETAILS

Freely downloadable software falls into the categories listed below:

- **Freeware**

    Software that is available fully functional, at no cost to users, and with no restrictions is called **freeware**. Freeware is sometimes described as open source software, which means that other program developers can look at and change the program code. Figure G-1 shows FreewareFiles.com, a Web site that allows Internet users to download freeware.

- **Shareware**

    Shareware is similar to freeware, but it is usually only available for free during a short evaluation period. After that evaluation period expires—usually after a specified number of days or a specific number of uses—shareware stops functioning. Shareware users are expected to stop using the shareware after the specified initial trial period and uninstall it from their computers. Otherwise, anyone who likes the program and wants to continue using it is requested to **license** it, which means to pay a fee for its use. Shareware is usually more reliable than freeware because the shareware developer is sometimes willing to accept responsibility for the program's operation. Usually, shareware developers have an established way for users to report any bugs and receive free or low-cost software upgrades and patches.

- **Evaluation Software**

    Evaluation software, sometimes called **limited edition** (**LE**) **software**, is a free, but restricted version of software. Sometimes, the restriction is that you can use the evaluation software for a limited number of days. Other times, the evaluation software provides most of the functionality of the full version of the program with one or more useful features of the full version omitted. If you like the software, you can purchase the full version of the program.

- **Licensed (or Full) Version Software**

    Purchasing a license involves paying a fee to get a code to unlock the software and render it fully functional. Usually this means that you click a button or link somewhere in the program interface that says "Buy Now" or "Register Now." When you click this button or link, you are connected to the programmer's Web site and you are asked to pay a fee to license the software. Figure G-2 shows the screen that appears when you try to start WS_FTP Home, a shareware program that allows you to use the FTP protocol to download and upload files, after the 30-day evaluation period. After you pay the fee, you usually receive the license in the form of a registration or serial number that you are then requested to enter the next time you start the program. Once you type in the license code, the software should work with no restrictions.

FIGURE G-1: FreewareFiles.com Web site

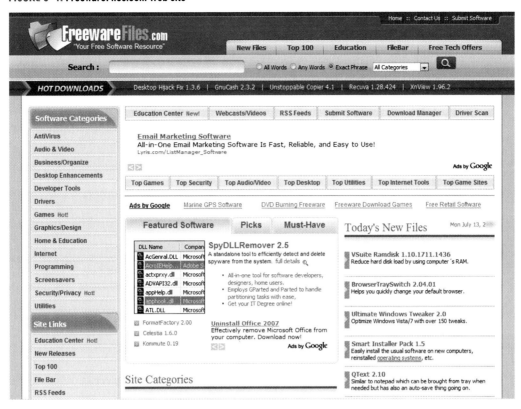

FIGURE G-2: Screen that appears in WS_FTP Home at the end of the evaluation period

Date evaluation period began (the first day you used the program) appears here

Date evaluation period ended appears here

Click to purchase the licensed version of the software

Understanding the risks of freeware

Freeware users must accept the implicit or explicit warning that the software might contain errors, called **bugs**, which could cause the program to halt, malfunction, or even damage the user's computer. The main risk associated with using freeware is that its limited testing sometimes results in a program that contains multiple bugs, and the software's developer is rarely liable for any damage that the freeware program might cause. On the other hand, a lot of good-quality commercial software started as freeware. Before you use freeware, you should use a Web search engine to locate reviews before you download, install, virus check, and use any freeware program to see what kinds of successes and problems its users have reported.

Internet

Downloading Programs and Files

You can download shareware and freeware from Web sites on which they are stored. To download programs, you can use HTTP or FTP. You can also transfer files over the Internet with **peer-to-peer** (**PTP**) file sharing, which is the process of transferring files directly from one computer to another. ▰▰▰ Before you download any programs for DigiComm, you investigate methods of downloading programs and sharing files.

DETAILS

Some of the methods for downloading programs and sharing files are:

- **Downloading Programs Using HTTP**

  Many Web sites are devoted to making programs available for downloading. You can use HTTP and your browser to download a program directly from the Web site of the company or programmer that developed the program or from a download site. A **download site** is a Web site that contains freeware and shareware programs organized in categories.

- **Downloading Programs Using FTP**

  You can also use FTP to download software from an **FTP server**, which is a server that uses FTP to transfer files rather than HTTP. An FTP server is also called an **FTP site**, **remote server**, or **remote site**; when you use FTP to download programs, your computer is called the **local computer** or the **local site**. An **FTP server program** runs on an FTP server, allows file transfer to and from the server by FTP, and manages FTP access to the server's files. You can use FTP with your browser by typing *ftp://* and then the URL for the FTP site, or you can use an **FTP client program**, which is a program that resides on your computer and allows you to transfer files between your computer and another computer connected to it using the rules for FTP.

- **Sharing Files Using PTP File Sharing**

  When you transfer files using PTP file sharing, you transfer files directly from one computer to another without going through a Web site, Web server, or FTP server. With PTP, users install a PTP program and then make files in certain folders on their computers available to other users of the PTP program. This is similar to the way computers on a LAN or WAN are configured to allow users to share files stored in certain folders.

- **Using Compressed Files**

  You use a **file compression program** to reduce a file to a fraction of its original size, creating a **compressed file** (sometimes called an **archived file**). The smaller file size of compressed files allows you to transfer files over a network more quickly than full-size files. Compressed files can save you significant time downloading, especially over an Internet connection with a slow modem. In order to access the compressed files, you need to use a file compression program to decompress the files.

- **Using Online Storage Providers**

  Another way to share files is to use a company that provides storage space on its servers. Some companies allow anyone to have access to these stored files, and others provide secure, password-protected access to these files. Users access online storage space using a program or other interface made available by the provider, an FTP client program, or a Web browser. Figure G-3 shows plans available on Live Mesh, which provides a variety of storage options. Some companies not only provide storage but allow users to create and edit documents stored on the server. In addition to using this service as a way to share files, many individuals use these online storage services to store backup files, sound files, personal Web sites, pictures, and other data. For example, to share photos online, Internet users can sign up for an account with companies such as Snapfish, Kodak Gallery, Flickr, and Shutterfly, which allow users to create online photo albums. Users upload digital photos to the company's Web server, then give other people a password so that they can see the uploaded photos. Figure G-4 shows the first page of a user's shared pictures on the Shutterfly Web site.

FIGURE G-3: Live Mesh home page

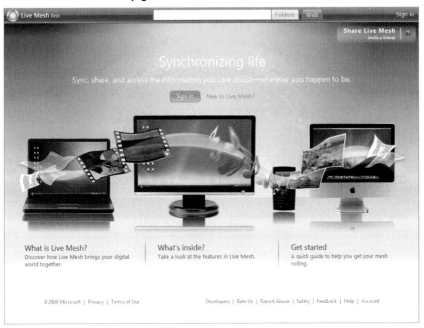

FIGURE G-4: Shared pictures on Shutterfly

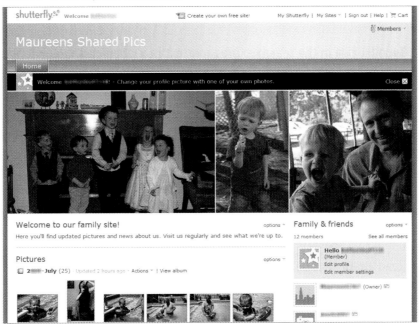

Downloading music files

Internet users can also download digital music from Web sites. To download music files, Internet users can register with a Web site such as Napster, iTunes, and Rhapsody; these sites have obtained the legal right to distribute the musical works they offer for sale. Some of these sites allow users to purchase and download songs that they can then store on a CD or a portable music player. Other sites charge a monthly subscription fee so that users can listen to an unlimited number of songs stored on the company's Web server via a streaming transmission. In a **streaming transmission**, the Web server sends the first part of the file to the Web browser, which begins playing the file; and while the browser is playing the first part of the file, the server is sending the next segment of the file. This file is not stored permanently on the subscriber's computer.

Using a Download Site

You can use your Web browser to download a program from the Web. You can download programs from a download site or you can often download a program directly from the Web site of the company or programmer that developed the program. To download and install some of the programs that DigiComm staff members need, you need an FTP client program. You decide to explore a download site, and then search for a free FTP client program.

STEPS

1. **Go to the Online Companion page for Unit G, then click one of the links to a download site**

   The download site that you chose opens. You can select a category in which to search, such as Games or Internet. Each category contains subcategories that allow you to narrow your search.

2. **If necessary, scroll down, click a category link, then scroll down again to view the available subcategories**

   Figure G-5 shows the subcategories in the Games category on Tucows.

3. **Click subcategory links to see the list of programs in those subcategories**

   The list of programs in the Games/Card games/Solitaire subcategory on the Tucows site is shown in Figure G-6. The results page includes a link from which you can download each program. It also might show the date when each file was uploaded, the number of times each file has been downloaded, or some other indication of the file's popularity, the size of the downloadable file, and the operating systems with which the program will work. You can usually click a program link to read a description of the program and to see reviews of the program. You want to download a free FTP program called FileZilla. You can type a search expression in most download sites.

4. **Type filezilla in the search expression text box, then click Go or something similar to start the search**

   A link to FileZilla is listed in the search results page.

TROUBLE

If a link to FileZilla does not appear in the search results, try a different download site.

5. **Click the FileZilla link, then, if there is one, click the More info link**

   The download page for FileZilla opens. Note that it is a very popular program. Many download sites include user ratings and reviews that you can read to help determine if you want to download the particular program. Figure G-7 shows the information page for FileZilla Client on FileHippo.com.

TROUBLE

If the link to the SourceForget.net site opens another page on the download site, look for a link to the publisher's site on that page.

6. **Click the SourceForge.net or FileZilla link near a "Publisher" or "Source" heading**

   The FileZilla page on SourceForge.net opens. The page might open in the same tab, a new tab, or in a new browser window. You can read more about a program at the publisher's Web site. You can also check to be sure that the version of the program on the download site is up-to-date.

7. **Read about the FileZilla program, then click the Close button in the tab or browser window title bar to close the window with the SourceForge.net page in it or click the Back button to return to the download site**

   The version of FileZilla on the SourceForge.net site might be a later version than the one on the download site. Usually, it is a good idea to download and use the latest version. However, many publisher's Web sites require you to enter personal information before you can download the program, so for the purposes of this lesson, you will download the version available on the download site. Some download sites include user reviews.

8. **Scroll down to see if there are any user reviews or ratings, click the See all user reviews and ratings link if one appears on the page, then read the user reviews**

FIGURE G-5: Subcategories in Games category on Tucows

Current Category

Subcategories

Search text box

Program rating

FIGURE G-6: Solitaire subcategory in Card games subcategory on Tucows

Solitaire subcategory

Solitaire games

FIGURE G-7: Download page for FileZilla on FileHippo.com

Link to publisher

File size

Version number on your screen might differ

Link to download file

Description of license

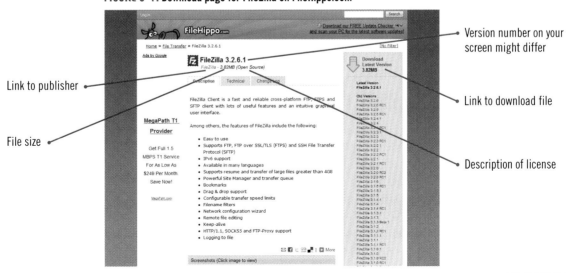

Downloading a Program Using Internet Explorer

After evaluating a program to determine if it meets your needs and is a reliable program, you can download the program. After you specify the program that you want to download, whether from a download site or a publisher's Web site, you will be prompted to save the program on your computer. It is a good idea to designate one folder on your computer for storing downloaded files so that you can easily find them later. When the download is complete, you can access the program file in Windows Explorer. You decide to download the FileZilla program to install on DigiComm computers.

STEPS

(STOP) *If you are using Firefox, skip to the next lesson.*

1. **If necessary, locate the download page for FileZilla on the download site you chose**

TROUBLE
If the name of the file ends in .zip, click Cancel and select another download site from the Online Companion.

2. **Click the Download link or something similar to start downloading the file**

Another page appears, telling you that the download should start automatically. Most sites also provide a link on this page to click if the download does not start. If the download does not start, you will probably see the yellow Information bar at the top of the browser window. See the Clues in the yellow box on this page for more information about the Information bar. Figure G-8 shows the FileZilla download page with the Information bar at the top of the window. Most download sites also have a link on the download page that you can click to download the software you requested if your browser blocks the download.

TROUBLE
If the File Download – Security Warning dialog box does not appear, the security level for Internet Explorer was changed on your machine. Skip Step 4.

3. **Click the If download does not start click here link or something similar**

The File Download - Security Warning dialog box appears, as shown in Figure G-9. Note that the name of the file must end in .exe in order to perform the steps in the next lesson. If you click Run, the program you selected installs while you are connected to the Web site and the installation program is not saved to your computer. You'll save the complete file to your computer so that you can run the installation program later.

4. **Click Save in the File Download – Security Warning dialog box**

The Save As dialog box opens, enabling you to specify the location where the file is saved.

5. **Navigate to the drive and folder where you store your Data Files, then click Save**

A dialog box that shows the progress of the download appears as the file downloads to your computer. See Figure G-10. When it has finished downloading, the dialog box changes to the Download Complete dialog box.

TROUBLE
If the dialog box already closed, a previous user selected the Close this dialog box when download completes check box. Skip Step 6.

6. **Click Close**

The dialog box closes and you are returned to the browser window.

7. **Exit your browser**

Working with the Information bar

The Information bar is a security feature in Internet Explorer. It appears when you try to download content from the Internet or when you click a link that tells your computer to start downloading content. It is turned on by default to protect your computer in case a malicious Web site tries to download content without your permission. You can override the security setting and download the content if you choose. To do this, click the Information bar, and then on the menu that appears, click Download File. The Information bar disappears and the File Download dialog box appears, from which you can save or run the file. The Information bar also appears if you have the Pop-up Blocker enabled and a Web site attempts to open a pop-up, if you try to display a Web page for which the security information does not match the security information stored on the Web site about that page, or if a Web page tries to download a potentially unsafe ActiveX control. (An ActiveX control is a small program written by a Web site designer that is designed to enhance the user's experience.)

FIGURE G-8: Download page on FileHippo.com

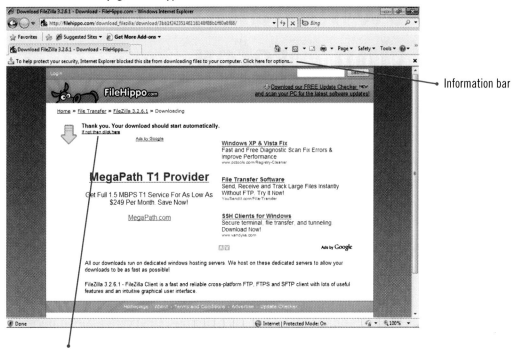

Information bar

Click this link to locate a download location and
start the download if it does not start automatically

FIGURE G-9: File Download - Security Warning dialog box

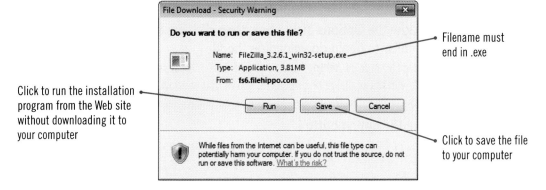

Filename must
end in .exe

Click to run the installation
program from the Web site
without downloading it to
your computer

Click to save the file
to your computer

FIGURE G-10: Dialog box showing progress of download

Select this option to
have the dialog box
close automatically
when download is
complete

Changes to Close
when the download
is complete

Internet

Downloading a Program Using Firefox

After evaluating a program to determine if it meets your needs and is a reliable program, you can download the program. After you specify the program that you want to download, whether from a download site or a publisher's Web site, you will be prompted to save the program on your computer. In Firefox, the **Download Manager** that opens when you download a file keeps track of your downloads. This is helpful if you need to find a list of recently downloaded files. Once the download is complete, you can access the program file in Windows Explorer. You decide to download the FileZilla program to install on DigiComm computers.

STEPS

If you are using Internet Explorer, skip to the next lesson.

1. **If necessary, locate the download page for FileZilla on the download site you chose**

2. **Click Tools on the menu bar, click Options, then click Main, if necessary**
   The Main page in the Options dialog box opens.

3. **If necessary, click the Show the Downloads window when downloading a file check box to insert a check mark, click the Close it when all downloads are finished check box to remove the check mark, then click the Always ask me where to save files option button**
   Now the Downloads window will open when your download starts and stay open until you close it, and you will be prompted to specify a location in which to save your downloaded files. Compare your screen to Figure G-11.

TROUBLE
If no dialog box opens after 15 seconds or so, click the If download does not start click here link or something similar to start the download.

4. **Click OK to close the Options dialog box, then click the Download Now link or something similar to begin downloading the file**
   The Download page appears, telling you to click a link if your download does not start. The Opening FileZilla_3.2.6.1_win32.exe dialog box opens on top of that window. Note that the numbers after "FileZilla" in the dialog box name indicate the version number, and might differ on your machine.

5. **Click the Save File option button**
   The Enter name of file to save to dialog box opens, enabling you to specify the location where the file is saved.

6. **Navigate to the drive and folder where you store your Data Files, then click Save**
   The Downloads window appears and shows the progress of the download as the file downloads to your computer. See Figure G-12. When it has finished downloading, the progress bar disappears and the filename is highlighted in the Downloads window. You can leave the file listing in the Downloads window, or you can remove it.

QUICK TIP
If there is more than one file listed in the Downloads window and you want to remove them all from the list, click Clear List in the Downloads window.

7. **Right-click FileZilla in the Downloads window, then click Remove From List on the shortcut menu**
   The file you downloaded is still on your computer, but it is removed from the list in the Downloads window.

8. **Click the Close button in the Downloads window title bar**
   The dialog box closes and you are returned to the browser window.

9. **Exit your browser**

FIGURE G-11: Main page in the Options dialog box

Click to see Main page in this dialog box

Select to set a default folder for downloads

Select to be prompted to specify a location for downloaded files

Options to configure downloads

FIGURE G-12: Downloads window showing progress of download

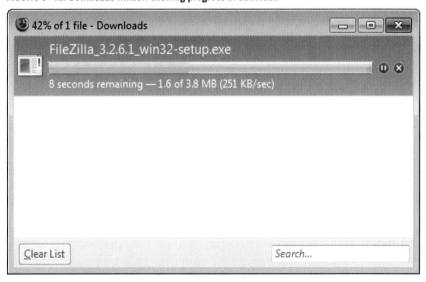

Designating a folder for downloaded programs

It is a good idea to create or designate a folder on your computer to where you download all files from the Internet, so that you can easily find them when you need to install them. In Firefox, you can set the Downloads options so that files are automatically saved to a specific folder. To do this, click Tools on the menu bar, click Options, and then click Main. In the Downloads section, click the Save files to option button, and then click Browse to open the Browse For Folder dialog box. In this dialog box, you can click the right-pointing triangle next to a folder to see subfolders in that folder, and then you can click the folder to which you want to download all of your program files.

UNIT
G
Internet

Installing a Downloaded Program

After you download a program from the Internet, you must install the program on your computer to use it. Usually, you can double-click a program file to install the program. The program file often facilitates installation by including an **installation wizard**, which is a series of dialog boxes that help you complete the installation process step-by-step. When you install a program, you must agree to the program's license agreement before the program will install. The **license agreement** is a contract between the publisher of the software and the person who is installing the software; it usually states that the software cannot be copied and resold, and it details restrictions for the software's use. ▓▓▓▓▓ You checked with Savan Chen, manager of technical services at DigiComm, to verify that it is okay to install FileZilla on the computers in your office. You install the program on your computer.

STEPS

 Before completing the steps in this lesson, ask your instructor if you may install the FileZilla program.

1. **Exit any programs that are running**
   You should always exit all programs before installing a new program.

> **TROUBLE**
> In Windows Vista, the Documents window opens.

2. **Click the Start button on the taskbar, then click Documents**
   The Documents Library window opens.

> **TROUBLE**
> If your computer is not set to display filename extensions, you will not see ".exe" at the end of the filename in the window.

3. **Navigate to the drive and folder where you store your Data Files, then double-click the file that starts with FileZilla and ends with .exe**
   The .exe file extension is an abbreviation for "executable," which means that the file is a program that you can run. The Open File - Security Warning dialog box might open.

4. **If the Open File - Security Warning dialog box opens, click Run**
   The User Account Control dialog box opens, asking if you want to allow a program to make changes to your computer.

5. **Click Yes, Allow, or Continue**
   The License Agreement appears, as shown in Figure G-13.

6. **Read the License Agreement, then click I Agree**
   The next dialog box asks if you want to make the software available to everyone who uses the computer or just the user who is currently logged in.

7. **Click the option button next to the option you want, click Next, click Next in the next dialog box to accept the default components, then click Next again to accept the default install location**
   When you click Install, the program will be installed on the computer using the choices you made in the previous dialog boxes with the default program name added to the Start menu.

8. **Click Install to complete the installation**
   After a moment, the final dialog box in the installation wizard appears. See Figure G-14.

9. **Click the Start FileZilla now check box to clear it, then click Finish**
   The dialog box closes.

Downloading Programs and Sharing Files

FIGURE G-13: FileZilla License Agreement

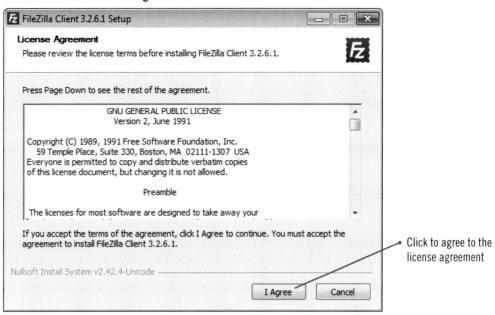

Click to agree to the license agreement

FIGURE G-14: Final dialog box in the FileZilla installation wizard

Click to deselect so that FileZilla does not start automatically when the installation is finished

Click to complete the installation

Checking files for viruses

After downloading anything from the Internet—even files from reputable sources—your first priority is to scan the file for viruses. Although you can configure antivirus software to regularly scan the files on your hard disk to find infected files, the most popular antivirus programs do not scan files while you are downloading them. However, you can set up antivirus software to scan programs and documents before you open them. To ensure the safety of your computer when you download files, you should use a combination of these methods. You can download many high-quality antivirus programs that are free for personal use. Alternatively, you can download an antivirus program that has a cost associated with it, and install and use it for a limited time to determine its appropriateness for your own security needs.

Internet

Establishing an FTP Session

To use an FTP client to download programs and files from another computer connected to the Internet, you need to create and save an **FTP session profile**, which is a collection of information about the FTP server. The FTP session profile includes the URL of the server you want to access as well as a user name and password that the client will use to log in to the FTP server. An **FTP session** is the interaction between your computer and the remote computer after you connect to the FTP server. Publicly accessible FTP servers allow you to use **anonymous FTP** to log in and use FTP without having a personal account. When you use anonymous FTP to connect to a publicly accessible FTP site, you are restricted to particular files and directories on the public server. The method of logging in to a computer on which you have an account (with a user name and password) and using that account to send and receive files is called **named FTP** or **full-privilege FTP**. Nancy has asked you to investigate file compression programs for use at DigiComm. A popular file compression program is WinZip. To download WinZip using FileZilla, you first need to create an FTP session profile for the FTP server where the WinZip program is stored.

STEPS

🛑 *These steps were written for FileZilla version 3.2.6.1. If you are using a different version, and these steps do not work with that version, see your instructor.*

> **TROUBLE**
> If you do not see FileZilla on the All Programs menu, make sure that you downloaded and installed the FileZilla program correctly. Ask your instructor or system administrator for help, if necessary.

1. **Click the** Start button, **point to** All Programs, **click** FileZilla FTP Client, **click** FileZilla, **then, if necessary, click** OK **in the Welcome dialog box**

   The FileZilla program starts and the main program window opens.

2. **Click the** Maximize button, **if necessary**

   See Figure G-15. The pane on the left shows the contents of the current folder on the local computer (the computer you are working on). The pane on the right will show the contents of the current folder on the remote computer (the computer at the FTP site). Now you will add a site to the site list in FileZilla.

3. **Click** File **on the menu bar, then click** Site Manager

   The Site Manager dialog box opens.

4. **Click** New Site **in the Site Manager dialog box**

   A new, untitled site is added to the site list on the left with the temporary name "New site" selected, ready to be replaced.

5. **Type** WinZip, **then press** [Enter]

6. **Click in the** Host text box, **then type** ftp.winzip.com

   Many FTP sites on the Internet use the prefix "ftp" followed by the domain name. For example, the FTP site for Mozilla is ftp.mozilla.org.

7. **If necessary, click the** Logontype list arrow, **then click** Anonymous

   When you select the Anonymous option, you do not need to type any information in the User or Password text boxes. See Figure G-16.

> **TROUBLE**
> If you receive an "access denied" message, the WinZip FTP site is busy. You can try again later.

8. **Click** Connect

   The Site Manager dialog box closes and FileZilla attempts to connect to the WinZip FTP site. The Windows Security Alert dialog box might open telling you that the Windows Firewall has blocked the program from accepting incoming network connections. In order to download the WinZip program from the FTP site, you need to unblock this program.

9. **If the Windows Security Alert dialog box opens, click** Unblock, **then click** Continue **in the User Account Control dialog box**

   FileZilla completes the connection to the WinZip ftp site.

FIGURE G-15: FileZilla program window

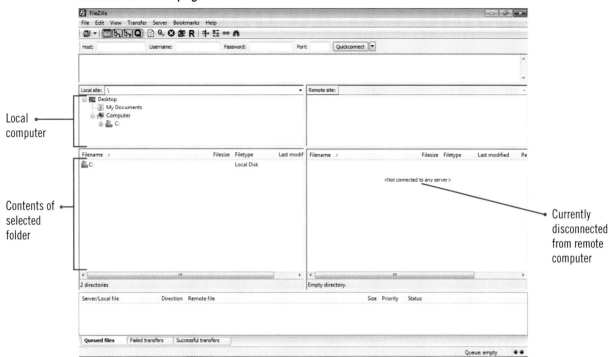

Local computer

Contents of selected folder

Currently disconnected from remote computer

FIGURE G-16: Site Manager dialog box in FileZilla

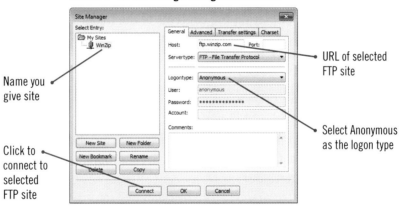

Name you give site

Click to connect to selected FTP site

URL of selected FTP site

Select Anonymous as the logon type

Using your browser to navigate an FTP site

You can use a browser to navigate an FTP site and to upload and download files to and from the site. For example, you can connect to the WinZip FTP site using your browser by typing **ftp.winzip.com** in the Address or Location bar. After you access the site, the URL in the Address or Location bar changes to ftp://ftp.winzip.com. This is because the protocol that FTP sites use is FTP instead of HTTP. If you have full-privilege access to an FTP site and have a user name and password, you can log in by typing the protocol, **ftp://**, followed by your user name, a colon, your password followed by the @ symbol, and then the URL of the FTP site. For example, if you had full-privilege access to the WinZip site with UserName and Password,

you would type **ftp://UserName:Password@ftp.winzip.com** in the Address or Location bar. When you access an FTP site using a browser, you will see the organization of the folders (also called directories) and files on the FTP site, similar to the organization of folders and files on a computer's hard drive. Each folder and file is formatted similar to a link. Click a folder link to open the folder and display its contents. Click a file link to open the file in the browser window, start the program associated with the file, and open the file in a program window, or begin downloading the file to your computer. To move up (or back) one folder, you click the Up to higher level directory link.

Internet

Using FTP to Download a File

After you create a session profile and connect to an FTP site, you can download available files from the FTP server. You can use the WinZip FTP site you logged in to in the previous lesson to download the WinZip file compression program. Now that you are connected to the WinZip FTP site, you use your FTP client to download the WinZip program.

STEPS

🛑 *Before completing the steps in this lesson, ask your instructor if you may complete Steps 4–10 and install the WinZip program.*

1. **Near the top of the left pane, click the plus sign next to the drive and folder where you store your Data Files or double-click the folder name in the middle pane on the left**

TROUBLE

If you do not see the filename winzip120. exe listed, look for any file that starts with "winzip" and has the filename extension "exe." If you cannot see the filename extensions, drag the column divider to the right of Filename to widen the Filename column. The number after "winzip" might differ as new versions of the software become available.

2. **In the right pane, click winzip120.exe, then drag the winzip120.exe file from the right pane to the left pane showing the contents of the folder containing your Data Files**
   Figure G-17 shows the winzip120.exe file being dragged from the right pane to the left pane. Once you release the mouse button, FileZilla begins to download the selected file (winzip120.exe) from the FTP server shown in the right pane to the selected folder on your computer shown in the left pane. A Progress bar appears at the bottom of the window, as shown in Figure G-18. When the Progress bar disappears, the file transfer is complete and the winzip120.exe program is saved on your computer.

3. **After the file has finished downloading, click the Close button in the FileZilla title bar**
   You disconnect from the WinZip FTP site and the FileZilla program closes. You should see the folder containing your Data Files open in a window on your desktop.

4. **In the window displaying the contents of the folder containing your Data Files, double-click winzip120.exe, then, if the Open File - Security Warning dialog box opens, click Run**
   The WinZip 12.0 Setup dialog box opens.

5. **Click Setup**
   Other programs are sometimes included with the WinZip program. Dialog boxes offering to install additional programs or components might appear.

QUICK TIP

If you do not want to install the Google Toolbar for Internet Explorer and Google Desktop or any other program offered, click the check boxes next to the program names to deselect them or click the option button next to the option that says Do not install the Google Toolbar.

6. **If any dialog boxes appear asking if you want to install additional programs or components, decide if you want to install them, click the appropriate check boxes or option buttons, then click Continue as needed**
   The first screen in the WinZip 12.0 Installation Wizard appears. See Figure G-19.

7. **Click Next to move to the License Agreement screen, read the license agreement, click the I accept the license agreement option button, then click Next three times to accept the license agreement and the default destination folder and configuration**
   The Default Compression Method dialog box appears. In WinZip 12.0, the compression method was improved so that compressed files are even smaller; however, this new compression is not compatible with previous versions of WinZip, so you can choose to use the new compression or the older one.

8. **Click the Optimize for best compression option button, click Next two times, then click Yes in the User Account Control dialog box that appears**
   Next you can choose to use WinZip in the classic mode or with a wizard.

9. **Click the Start with WinZip Classic option button, if necessary, click Next three times, click the Launch WinZip 12.0 check box to deselect it, then click Finish**
   The dialog box closes and the program is installed. Your browser starts and displays the Thank you for installing WinZip page on the WinZip Web site.

10. **Click the Close button in the browser window title bar**

FIGURE G-17: Dragging the WinZip program from the right pane to the left pane

Current path on local computer (yours might differ)

Contents of current folder on local computer

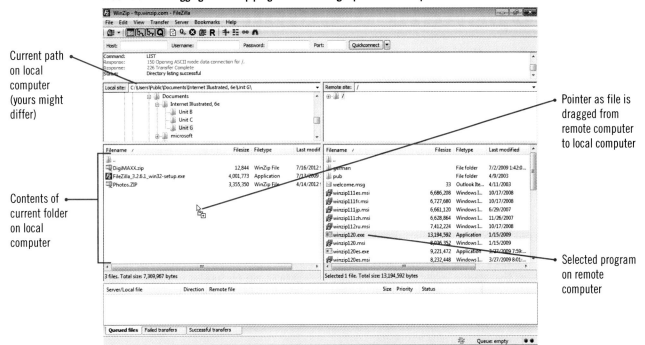

Pointer as file is dragged from remote computer to local computer

Selected program on remote computer

FIGURE G-18: Downloading a file using FileZilla

Name of file being downloaded

Progress bar

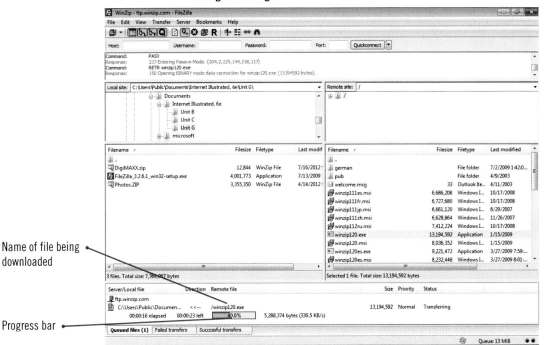

FIGURE G-19: First screen in the WinZip 12.0 Installation Wizard

Click to move to the next screen in the Installation Wizard

Opening a Compressed File

After you download a compressed file, you must restore the file to its original size before you can open or run it. The process of restoring a compressed file to its original form is called **file decompression**, **file extraction**, or **file expansion**. To open a compressed file, you need a file compression program, such as WinZip. ▰▰▰▰▰ Nancy wrote a memo for the DigiComm sales staff instructing them to learn more about DigiComm's new wireless router, DigiMAXX. She used WinZip to compress her memo and a sales information sheet into one file. She asked you to open the compressed file and look over the information.

STEPS

1. **In the open Windows Explorer window, navigate to the drive and folder where you store your Data Files, if necessary, then double-click** DigiMAXX.zip

   The WinZip dialog box opens, as shown in Figure G-20.

2. **Click** Use Evaluation Version

   The .zip file opens and the files in the DigiMAXX.zip file are listed in the WinZip (Evaluation Version) window, as shown in Figure G-21.

> **QUICK TIP**
> To extract a specific file in a zip file, click the file that you want to extract, then click the Extract button on the toolbar.

3. **Click the** Extract button **on the toolbar**

   The Extract dialog box opens.

4. **In the list of drives and folders, click the** plus signs **next to the appropriate drive and folders to navigate to the drive and folder where you store your Data Files**

   Your screen should look similar to Figure G-22.

5. **Click** Extract

   The two files are extracted to your computer. You could open the documents in any word processor that reads .rtf files (rich text files). A new window might open on your desktop.

6. **If a new window opens on your desktop, click the** Close button **in the title bar to close it**

FIGURE G-20: WinZip opening dialog box for the Evaluation Version

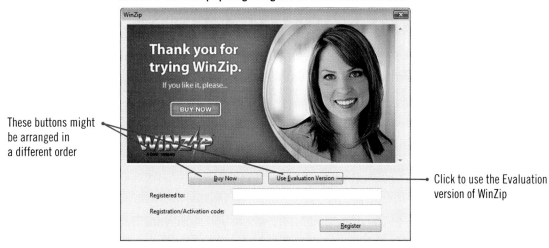

These buttons might be arranged in a different order

Click to use the Evaluation version of WinZip

FIGURE G-21: Contents of DigiMAXX.zip

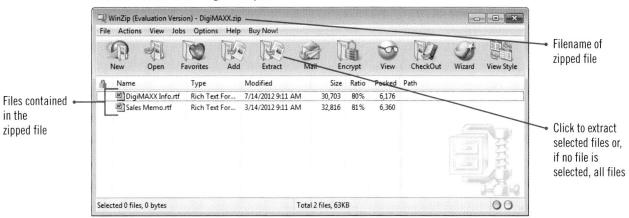

Filename of zipped file

Files contained in the zipped file

Click to extract selected files or, if no file is selected, all files

FIGURE G-22: Extract dialog box

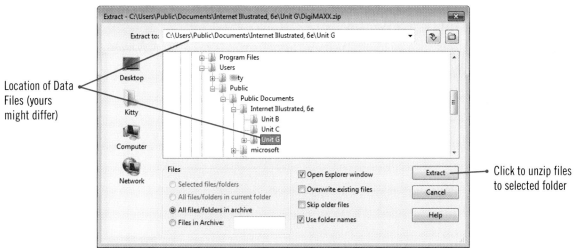

Location of Data Files (yours might differ)

Click to unzip files to selected folder

Internet

Compressing Files

If you need to transfer large files over the Internet, you should compress them to make the upload and download times shorter. To compress files, you need a file compression program, such as WinZip. When you add a file to a compressed file, you do not remove the original file from its location; rather you add a copy of the file to the compressed file. Nancy wants you to re-compress the two files she sent to you and make them available for the sales representatives to download from DigiComm's network server.

STEPS

1. **Click the New button on the WinZip toolbar**

   The New Archive dialog box opens. Compressed files are referred to as **archives** in WinZip.

2. **Navigate to the drive and folder where you store your Data Files if necessary, type Info from Nancy in the File name text box, then click OK**

   The New Archive dialog box closes, and the Add dialog box opens. Note that in the lower right the Compression method is Optimize for best compression.

3. **Navigate to the drive and folder where you store your Data Files, then click Sales Memo.rtf**

   See Figure G-23.

4. **Click Add**

   The WinZip Caution dialog box opens telling you that the Best method compression may not be compatible with older versions of WinZip and with other compression programs. Although you and Nancy have WinZip 12.0, you are not sure if all the sales representatives do, so you decide to change the compression method.

5. **Click No, then in the Add dialog box, click Change Compression**

   The Change Compression dialog box opens. See Figure G-24.

6. **Click the Legacy compression (Zip 2.0 compatible) option button, then click OK**

   The Change Compression dialog box closes and the Compression method listed in the Add dialog box is now Legacy (Zip 2.0 Compatible).

7. **With Sales Memo.rtf still selected in the Add dialog box, click Add**

   The Add dialog box closes and the Add Complete dialog box appears showing you how much space you saved by compressing the file. See Figure G-25.

8. **Click OK**

   The Add Complete dialog box closes, and Sales Memo.rtf is listed in the WinZip (Evaluation Version) – Info from Nancy.zip window.

   QUICK TIP
   To add more than one file to a WinZip archive at a time, press and hold the Ctrl key while you click the files you want to add in the Add dialog box.

9. **Click the Add button on the toolbar, click DigiMAXX Info.rtf in the Add dialog box, click Add, then click OK in the Add Complete dialog box**

   DigiMAXX Info.rtf is added to the list of files in the Info from Nancy compressed file.

10. **Click the Close button in the WinZip title bar**

    The WinZip program closes.

FIGURE G-23: Add dialog box

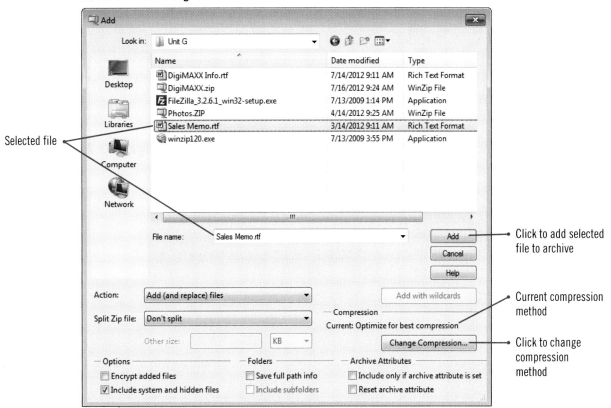

Selected file

Click to add selected file to archive

Current compression method

Click to change compression method

FIGURE G-24: Change Compression dialog box

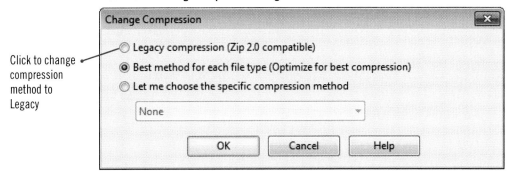

Click to change compression method to Legacy

FIGURE G-25: Add Complete dialog box

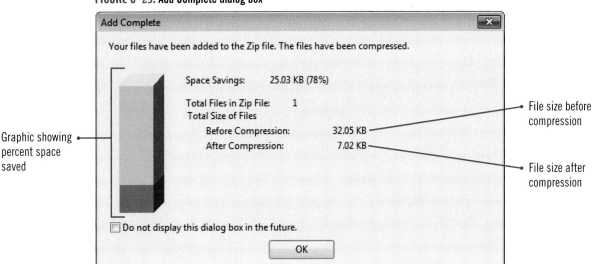

Graphic showing percent space saved

File size before compression

File size after compression

Internet

Practice

For current SAM information including versions and content details, visit SAM Central (http://samcentral.course.com). If you have a SAM user profile, you may have access to hands-on instruction, practice, and assessment of the skills covered in this unit. Since we support various versions of SAM throughout the life of this text, you will want to check with your instructor for instructions and the correct URL/Web site to access those assignments.

▼ CONCEPTS REVIEW

Identify each element of the FTP client program window shown in Figure G-26.

FIGURE G-26

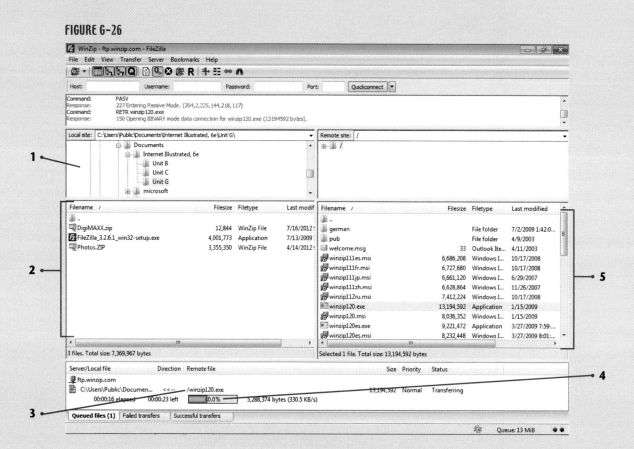

Match each term with the statement that best describes it.

6. Upload

7. Download

8. Download site

9. Anonymous FTP

10. FTP client program

11. PTP

12. Freeware

13. Shareware

a. Acronym for peer-to-peer file sharing

b. A program that allows transfer of files between computers using FTP

c. A method used to log in to public FTP sites

d. To transfer files from a remote computer to your computer

e. To transfer files from your computer to a remote computer

f. Software that you can download for free to use for a short evaluation period

g. A Web site that contains freeware and shareware programs organized in categories

h. A type of software that you can download for free with no restrictions on its use

Select the best answer from the list of choices.

14. To use full-privilege FTP, you must:
   a. log in with the user name "anonymous."
   b. enter your email address as your password.
   c. have an account on the FTP server to which you are connecting.
   d. use a specific FTP client program.

15. What is the name of the process you use to log in to a publicly accessible remote FTP server when you do not have a personal account?
   a. Unknown FTP
   b. Anonymous FTP
   c. Guest FTP
   d. FTP.COM

16. Evaluation software is:
   a. a free, restricted version of shareware that provides most of the functionality of the full commercial version.
   b. usually available at no cost for a short evaluation period, after which users are requested to pay for its use.
   c. fully functional software that is available to anyone at no cost and with no restrictions attached to its use.
   d. the commercial version of a software program.

17. To use an FTP client program to download files and programs from a given server, you need to:
   a. start WinZip.
   b. start Internet Explorer.
   c. view the server's contents in a Web browser.
   d. create an FTP session profile for the server.

18. FTP works:
   a. only between computers connected via a local network.
   b. between any connected computers.
   c. only between connected computers that are near one another.
   d. only between computers connected via the Internet.

19. Which of the following program types do you use to reduce a file to a smaller size?
   a. FTP client program
   b. File compression program
   c. PTP program
   d. Downloaded program

20. Which of the following types of software allows you to use the program for an unlimited amount of time with no program restrictions for free?
   a. Freeware
   b. Shareware
   c. Limited Edition software
   d. Licensed software

Internet

▼ SKILLS REVIEW

1. **Locate a program using a download site.**
   a. Go to the Online Companion page for Unit G, then click one of the links to a download site.
   b. Search on the term zip.
   c. Examine the search results, and read the reviews, if available, for at least three file compression programs.

2. **Download a program using a browser.**
   a. Go to the Online Companion page for Unit G, then click one of the links to a download site.
   b. Click category and subcategory links to look for personal information manager programs.
   c. Look for freeware versions of personal information managers (such as Debrief or Debrief Notes). If you cannot find any by browsing the categories, use the Search box. If you cannot find any on the download site you chose, try another one.
   d. Download the software and save the file to the drive and folder where you store your Data Files.
   e. If necessary, close any open dialog boxes when the download is complete.

3. **Install a downloaded program.**
   a. Check with your instructor or system administrator for permission to install the program you download in Step 2d.
   b. Exit all open programs.
   c. If you have permission, open Windows Explorer, then navigate to the drive and folder where you store your Data Files.
   d. Install the program.

4. **Establish an FTP session.**
   a. Start FileZilla.
   b. Display the Site Manager dialog box.
   c. Add the Mozilla ftp site, as shown in Figure G-27.
   d. Connect to the Mozilla FTP site.

5. **Use FTP to download a file.**
   a. In the Mozilla FTP site, double-click the pub folder.
   b. Double-click the mozilla.org folder.
   c. In the left pane, navigate to the drive and folder where you store your Data Files.
   d. Scroll down in the right pane, then download the README file to your computer. This is a text file that explains the purpose of the Mozilla.org FTP site.
   e. When the file has downloaded, close FileZilla.

6. **Open a compressed file.**
   a. Open the Photos.zip file from the drive and folder where you store your Data Files.
   b. Press and hold the Ctrl key, click Jerusalem.jpg and Prague.jpg, then release the Ctrl key.
   c. Extract the two selected files to the drive and folder where you store your Data Files.

7. **Compress files.**
   a. Create a new WinZip archive named City Images.zip stored in the drive and folder where you store your Data Files.
   b. Add Jerusalem.jpg and Prague.jpg from the location where you store your Data Files to the City Images.zip archive file.
   c. Exit WinZip.

FIGURE G-27

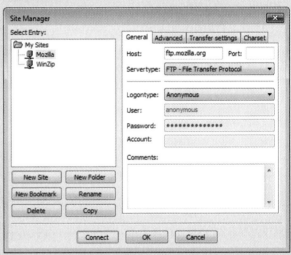

▼ INDEPENDENT CHALLENGE 1

You own Internet Adventures, a one-person consulting company that provides a variety of consulting services to small and medium-size companies. You charge an hourly rate to help companies find and download information on the Internet. You are working for a large CPA firm that wants you to create bookmarks and favorites for Web sites that are of interest to tax pre-parers. Some members of the tax-preparation team use Microsoft Internet Explorer, whereas others use Mozilla Firefox. When team members find interesting Web sites, they use their Web browser to create either an Internet Explorer favorite or a Firefox bookmark. The team members do not always have time to create a bookmark for the Web site in the other Web browser, so they end up losing some of the URLs. You remember reading a review about several shareware products that can convert Internet Explorer favorites to Firefox bookmarks.

    a. Start your Web browser.

    b. Go to the Online Companion page for Unit G, then click one of the links to a download site.

    c. Type **convert bookmarks** in the search expression text box, then click **Go** (or something similar) to start the search.

    d. Scroll down the list of results and look for a bookmark program whose description indicates that it can convert bookmarks between Internet Explorer and Firefox, such as the program Bookmark Converter.

    e. Download the bookmark converter program, and save it to the drive and folder where you store your Data Files.

    f. Open Windows Explorer, navigate to the drive and folder where you store your Data Files, install the program you downloaded, then open it and examine its features.

    g. Close all open programs.

▼ INDEPENDENT CHALLENGE 2

As the director of computing at Baseline High School, you and a staff of three people ensure that the school's computer lab of 45 PCs functions properly. Last week, a virus infected every computer in the lab, and you had to close the lab to prevent the virus from spreading to students' disks and other computers. Each lab computer has McAfee Virus Scan software installed, but the installed version does not recognize and cannot eradicate the new virus pattern. You need to download the latest virus data file from McAfee.

    a. Start FileZilla.

    b. Create a new session profile using the profile name McAfee, the host address ftp.mcafee.com, and the anonymous login method.

    c. Connect to McAfee's FTP site.

    d. To see the antivirus data files on the remote computer, use the following pathname: /pub/antivirus/datfiles/4.x.

    e. Change the local folder in FileZilla to display the location of your Data Files.

    f. On the remote computer, select the filename that begins with dat and ends with the filename extension .zip.

    g. Download the file.

Advanced Challenge Exercise

    ■ Open FileZilla help, then search for information about changing the interface settings.

    ■ Change the interface settings so that the icons are displayed using any theme except Classic.

    ■ View the FileZilla window with the change, then change the theme back to Classic.

    h. Exit all open programs.

▼ INDEPENDENT CHALLENGE 3

You work for PCD Resources, a company that supplies human resources services to other companies. They recently added a new computer system to the office, and you have been hired to help the staff find and download programs they might find useful. Your manager told you that several people have complained that they are confused about the difference between downloading files using a browser and downloading files using an FTP client program. He asked you to create a short report on the similarities and differences between FTP and HTTP. He also wants you to include a brief explanation of archiving programs and why it can be a good idea to archive files before you transfer them.

    a. Use a search engine and find information describing what each protocol was originally designed for.

    b. Find information describing each protocol's most common uses today.

    c. Find information describing any overlapping uses between the two protocols.

    d. Start a new word processing document, then write at least two paragraphs summarizing your findings.

    e. Write another paragraph describing archiving programs, and then explain why it is helpful to archive files before transferring them.

    f. Save the file. Start WinZip, create a new archive, then add the word-processed document you created to the archive using the Optimize for best compression method.

    g. Use email to send this information to your instructor.

    h. Exit all open programs.

▼ REAL LIFE INDEPENDENT CHALLENGE

The Macintosh computer runs the Mac OS operating system rather than Windows. The most prevalent type of compressed files for Macintosh users is the .sit file, rather than .zip. .sit is an abbreviation for StuffIt, the name of the program that creates these files. You or a friend might need a program to open a .sit file one day. You can locate a program that can open a .sit file on a download site.

a. Go to the Online Companion page for Unit G, then click one of the links to a download site.

b. Search for an archive program called StuffIt for the Macintosh operating system (Mac OS). You might need to click a list arrow and select the Mac OS from the list.

c. In the search results list, identify the most recent version of StuffIt for the Mac OS (this is the program name with the highest number and with Mac OS listed next to OS under the program name), then click the link.

d. Read the information about the program.

e. Send an email message to your instructor that includes the URL for the Web page on the download site where you can download the program.

Advanced Challenge Exercise

- Your friend wants to download a program that will help her create lists. Go to the Online Companion page for Unit G, click one of the links to a download site, then search for a To-do list manager program for the Macintosh operating system.

- Click the link for a file that you find, then click the link to go to the developer's Web site.

- Explore the developer's Web site and see if that developer has any other programs that your friend might find useful.

- Send an email message to your instructor that includes the URL for the developer's Web site and a sentence explaining the to-do list manager program you found, as well as a sentence identifying any other programs on the developer's Web site that your friend might find useful.

f. Exit your Web browser.

▼ VISUAL WORKSHOP

Start FileZilla, then complete the Site Manager dialog box. Enter the information shown in Figure G-28. Log in to the Netscape FTP site, then explore the contents of the pub folder.

FIGURE G-28

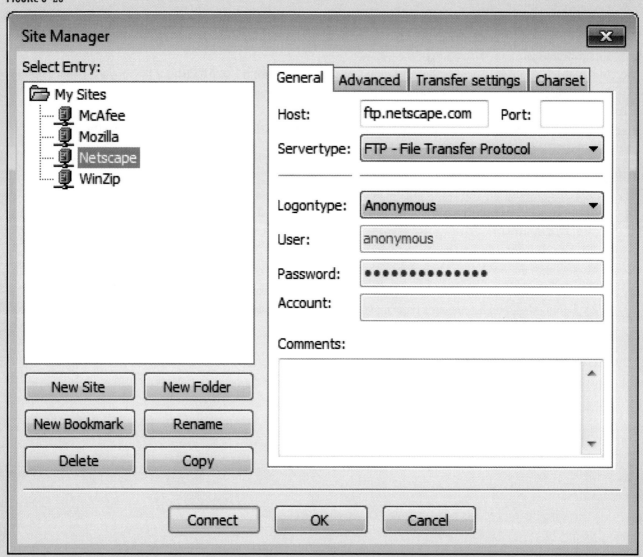

UNIT
H
Internet

Extending Browser Capabilities

Files You Will Need:

No files needed.

Many Web sites include files in file formats that Web browsers cannot display by default. These file formats are used primarily for elaborate graphics and multimedia content. Most browsers can display graphics on Web sites, but in order to properly display audio and video files, you need another program. You can enable a Web browser to interpret almost any file format on the Web by installing programs for the Web browser. These programs are often small and can be downloaded for free. In this unit, you will download, install, and use these programs. ████ Remes Video Productions (RVP) is a video production company that specializes in producing training and safety videos. Mark Remes, the company's founder, wants to expand his business outside the Minneapolis/St. Paul area and he has hired you to market the company on the Web. He wants you to create a Web site that includes samples of the company's video work.

OBJECTIVES

Understand graphics

Understand multimedia

Understand browser extensions

Locate browser extensions

Download and install extensions
  with Internet Explorer

Download and install extensions
  with Firefox

Use browser extensions

Understanding Graphics

In addition to basic text, most Web sites incorporate images or art, known as **graphics**, into their designs. Graphics can help Web site users find information more easily, and they can strongly influence the Web site's look and feel. ⬛⬛ Before you research the best way to incorporate graphics into the RVP Web site, you ask Franco, the company's Webmaster, to give you an overview of common graphic file formats used in Web pages.

DETAILS

Common file formats used in Web pages are described below:

- **GIF**

  GIF, an acronym for Graphics Interchange Format, is a file format that can contain up to 256 colors. GIF is a popular file format because it is compressed, which means that the browser downloads the images quickly. GIF uses **lossless compression** technology, which reduces the file size without any loss of data. The algorithm that compresses GIF files is owned by Unisys, and programs that create GIF files must pay a licensing fee to Unisys to use this file format. An **animated GIF** file combines several images into a single GIF file so that the images can be displayed one after the other to simulate movement.

- **JPEG**

  JPEG, an acronym for Joint Photographic Experts Group, is a file format that can store over 16 million colors, which is particularly useful for photographs. JPEG is also a compressed file format, but it uses **lossy compression** technology, which eliminates redundant and unnecessary data in an image to reduce the file size. The discarded data is not usually noticeable to the human eye. The greater the level of compression, the more data is lost and the smaller the file size gets. Figure H-1 shows the page for Vincent van Gogh's self-portraits on the WebMuseum site. The images of the paintings are in JPEG file format to preserve the colors of the paintings and to reduce the file sizes to manageable sizes for viewing on the Web. Most graphics on the Web are saved in the GIF or JPEG file formats.

- **PNG**

  The PNG format is a license-free compressed format that is similar to GIF, but it cannot be used to create animations. The PNG format was designed specifically for use on the Web in the mid-1990s and has become more common in recent years.

- **Uncompressed File Formats**

  Other file formats used on the Web are Windows bitmap file format (.bmp), Tagged Image File Format (or TIFF) format (.tif), and PC Paintbrush format (.pcx). These formats are all uncompressed graphics formats. Web page designers usually avoid these formats because a Web browser takes too long to download them.

FIGURE H-1: Vincent van Gogh self-portrait page on WebMuseum site

 WebMuseum, Paris

Gogh, Vincent van: Self-Portraits

In the most limited definition of the term, Impressionism as the objective study of light did not encourage so essentially a subjective study as the self-portrait but in the later expansion of the movement this self-representation was given renewed force by Cézanne and van Gogh. The latter has often been compared with Rembrandt in the number and expressiveness of his self-portraits but while Rembrandt's were distributed through a lifetime, van Gogh produced some thirty in all in the short space of five years --- from the end of the Brabant period (1885) to the last year of his life at St Rémy and Auvers. In each there is the same extraordinary intensity of expression concentrated in the eyes but otherwise there is a considerable variety. From the Paris period onwards he used different adaptations of Impressionist and Neo-Impressionist brushwork, separate patches of colour being applied with varying thickness and direction in a way that makes each painting a fresh experience.

 Self-Portrait Dedicated to Paul Gauguin
1888 (130 Kb); Oil on canvas, 60.5 x 49.4 cm (23 3/4 x 19 1/2 in); Fogg Art Museum, Harvard University, Cambridge, MA

 Self-Portrait in front of the Easel
1888 (200 Kb); 65 x 50.5 cm

JPEG images

 Self-Portrait with Bandaged Ear
1889 (250 Kb); Oil on canvas, 60 x 49 cm; Courtauld Institute Galleries, London

Self-Portrait

Using clip art

A collection of individual icons, shapes, and other graphics is known as **clip art**. Clip art is available for free use or for purchase on many Web sites. Some Web sites offer clip art or tools for helping you find clip art. Often you can browse clip art by subject category or search for images associated with a keyword you specify. Clip art files are often GIF or BMP files. Figure H-2 shows the Concepts category in the Microsoft Office Online Clip Art and Media collection of clip art. When you use graphics that you download from a Web site, you must be careful not to violate the image owner's rights. Check the Web site copyright notices and conditions-of-use statements for information about using the images.

FIGURE H-2: Concepts category on the Microsoft Office Online Clip Art and Media Web site

Clip art images

Understanding Multimedia

In addition to graphics, some Web sites incorporate sound, animation, and video, known collectively as **multimedia**. Web pages can communicate information by playing music or showing a video. A popular technique for transferring both sound and video files on the Web is called streaming transmission. In a **streaming transmission**, the Web server sends the first part of the file to the Web browser, which begins playing the file. While the browser is playing the first part of the file, the server is then sending the next segment of the file. Some Web sites play music and video using built-in video players, and others require you to have a music or video player on your computer. You know that Mark wants to add multimedia elements to the RVP Web site. You ask Franco to give you an overview of multimedia file formats used on Web pages.

DETAILS

Common multimedia formats are described below:

- Audio File Formats

QUICK TIP

In order for your computer to play sounds, it must also be equipped with a sound card and either speakers or earphones.

  - The **Wave (WAV) format** digitizes audio waveform information at a user-specified sampling rate and can be played on any Windows computer that can play sounds. WAV files can be very large; a WAV file that stores one minute of CD-quality sound can be more than 1 megabyte in size.

  - The **MIDI (Musical Instrument Digital Interface) format** does not digitize the sound waveform; instead, it digitally records information about each element of the sound, including its pitch, length, and volume. MIDI files are much smaller than WAV files and are therefore often used on the Web. Figure H-3 shows a Web page that offers MIDI files that you can download to use as ringtones on a cell phone.

  - The **AU format** is the audio file format used by the UNIX operating system. Browsers need to be able to recognize this file format because many of the pages available on the Web were originally created on computers running the UNIX operating system. These files are approximately the same size as WAV files.

QUICK TIP

The MP3 file format is the most popular for music on the Web today.

  - The **MPEG Audio Layer 3 (MP3) format** is the audio portion of a compressed video format developed by the International Standards Organization's **Moving Picture Experts Group (MPEG)**. Files in the MP3 format are somewhat lower in quality than WAV files, but they are 90 percent smaller.

- Video File Formats

  AVI and **MPEG** are common formats used for video on the Web, and they can be played using the same software that plays many other multimedia file types, including the players that come with Windows. AVI files are uncompressed files and can be very large. MPEG files use lossy compression.

- Proprietary File Formats

  - **RealAudio format** for audio files and the **RealVideo format** for video files are file formats developed by RealNetworks, Inc. These files have filename extensions of .ra, .ram, or .rmj. To play these files, you must download and install one of the Real file players from Real.com.

  - Proprietary Windows Media Player file formats include **Windows Media Audio (wma)**, **Windows Media Video (wmv)**, and **Advanced Systems Format (asf)**. These files will play only in Windows Media Player and Windows Media Center, which is shown in Figure H-4.

  - **QuickTime** is a proprietary video format developed by Apple Computer. It works equally well on Windows and Macintosh computers. You need to download the QuickTime player to play a QuickTime video.

FIGURE H-3: Web site with MIDI files

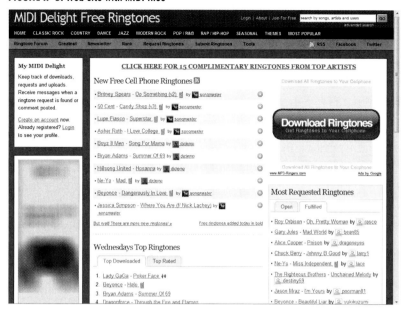

FIGURE H-4: Windows Media Player displaying sample music installed with Windows 7

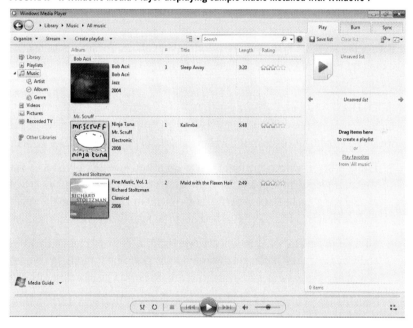

Sharing MP3 files

MP3 files became wildly popular just as disk storage on personal computers dropped in price and CD writers (also called CD burners) became affordable for home use. Their smaller size made MP3 files easy to send from one person to another over the Internet, and file-sharing software, such as Napster and Kazaa, became very popular. Companies in the recording industry and the recording artists themselves were not happy. Recording companies and artists filed suits against Napster and other file-sharing sponsors for violating copyright laws. The recording companies were generally successful in obtaining court orders or out-of-court settlements to prevent further copyright violations in many cases. Many individuals, however, still violate the law and share MP3 files that contain copyrighted works. Over the past several years, the Recording Industry Association of America (RIAA) has threatened individual users who have downloaded songs using file-sharing software with lawsuits unless they settle for a specified amount, usually approximately $3,000. The RIAA recently won a case they brought against a college student in Boston who refused to settle, the jury awarded the RIAA $22,500 per song for 30 songs, a total of $675,000. In another case in which a woman in Minnesota refused to settle, the jury awarded the RIAA $80,000 per song for 24 songs, a total of $1.92 million.

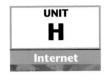

Understanding Browser Extensions

Browser extensions enhance the capabilities of Web browsers by allowing a Web browser to perform tasks that it was not originally designed to do. There are three categories of browser extensions. **Plug-in** browser extensions are programs that a Web browser starts to display or play a specific file type. Plug-ins can start only from within a Web browser. **Helper application** or **helper app** browser extensions are separate programs, such as a spreadsheet program, that are launched to display or play some files, such as a spreadsheet, that can start independently of Web browsers. **Add-ons** are browser extensions that enhance your browsing experience, such as toolbars that let you access a search engine without opening its Web site. Although all extensions are not, technically, add-ons, Internet Explorer refers to all browser extensions as add-ons. You want to include video clips on the RVP Web site, and you need to decide on a format that users can easily view with a Web browser. You begin the process by reviewing some of the types of browser extensions that are available.

DETAILS

Categories of browser extensions are discussed below:

- **Document and Productivity**

  Document and productivity browser extensions let you use a Web browser to read documents, such as documents saved in **PDF format**, a format that allows documents to maintain a consistent layout and format on different computers when viewed using Adobe Reader. Figure H-5 shows the PDF version of a commonly used tax form on the IRS Web site.

- **Animation**

  Animation browser extensions allow you to play interactive games, view animated interfaces, listen to streaming CD-quality audio music and speech, and view instructional presentations.

  - **Flash® Player:** One of the most popular animation extensions is Adobe's **Flash Player**, which lets your Web browser display simple animations, user interfaces, static graphics, movies, sound, and text that was created using Adobe Flash software. Flash content usually appears in the same browser window as the page you are viewing. In fact, Flash has become so popular that it is installed automatically with some browsers.

  - **Silverlight:** Microsoft developed **Silverlight**, a browser plug-in that delivers high-definition audio and video, high-resolution graphics, and interactive applications, to compete with Adobe's Flash. It is a new application and therefore many users have not yet installed the Silverlight player.

  - **Shockwave® Player:** A more fully featured browser plug-in is Adobe's **Shockwave Player**, which lets you view animated, three-dimensional interfaces, interactive advertisements and product demonstrations, multiuser games, streaming CD-quality audio, and video that was created using Adobe Director software. Because Shockwave uses streaming technology, you do not need to wait for an entire file to download before playing it—the animation or sound plays almost immediately after you click the link to access the content. Shockwave content usually appears in a new browser window. Some instructors use Shockwave to deliver audio instruction and interact with students over the Internet just as they would in the classroom. Figure H-6 shows a page that demonstrates a biology lesson that requires the Shockwave player.

- **Sound Player**

  Sound player browser extensions let your Web browser play nonstandard audio file formats. Many sound player extensions are available, including Beatnik and RealPlayer.

- **Video Player**

  Video player browser extensions deliver movies to Web browsers over the Internet. When you click a movie link, the movie downloads and begins playing in its own window. Popular video players include QuickTime, RealPlayer, and Windows Media Player.

> **QUICK TIP**
>
> According to Adobe, 96 percent of all desktop computers connected to the Internet have the Flash Player installed and can use the Flash Player to view enhanced content on the Web.

> **QUICK TIP**
>
> QuickTime was one of the first video players developed.

FIGURE H-5: W-9 form on the IRS Web site in PDF format in Internet Explorer

Adobe
Reader
plug-in
toolbar

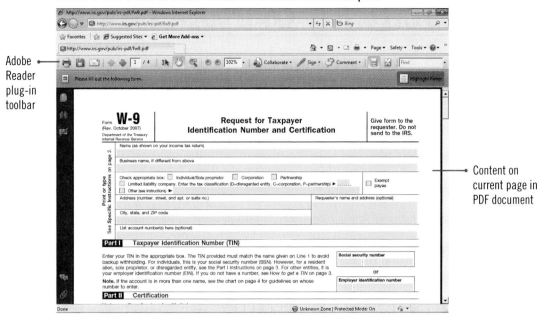

Content on
current page in
PDF document

FIGURE H-6: Shockwave animation

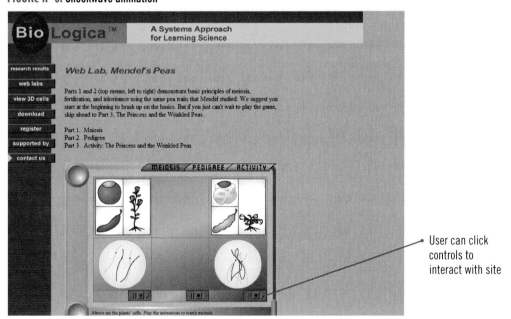

User can click
controls to
interact with site

Understanding Java

Java is a programming language that can be used to write programs that add interactivity to a Web page. These programs are sometimes called Java applets. There are many Web sites that offer games and other interactive content through the use of Java. When a Web page contains Java content, it requires a Java plug-in for your browser in order to display the content. Because Java does not come with Windows, you must download it to access all of the content on Web pages that require it. As with other types of extensions, most Web sites that require Java display a message informing you that you need Java installed or enabled. Because Java can be used to write malicious programs that can execute on a user's computer, you can choose to not allow Java applets to run. You will learn more about enabling and disabling Java content in Unit I.

Locating Browser Extensions

You can find and download browser extensions from different Web sites. Some download sites include a list of links to browser extensions, which are grouped by category or function. Before deciding on a video format for displaying samples of RVP's work on the Web site, you want to see which file formats are handled by the most popular and highest-rated browser extensions. You review the audio and video extensions listed on a couple of download sites.

STEPS

1. Go to the Online Companion page for Unit H, then click one of the links to a download site under Lesson 4

2. Type plug-ins in the search expression text box, then click Go, Search, or press [Enter]

   A search results page opens with various plug-ins listed in descending order by the date the software was added to the list. Some download sites allow you to sort the results list.

   TROUBLE
   You will not be able to sort the results on all the download sites.

3. If possible, click a list arrow or a button to re-sort the list by popularity or by the number of times the plug-in has been downloaded

4. Scroll down to view the available downloads

5. Select the text in the search expression text box, type add-ons, then click Go, Search, or press [Enter]

   A search results page opens with programs labeled as "add-ons."

6. If possible, sort the list by popularity or the total number of times the add-on has been downloaded, then scroll through the list

   TROUBLE
   Your results page might look different because the plug-ins and their statistics change over time.

7. Type shockwave player in the search expression dialog box, then click Go, Search, or press [Enter]

   The search results page that opens displays a Shockwave Player link followed by a version number at the top of the list. Figure H-7 shows the link to Shockwave Player on filehippo.com. You want to make sure you download the most recent version of Shockwave Player, so you go to Adobe's site rather than using a download site.

   TROUBLE
   If you don't see a link to the Adobe Web site, go to the Online Companion page for Unit H, then click the Adobe Shockwave link.

8. Click the Shockwave Player link, then click the link to the Adobe Web site

   The download page for Shockwave Player opens. If Shockwave has been installed on your computer in the past, you might see the screen shown in Figure H-8. If Shockwave has never been installed on your computer, you might see the screen shown in Figure H-9.

How do you know when you need an add-on?

When you are browsing the Web, you might encounter Web pages that indicate you need a specific add-on to view or hear the Web page's content. If you do not have the required add-on to play the content, sometimes nothing happens and you see only what your Web browser can display and you do not hear sound, for example, or you do not see a video. The Web page might also display an icon or empty frame, indicating that you are missing an add-on. Some Web pages might contain a link to the Web site where you can download the required add-on or display a dialog box that provides information about the missing add-on and where to obtain it. When you click the link, the developer's Web site opens so you can download the add-on. Finally, some pages might try to install the missing add-on and the User Account Control dialog box or the Information bar will appear. After you install the missing add-on, the full Web page content will be available in your Web browser.

FIGURE H-7: Link to Shockwave Player on filehippo.com

List of search
results

Search expression

Link to
Shockwave
Player download

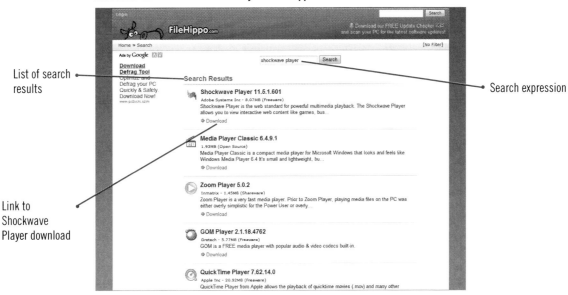

FIGURE H-8: Shockwave Player download page on Adobe's Web site if Shockwave has been previously installed

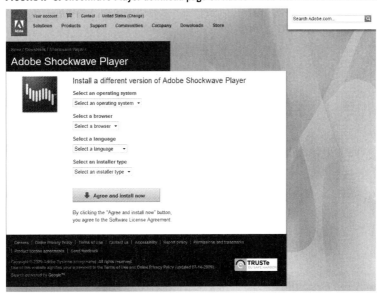

FIGURE H-9: Shockwave Player download page on Adobe's Web site if Shockwave has not been previously installed

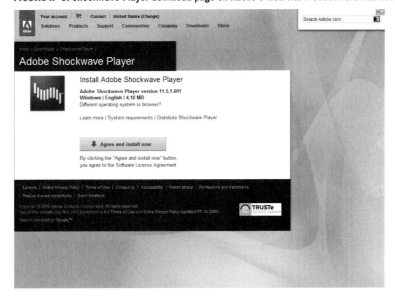

UNIT
H
Internet

Downloading and Installing Extensions with Internet Explorer

You download and install browser extensions just as you would other software for your computer. Internet Explorer allows you to automatically download and install some browser extensions by simply clicking a link on a Web page. Add-ons are generally small programs that do not require a lot of system resources. Although many add-ons are available, you should limit yourself to installing only add-ons that you will use often. You investigate how easy it would be for potential Web site users to install a required add-on by adding the Shockwave add-on to your Web browser.

STEPS

 Check with your instructor or technical support person before installing this add-on. If you do not get approval to install it, read the instructions without performing the steps. If you are using Firefox, skip to the next lesson.

1. **If your screen matches Figure H-8, click the** Select an operating system list arrow, **click** Windows, **click the** Select a browser list arrow, **click** Internet Explorer, **click the** Select a language list arrow, **click** English, **click the** Select an installer type list arrow, **then click** Slim; **if your screen matches Figure H-9, skip this step**

2. **Click** Agree and install now
   The Information Bar might appear at the top of the browser window.

> **TROUBLE**
> If you are using Windows Vista, the Internet Explorer Add-on Installer - Security Warning dialog box might open. If it does, click **Install**. Skip Step 4.

3. **If the yellow Information bar appears at the top of the browser window, click it, then click** Install This Add-on for All Users on This Computer **on the menu that appears**
   The User Account Control dialog box opens. This dialog box may appear several times when you are installing new software, depending on the security settings on your computer.

4. **Click** Yes, Allow, **or** Continue
   The Web site shows the progress of the download, as shown in Figure H-10. After a moment, the Installing Shockwave Player dialog box might open asking if you want to install another program, such as the Google Toolbar.

> **TROUBLE**
> If the installation seems to stall, point to the buttons on the Windows taskbar to see the ScreenTips, then click the Installing Adobe Shockwave Player button to make the Installing Adobe Shockwave Player dialog box the active window.

5. **If you do not want to install this additional program, deselect the check box next to the option to install the program, then click** Next
   You might need to click Yes, Allow, or Continue in several dialog boxes as you install the program, depending on the security settings on your computer. When the installation is complete, a message informing you of this appears, as shown in Figure H-11.

Extending Browser Capabilities

FIGURE H-10: Progress of Shockwave Player download on Adobe Web site

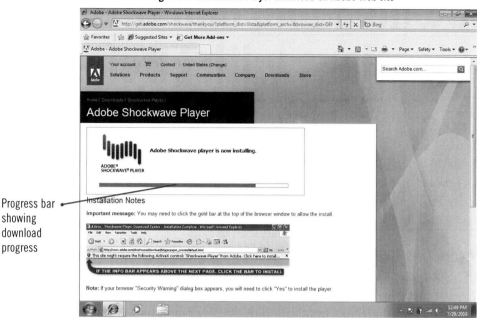

Progress bar
showing
download
progress

FIGURE H-11: Message on Adobe Web site when Shockwave installation is complete

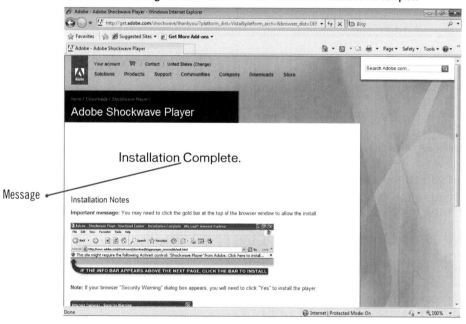

Message

Managing and finding new add-ons

In Internet Explorer, you can add, enable, and disable add-ons in the Manage Add-ons dialog box. To open this dialog box, click the Tools button on the Command bar, and then click Manage Add-ons. The Manage Add-ons dialog box opens with Toolbars and Extensions selected in the Add-on Types list in the left pane and the list of add-ons currently loaded in Internet Explorer in the right pane. If you want to disable an add-on, you would click it in the list, and then click Disable in the bottom section of the dialog box. To explore and install additional add-ons, click the Find more toolbars and extensions link in the bottom pane in the Manage Add-ons dialog box. A new browser window opens to the Internet Explorer 8 Add-ons Gallery at www.ieaddons.com. You can browse through the various categories looking for add-ons, or you can type keywords in the Search text box to search for specific add-ons. To install an add-on, click Add to Internet Explorer next to the add-on you want to install.

Downloading and Installing Extensions with Firefox

You download and install browser extensions just as you would other software for your computer. You first download the browser extension to your computer, and then double-click it to run the installation wizard. Plug-ins are generally small programs that do not require a lot of system resources. Although many plug-ins are available, you should limit yourself to installing only plug-ins that you will use often. You investigate how easy it would be for potential Web site users to install a required plug-in by adding the Shockwave plug-in to your Web browser.

STEPS

🛑 *Check with your instructor or technical support person before installing this plug-in. If you do not get approval to install it, read the instructions without performing the steps. If you are using Internet Explorer, skip to the next lesson.*

TROUBLE

If the Enter name of file to save to dialog box does not open, click Tools on the menu bar, click Options, click the Main button on the toolbar, look at the path in the Downloads section of the dialog box next to the Save files to option button to see this location, then skip Step 4.

1. **If your screen matches Figure H-8, click the** Select an operating system list arrow, **click** Windows, **click the** Select a browser list arrow, **click** Firefox, **click the** Select a language list arrow, **click** English, **click the** Select an installer type list arrow, **then click** Slim; **if your screen matches Figure H-9, skip this step**

2. **Click** Agree and install now
   The Opening Shockwave_Installer_Slim.exe dialog box opens. See Figure H-12.

3. **Click** Save File
   The Enter name of file to save to dialog box opens.

4. **Navigate to the drive and folder where your data files are stored, then click** Save
   The file downloads and a Downloads Complete alert box briefly appears in the lower-right corner of the screen.

TROUBLE

If your computer is not set to display filename extensions, the file will appear as Shockwave_Installer_Slim instead.

5. **If the Downloads dialog box is still open, click its** Close button **to close it, exit Firefox, open Windows Explorer and display the contents of the folder containing your data files, then double-click the** Shockwave_Installer_Slim.exe file
   The Open Executable File dialog box might open.

6. **If the Open Executable File dialog box opens, click** OK
   The User Account Control dialog box opens.

TROUBLE

If the Program Compatibility Assistant dialog box opens telling you that the program might not have installed correctly, click This program installed correctly.

7. **Click** Yes, Allow, **or** Continue
   The Installing Shockwave Player dialog box might open asking if you want to install another program, such as the Google Toolbar for Internet Explorer (even though you are using Firefox).

8. **If you do not want to install the additional program, deselect the check box next to the option to install the program, then click** Next
   After a few moments, the dialog box tells you that the installation was successfully completed.

9. **Click** Close, **then close the Windows Explorer window**
   The dialog box closes. You can test the Shockwave installation at the Test Adobe Shockwave & Flash Players Web page.

10. **Go to the Online Companion page for** Unit H, **then click the** Test Adobe Shockwave & Flash Players link **below Lesson 6**
    After a moment, you see a message in the Adobe Shockwave Player section telling you that the Installation is complete. See Figure H-13.

FIGURE H-12: Opening Shockwave_Installer_Slim.exe dialog box

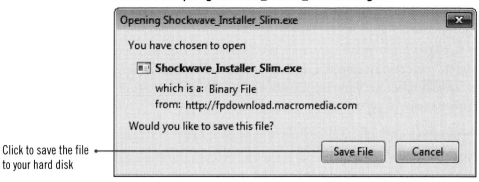

Click to save the file to your hard disk

FIGURE H-13: Test Adobe Shockwave & Flash Players Web page

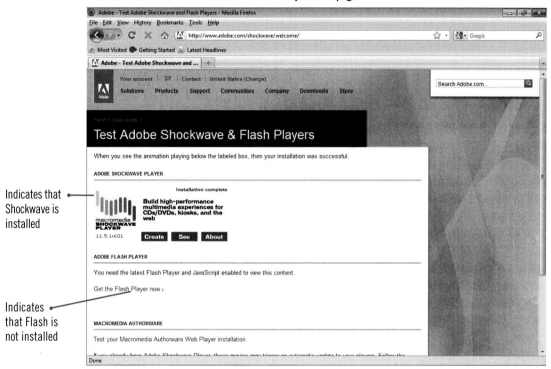

Indicates that Shockwave is installed

Indicates that Flash is not installed

Managing and finding new Firefox add-ons

In Firefox, you can manage add-ons in the Add-ons window. To open this window, click Tools on the menu bar, and then click Add-ons. In the Add-ons window, click a button on the toolbar to see the list of add-ons in that category. To disable an add-on, click it to select it, and then click Disable. To change how the add-on works, click the add-on in the list, and then click Options, if available. Firefox was designed to give programmers an easy way to write add-ons. Anyone who writes a Firefox add-on can submit it to the site administrator of the Mozilla Development Center. To install an add-on from this site, click Tools on the menu bar, click Add-ons to open the Add-ons window, and then click the Get Add-ons button on the toolbar at the top of the window, if necessary,

to see a short list of recommended add-ons in the window. To see all the add-ons available, click the Browse All Add-ons link at the top of the window to open the Add-ons for Firefox page on the Mozilla Web site. After you find the add-on you want to install, click Add to Firefox next to the add-on. The Software Installation dialog box opens. Click Install Now in that dialog box. The dialog box closes and the Add-ons window appears again, displaying the progress of the add-on as it is installed. After the installation is complete, the new add-on is added to the bottom of the list in the Add-ons window. Read the description of the add-on. Many add-ons will not be completely installed until you restart Firefox.

Using Browser Extensions

If the required browser extension is installed, you do not have to do anything special to view content on a Web page that requires that particular browser extension; the Web page will display the content as it was designed. Mark asks if you can show him some Web sites that use the Shockwave and Flash Players so he can get a sense of the kind of content they can display.

STEPS

TROUBLE
If a dialog box opens telling you that you need to install or update the Flash Player, or if you do not see any content on the page, follow the on-screen instructions to install it. If you are working in a lab, check with your instructor or technical support person first.

1. **Go to the Online Companion page for Unit H, click the National Institutes of Health—Flash Demo link under Lesson 7, then click the Click to Start control at the bottom of the blue box**

   The browser loads the page and displays the content, similar to Figure H-14. This page contains an interactive sound ruler.

2. **Point to one of the bars on the ruler**

   A sound plays, and a description of the sound and its typical decibel level appears below the ruler.

3. **Point to several other bars on the ruler**

4. **When you are finished viewing the Flash demonstration, return to the Unit H page on the Online Companion**

TROUBLE
If the User Account Control dialog box opens, click Yes, Allow, or Continue.

5. **Click the Bow Master—Shockwave Demo link under Lesson 7, click Play twice in the pages that load, then click anywhere in the game window**

   The browser loads the page and displays the Shockwave content, similar to Figure H-15.

6. **Press and hold the left mouse button**

   The bow string on the bow is drawn back.

7. **Move the pointer up and to the left and right to aim at a target, then release the left mouse button**

   The arrow releases, and, if you aimed correctly, hits a target.

8. **When you are finished, exit your browser and close any open windows**

FIGURE H-14: Flash animation

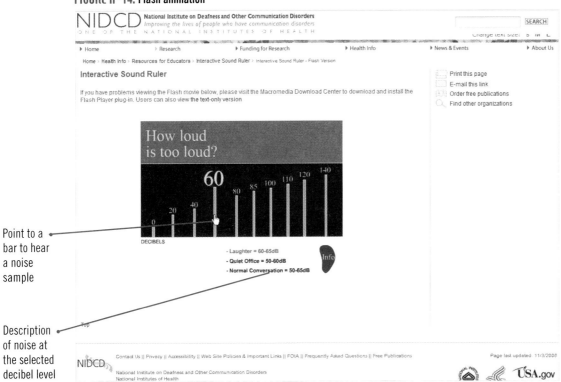

Point to a bar to hear a noise sample

Description of noise at the selected decibel level

FIGURE H-15: Shockwave animation

Internet

Practice

For current SAM information including versions and content details, visit SAM Central (http://samcentral.course. com). If you have a SAM user profile, you may have access to hands-on instruction, practice, and assessment of the skills covered in this unit. Since we support various versions of SAM throughout the life of this text, you will want to check with your instructor for instructions and the correct URL/Web site to access those assignments.

▼ CONCEPTS REVIEW

Match each term with the statement that best describes it.

1. **QuickTime**
2. **Multimedia**
3. **Browser extension**
4. **Plug-in**
5. **Animated GIF**
6. **MIDI format**
7. **Graphics**
8. **JPEG**
9. **MP3**
10. **Lossy compression**

a. Graphic file format that is good for photographs
b. A program you install to expand your Web browser's capabilities
c. File compression technique that deletes unnecessary information from a file to reduce its size
d. A browser extension that starts from within a browser
e. Sound, animation, and video on a Web page
f. Proprietary file format that works on both Windows and Macintosh systems
g. Audio file format that digitally records information about each element of the sound
h. Audio files that are 90 percent smaller than WAV files
i. Images or art used in Web pages
j. Several images combined into a single GIF file displayed one after the other to simulate movement

Select the best answer from the list of choices.

11. **A browser extension:**
    a. expands the width of the browser window.
    b. is a program that you can only open from your Web browser.
    c. is an executable file that causes harm to a computer.
    d. enhances the capabilities of a Web browser by allowing the browser to perform tasks that it was not originally designed to do.

12. **The technique for transferring sound and video on the Web in which the server sends part of the file to the browser to begin playing it while the server sends the next part of the file is called:**
    a. plugging in.
    b. multimedia transmission.
    c. streaming transmission.
    d. extensibility.

13. **Which of the following is such a popular add-on that it is now included in many browsers?**
    a. RealPlayer
    b. QuickTime
    c. Flash
    d. Shockwave

14. **Which of the following is a separate program that launches independently of the Web browser to display or play some files?**
    a. Plug-in
    b. Helper application
    c. Flash
    d. Shockwave

15. **Which of the following file formats uses lossy compression?**
    a. AU format
    b. GIF
    c. JPEG
    d. WAV

16. **Which of the following file formats uses lossless compression?**
    a. AU format
    b. GIF
    c. JPEG
    d. WAV

17. **Which of the following is a file format that allows documents to maintain a consistent layout and format on different computers?**
    a. AU format
    b. MPEG
    c. PDF
    d. WAV

18. **Which of the following is an uncompressed video file format?**
    a. AU format
    b. AVI
    c. MPEG
    d. MP3

▼ SKILLS REVIEW

1. **Locate browser extensions.**
    a. Go to the Online Companion page for Unit H, then click one of the links under Download Sites in Skills Review 1.
    b. Filter the list to browse for plug-ins in the browser category. (If you can't filter by category, select a different download site from the Online Companion page for Unit H.)
    c. Scroll through the list to view the available downloads.
    d. Return to the Unit H page on the Online Companion, then click the Google Pack link under Skills Review 1.
    e. Read the descriptions of the various downloads available from Google.
    f. Scroll down, click the Learn more about Google Pack Software link, then click the link that will provide you with more information about the Google Toolbar for your browser.

2. **Download and install a browser extension with Internet Explorer.**
    a. Return to the Unit H page on the Online Companion, then click the Snap Shots link under Skills Review 2.
    b. Click the Learn More link in the End Users section.
    c. Check with your instructor, then click Download Now, then click Accept & Download to accept the license and start the download. You will need to run the software and click Yes, Allow, or Continue in the User Account Control dialog box when it appears.
    d. After the installation is complete, a Web page appears thanking you for installing Snap Shots Add-On. Click one of the links listed.
    e. Point to several of the search results to see the snapshot of the results page.
    f. If you want to disable the add-on, open the Manage Add-ons dialog box, locate and select each Snap Shot component, then click Disable. If you want to uninstall the add-on, open the Windows Control Panel, click the Uninstall a program link, select Snap Shots in the list, then click Uninstall.

3. **Download and install a browser extension with Firefox.**
    a. Return to the Unit H page on the Online Companion, then click the Snap Shots link under Skills Review 3.
    b. Click the Learn More link in the End Users section.
    c. Check with your instructor, then click Download Now. Follow the instructions to allow add-ons to be installed from Snap.com. Click Yes, Allow, or Continue in the User Account Control dialog box when it appears.

Internet

▼ SKILLS REVIEW (CONTINUED)

d. After the installation is complete, a Web page appears thanking you for installing Snap Shots Add-On. Click one of the links listed.

e. Point to several of the search results to see the snapshot of the results page.

f. If you want to disable or uninstall the add-on, click Tools on the menu bar, click Add-ons, locate and select Snap Shots in the Add-ons window, then click the appropriate command.

4. Use browser extensions.

a. Return to the Unit H page on the Online Companion, then click one of the links under Flash Sites in Skills Review 4.

b. Watch the animation and interact with the site, if possible.

c. Return to the Unit H page on the Online Companion, then click one of the links under Shockwave Sites in Skills Review 4.

d. Interact with the site.

e. Exit your browser.

▼ INDEPENDENT CHALLENGE 1

You work as a technology consultant specializing in helping small businesses and independent contractors take full advantage of the Internet in their work. You generally install a couple of useful browser extensions for your clients. You want to identify other useful extensions that your clients might find helpful in their work.

a. Start your Web browser.

b. Go to the Online Companion page for Unit H, then click one of the links under Independent Challenge 1 to locate and research a browser extension not already used in this unit.

c. Write a paragraph describing how the browser extension extends a Web browser's capabilities (what it does that a Web browser cannot do alone).

d. Include the URL of the Web page on the publisher's Web site from where you can download this browser extension. Also include the URL of a Web page that makes use of this browser extension. (*Hint*: Such Web pages are often listed on the Web site of the company that makes the browser extension.)

Advanced Challenge Exercise

- If you use Internet Explorer, locate IESpell, which checks your spelling as you type in text boxes on Web pages, on the download site you chose; if you use Firefox, locate FoxyTunes, which allows you to control media players without leaving the browser.
- Visit the publisher's Web page and make sure you are downloading the most current version of the program.
- Download and install the program you found for your browser.

e. Exit your Web browser and close any open windows.

▼ INDEPENDENT CHALLENGE 2

A friend of yours is a third-grade language skills teacher at Midland Elementary School. The school is closing its music program because the state has cut its budget severely over the past several years. Your friend believes that it is important to expose third-graders to the music of the great composers, such as Beethoven and Mozart. She does not have a budget for buying CDs, so she asked you to help her find some music files to play on the computer. You have heard that single musical instruments, particularly pianos, sound realistic in the MIDI format.

a. Go to the Online Companion page for Unit H, then click one of the links under Independent Challenge 2.

b. Examine the MIDI files available on the site you chose.

c. Return to the Unit H page on the Online Companion, then examine the MIDI files available on two other sites listed under Independent Challenge 2.

▼ INDEPENDENT CHALLENGE 2 (CONTINUED)

d. Evaluate the files offered on these Web pages or the pages to which they lead, then note the URLs of the best site for your friend. Explain why this site is the best choice for her.

e. Exit your Web browser.

▼ INDEPENDENT CHALLENGE 3

Jon Sagami is the manager of the Ski-Town Ski and Snowboarding School at Arrowhead Mountain in the Colorado Rocky Mountains. Jon wants to expand the school's marketing efforts with a Web site that lets visitors to Arrowhead Mountain learn more about the school and its merchandise. To make the Web site more fun to use, Jon wants to use virtual reality, motion, and sound to create a virtual reality ski slope on the Web site for entertainment purposes.

a. Go to the Online Companion page for Unit H, then click one of the links under Independent Challenge 3.

b. Search for 3D plug-ins on the download site you chose. (Make sure you search for "plug-ins," not "add-ons.")

c. Click several of the links to programs on the results pages and read their descriptions to see if one might be appropriate for an on-screen simulated race. Print the description of each plug-in you think might work (make sure you find at least three).

d. Visit the Web site of at least one of the publishers and see if you can view a demonstration of the plug-in.

e. Write a brief description of the plug-ins you chose and explain why you chose them.

f. Exit your browser.

▼ REAL LIFE INDEPENDENT CHALLENGE

Looking for a new home or apartment can be time consuming. Using the Internet can help you in your search. Some realty sites offer virtual tours of homes for sale. To get a feel for how these tours work, research a few sites that offer software to realtors for creating tours, and view their demos.

a. Go to the Online Companion page for Unit H, then click one of the links under Real Life Independent Challenge.

b. On the Web site you chose, find the link to view a sample virtual tour.

c. Return to the Unit H page on the Online Companion, then view the sample tours on two other Web sites listed under Real Life Independent Challenge.

d. Note whether an add-on is required to view the virtual tours on any of the sites you visit.

Advanced Challenge Exercise

- Go to a download site of your choice, then search for software you can buy to create your own virtual tour.
- Find out whether users will need an add-on to view tours created using that software.
- Find one freeware program that you think would work well, and download it.

e. Exit your Web browser.

Extending Browser Capabilities   Internet 211

Internet

Go to the Online Companion page for Unit H, then click the **Just Solitaire link** under Visual Workshop. Find the page for the Beleaguered Castle solitaire game, as shown in Figure H-16. Play the game.

FIGURE H-16

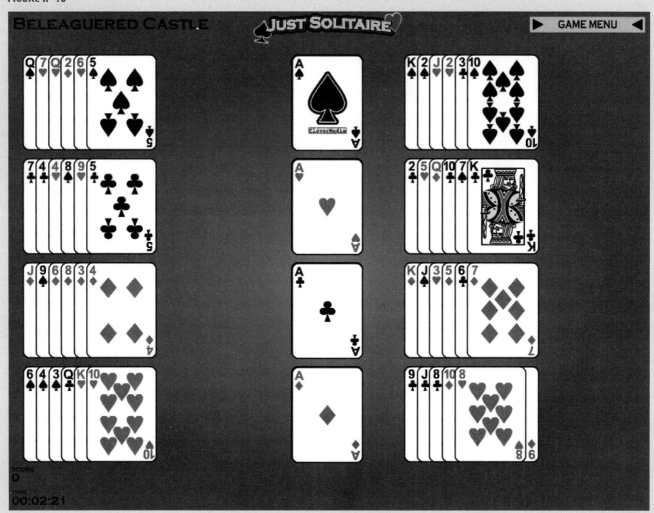

Increasing Web Security

When an individual or organization creates a Web site and publishes it on the Internet, the Web site becomes vulnerable to security threats. **Security** is broadly defined as the protection of assets from unauthorized access, use, alteration, or destruction. Individuals and organizations must secure their Web servers so that the data stored on them is protected from being stolen or altered and so that the connections to them are protected from being intercepted. Individuals and organizations must also secure their own computers with adequate safeguards against potential security and privacy threats that occur when they use them to access the Internet using a Web browser and an email program. Riverview Rowing Club in Victoria, British Columbia, has experienced a tremendous growth in membership over the past two years. The members have been asking the board of directors to provide t-shirts, jackets, and memorabilia, such as coffee mugs and pens, with the club's logo on it. The board decided to make these items available via their Web site in the hopes that they will sell to the general public as well. Because you have some experience with Web site design, the board has asked you to set up the site so that they can accept payments via the Web. You decide to research how to make transactions secure and how to maintain customers' privacy over the Internet.

OBJECTIVES

Understand security threats on the Internet

Minimize security risks on the Internet

Use the SmartScreen Filter in Internet Explorer

Use Phishing and Malware Protection in Firefox

Strengthen security in Internet Explorer

Strengthen security in Firefox

Check security features on a Web Site

Understand how Web sites track users

Manage browsing tracks in Internet Explorer

Manage browsing tracks in Firefox

Protect email from viruses and interception

Understanding Security Threats on the Internet

Internet sites and users are vulnerable to security threats, such as stealing users' identities, files, and hard drive space; misdirecting or intercepting email messages; or illegally obtaining and using passwords to access private accounts, such as online bank services. If you understand how security on the Internet can be compromised, you can then take steps to minimize your risks when you are online. You begin your research by investigating basic security concerns for Internet users.

DETAILS

Some of the security risks to which Internet users are exposed are described below:

- **Data Confidentiality**

  Many Web sites include forms in which users can efficiently supply information, such as their names and addresses, to an organization. If security features are not deliberately put into place by a Web site administrator, submitting information over the Web is about as secure as sending the same information on a postcard.

- **Sniffer Programs**

  At any point along a data packet's trip from source to destination, anyone can use a tool known as a **packet sniffer** or **sniffer program** to monitor and analyze it. Used illegally, a packet sniffer can capture user names, passwords, and other personal information.

- **Phishing**

  Phishing occurs when an individual tries to obtain confidential information from people via email by pretending to be a familiar organization or institution, such as a bank. The email message might ask the recipients to click a link in the message and use the form that opens to "confirm" personal information, such as names, account numbers, and Social Security numbers, or to reset their passwords by supplying their current passwords and new passwords. Any information provided by users is then stolen by the phisher.

- **Spoofing**

  Web sites that look like they belong to one organization but actually belong to someone else are **spoofed sites**, or **phishing sites**. Phishers use spoofed Web sites to make their victims believe that they are visiting the organization's real Web site. The site looks like the organization's real Web site, and the URL in the Address or Location bar starts with the name of the company (such as www.ebay.com). The underlying IP address, however, will not match the real one that belongs to the company being spoofed.

- **Port Scan**

  A **port** on a computer is like a door; it permits traffic to enter and leave a computer. A computer has over 65,000 ports for different processes, such as HTTP/World Wide Web traffic (port 80) and FTP traffic (port 21). A **port scan** occurs when one computer tests all or some of the ports on another computer to determine whether its ports are open, closed, or stealth (the user has hidden its state). Someone could use open ports on your computer to access data on your computer.

- **Malware**
  - **Malware** (short for *malicious software*) is a broad term that means any program that runs on your computer without your permission and usually performs undesired tasks. Viruses, worms, and Trojan horses are examples of malware. Many Web sites, such as the one shown in Figure I-1, provide news and information about viruses. In addition, malware includes **key loggers**, programs that run in the background and send your keystrokes to someone else so they can discover your user names and passwords.
  - Malware also includes programs that turn your computer into a a **bot** (short for *robot*) or a **zombie**, which is a computer that sends malware to or communicates with other computers without the owner's knowledge to harm those computers or act with other zombies to harm Web servers.

QUICK TIP
Another form of phishing is **pharming**, in which users are redirected to a spoofed site without their knowledge or consent and without clicking a link in an email message.

QUICK TIP
When a computer is connected to the Internet, it receives traffic through a port from other computers without its user even realizing it.

QUICK TIP
A **distributed denial of service (DDoS)** attack is when an attacker uses his or her own computer as well as zombie computers to bombard a server or other computer with so many messages that the network's bandwidth resources are consumed and the organization's computer communications are disabled.

FIGURE I-1: Web page on Trend Micro's Web site containing information about viruses

Names of viruses listed in this column

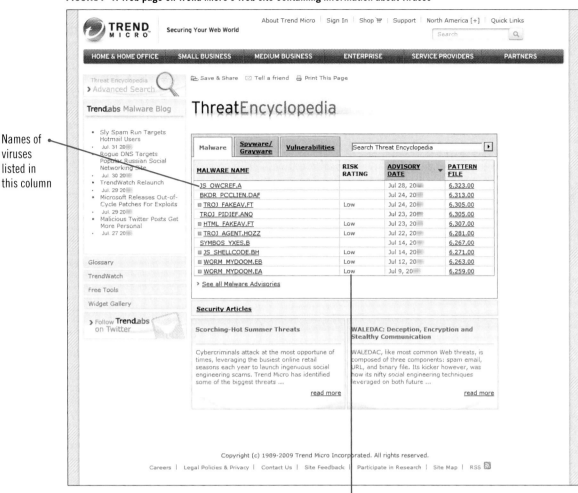

Column describes relative seriousness of virus threat

Brute force attacks

A **brute force attack** occurs when someone uses a program to enter character combinations until the system accepts a user name and password, thereby gaining access to the system. Some systems will send a warning to the computer's operator or lock out a user name when someone attempts to log in to a system a predetermined number of times without succeeding. Depending on the system to which the person gains access, the damage can range anywhere from reading a person's email messages to gaining access to accounts at financial institutions. Another example of a brute force attack is when someone submits combinations of numbers to a Web site that accepts credit card payments until the site accepts a valid credit card number. In this case, the person can then charge goods and services using the credit card number that he has discovered and stolen. People who create and use strong passwords and avoid using the same password for multiple logins are less likely to have their accounts threatened in this manner.

Minimizing Security Risks on the Internet

As you have seen, the Internet can expose users to many types of security risks. Fortunately, informed users can take simple **countermeasures**, which are procedures, programs, and hardware that detect and prevent each type of computer security threat. You continue your research for Riverview Rowing Club's Web site by researching popular countermeasures to common security threats.

DETAILS

Some common countermeasures are described below:

- Encryption
  - **Encryption** is the process of scrambling and encoding data transmissions using a mathematically-based program to produce a string of characters that are unreadable except by the person with the key. A **key** is the mathematical code used to **decrypt**, or reverse the encryption of the data. Without the key, anyone using a sniffer program or other program won't be able to read the data they are intercepting.
  - The resistance of an encrypted message to attack attempts (its strength) depends on the size of the key used in the encryption procedure. The size of the key is measured in bits (a **bit** is the single unit of data stored in a computer). Keys that are 128 bits or longer are called **strong keys**. Most Web browsers use 128-bit encryption, and some browsers and Web servers are equipped to use 256-bit and even longer keys.

- Digital Certificates
  - A **digital certificate** is an encrypted and password-protected file that contains information to authenticate and prove a person's or organization's identity. Usually, a digital certificate contains the certificate holder's name, address, and email address; a key; the certificate's expiration date or validity period; and a **certificate authority** (**CA**), an organization that verifies the certificate holder's identity and issues the digital certificate.
  - A **server certificate** is a digital certificate that authenticates a Web site for its users so the user can be confident that the Web site is not spoofed. A server certificate also ensures that the transfer of data between a user's computer and the server with the certificate is encrypted so that it is both tamper-proof and free from being intercepted. Figure I-2 shows a basic representation of how digital certificates work.

QUICK TIP

A **strong password** contains many characters consisting of random strings of letters not found in a dictionary, including numbers and special characters, and combinations of uppercase and lowercase letters; for example, using your first name or birthdate is not a strong password, but Rfp*^h90 is.

- User Identification
  Many Web sites let returning customers log on to an account that they have created on the server to make it easy for them to schedule services and check on their account status. **User identification** is the process of identifying a user to a computer. Most computer systems implement user identification with user names and passwords; the combination of a user name and password is sometimes called a **login**.

- User Authentication
  User authentication is the process of associating a person and his identification with a very high level of assurance. One method of user authentication is asking one or more questions to which only the authentic user could know the correct answers.

- Antivirus Software
  As you learned in an earlier unit, **antivirus software** is software that protects your computer from viruses, worms, and Trojan horses by blocking these programs from being downloaded from the server.

- Firewalls
  A **firewall** is a software program or hardware device that controls access between two networks, such as a local area network and the Internet or the Internet and a computer. A firewall can control port scans and other incoming traffic by rejecting it unless you have configured it to accept the traffic. A firewall on an individual's computer that is connected to the Internet might be a dedicated hardware device, as illustrated by Figure I-3, or it might be a program running on that computer.

FIGURE I-2: Processing a certificate

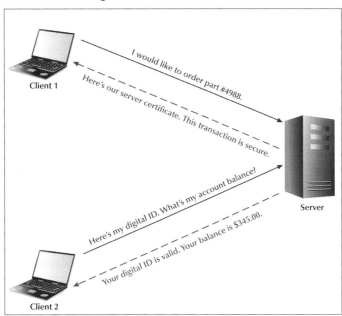

FIGURE I-3: Basic firewall architecture

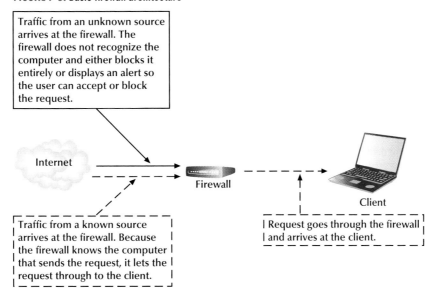

Traffic from an unknown source arrives at the firewall. The firewall does not recognize the computer and either blocks it entirely or displays an alert so the user can accept or block the request.

Internet

Firewall

Client

Traffic from a known source arrives at the firewall. Because the firewall knows the computer that sends the request, it lets the request through to the client.

Request goes through the firewall and arrives at the client.

Securing a wireless network and devices

By default, most wireless networks are unsecured. **Wired Equivalent Privacy (WEP)** is a security protocol for Wi-Fi networks that works by encrypting data sent over the network. **Wi-Fi Protected Access (WPA)** is a newer standard that provides better encryption than WEP by encrypting individual data packets with different keys so that if someone is able to intercept a data packet, that person won't gain access to the entire message automatically. If you access the Internet at a public hotspot, be wary of an **evil twin attack** (sometimes called a **café latte attack** because the attack often occurs at coffeehouses). In this type of attack, a hacker gathers information about an access point, and then uses that information to set up his own computer to use the real access point's signal to impersonate the real access point. Devices that use Bluetooth, a technology that provides short-wave radio links between electronic devices, are also susceptible to security threats.

Bluejacking occurs when the bluejacker sends an anonymous message in the form of a phone contact that is displayed as a text message to a Bluetooth device in an attempt to surprise the owner, express a comment or opinion, or contact the owner to make a social connection. One way to protect a Bluetooth device is to disable it from broadcasting its signal (a setting known as **undiscoverable mode**) to other Bluetooth devices. **Bluesnarfing** occurs when a hacker is able to detect the signal from a Bluetooth device and gain access to its data, listen in on phone calls, and send email messages from the victim's device. **Bluebugging** occurs when a hacker gains access to the device and all of its functions without the owner's consent. Most manufacturers of Bluetooth devices have released patches to fix the security flaws that make bluesnarfing and bluebugging possible.

UNIT
I
Internet

Using the SmartScreen Filter in Internet Explorer

The Internet Explorer SmartScreen Filter checks to see if the Web site you are visiting is a phishing site. It also works with other Windows programs, such as Windows Defender, to identify and block harmful programs that try to download to your computer. When the SmartScreen Filter is turned on, the URLs of Web sites you visit are sent to Microsoft to be compared against the latest list of known phishing sites. When the SmartScreen Filter is turned off, Internet Explorer checks Web sites you visit against a list of phishing sites stored on your computer, but it doesn't send any information to Microsoft. Whether the SmartScreen Filter is turned on or off, Internet Explorer checks the URLs of visited Web sites to see if they have characteristics of phishing sites. When the SmartScreen Filter is turned on, it also detects when suspected malware is being downloaded. You decide to explore the SmartScreen Filter settings in Internet Explorer.

STEPS

 If you are using Firefox, skip to the next lesson.

1. **Start Internet Explorer, go to your browser's home page, click the Safety button on the Command bar, then point to SmartScreen Filter**
    A submenu opens with commands that allow you to check to see if the current Web site is a phishing site or report the current Web site as a possible phishing site. Notice that the second command in the menu is either Turn Off SmartScreen Filter or Turn On SmartScreen Filter.

2. **Click Turn Off SmartScreen Filter or Turn On SmartScreen Filter**
    The Microsoft SmartScreen Filter dialog box opens. See Figure I-4.

3. **Click the Close button in the upper-right corner of the dialog box**
    The dialog box closes and the status of the SmartScreen Filter is unchanged.

TROUBLE
If a dialog box opens telling you that information will be sent to Microsoft, click the Don't show this message again check box to deselect it, then click OK.

4. **Click the Safety button on the Command bar, point to SmartScreen Filter, then click Check This Website**
    A dialog box opens telling you that this is not a reported phishing site. If the URL of the Web site you are trying to visit matches one of the sites listed as a phishing site, the browser window is colored red, and a message informing you that this Web site has been reported as unsafe appears. See Figure I-5. If a Web site is not on the list of known phishing sites, but the URL has the characteristics of a phishing site, the message "Are you trying to visit this site?" is displayed along with an option to provide feedback about the site to Microsoft. If the Web site attempts to download a program that has been identified as unsafe, the download is blocked and a dialog box with a red bar appears warning you that the download has been reported as unsafe.

5. **Click OK**
    The dialog box closes. To help users identify possible phishing sites, the domain name in the URL in the Address bar is in bold. For example, in Figure I-6, you can easily see that the page shown in the figure is stored on the MSN.com Web site, even though the URL is very long.

Commonsense precautions

If you receive an email purporting to be from your bank, credit card company, or any company with which you do business, and the email asks you to click a link to verify your personal identification information, don't click the link. Instead, open a new browser window, type the URL of the company directly into the Address bar, and check your account information in the usual way. If you receive an

email from a company with whom you do not do business telling you that your account has been compromised or asking you to check your account status, again, do not click the link in the email. If you want to follow up with the company, open a new browser window and contact them using a Contact link on the company's Web site, or contact them by phone.

FIGURE I-4: Microsoft SmartScreen Filter dialog box

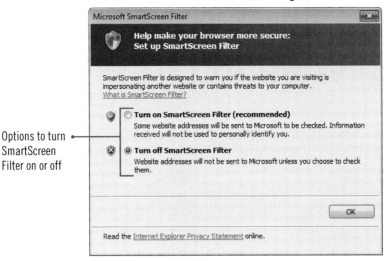

Options to turn
SmartScreen
Filter on or off

FIGURE I-5: A known phishing site caught in the Internet Explorer SmartScreen Filter

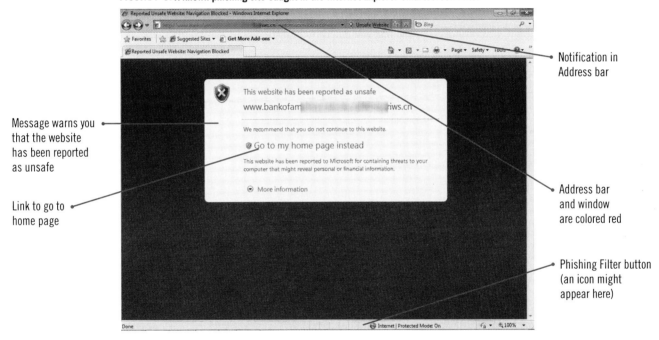

Message warns you
that the website
has been reported
as unsafe

Link to go to
home page

Notification in
Address bar

Address bar
and window
are colored red

Phishing Filter button
(an icon might
appear here)

FIGURE I-6: Domain name in bold in Address bar

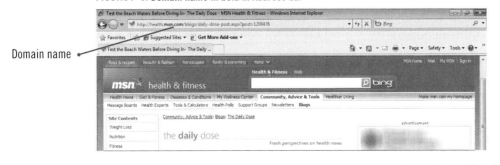

Domain name

Using Phishing and Malware Protection in Firefox

Firefox's Phishing Protection feature checks to see if the Web site you are visiting is a phishing site. The Malware Protection feature checks to see if the Web site you are visiting is an attack site that will attempt to download malware onto your computer. When Phishing and Malware Protection is turned on, the URLs of Web sites you visit are compared against the latest list of known phishing and malware sites. This list of known sites is updated on a regular basis. You decide to explore the Phishing and Malware Protection features in Firefox.

STEPS

(STOP) **If you are using Internet Explorer, skip to the next lesson.**

1. **Start Firefox, click** Tools **on the menu bar, click** Options, **then click the** Security icon **at the top of the Options dialog box**

   The Security panel of the Options dialog box appears.

2. **If necessary, click the** Block reported attack sites check box **and** Block reported web forgeries check box **to select them**

   See Figure I-7. When the Block reported web forgeries check box is selected, Phishing Protection is turned on. When the Block reported attack sites check box is selected, Malware Protection is turned on.

QUICK TIP
If the Block reported web forgeries check box in the Security panel of the Options dialog box is unchecked before you execute Step 4, and you want to see the warning page, select the check box. Then you must clear your history by clicking Tools on the menu bar, Clear Recent History, then clicking Clear Now.

3. **Click** Cancel

   The dialog box closes and the status of Phishing and Malware Protection is unchanged.

4. **Go to the Online Companion page for** Unit I, **then click the** Firefox Phishing Test site link **under Lesson 4**

   If Phishing Protection is turned on, a Web page with the message "Reported Web Forgery!" appears in the browser window. See Figure I-8. If Phishing Protection is turned off, the Web page stored on the server (announcing "It's a Trap!") appears instead. If you click Get me out of here!, you return to your browser's home page. You can click the Ignore this warning link to visit the Web site despite the warning, or click Why was this site blocked? to go to a Web page that provides information about phishing and malware and the Phishing and Malware Protection features in Firefox, as well as links you can use to let Mozilla know that you think the Web site is a safe site.

TROUBLE
If nothing seems to happen, note that the process of checking a Web site to see if the URL matches the characteristics of a phishing site can take several minutes.

5. **If the Reported Web Forgery! page is open in your browser window, click** Get me out of here!; **if the It's a Trap! Web page is open in your browser window, click the** Home button **on the toolbar**

   Your browser's home page appears in the window.

6. **Return to the Online Companion page for** Unit I, **then click the** Firefox Malware Test site link **under Lesson 4**

   If Malware Protection is turned on, a Web page with the message "Reported Attack Site!" appears in the browser window. If Malware Protection is turned off, the Web page stored on the server (announcing "It's an Attack!") appears instead.

7. **If the Reported Attack Site! page is open in your browser window, click** Get me out of here!; **if the It's an Attack page appears in your browser window, click the** Home button **on the toolbar**

   Your browser's home page appears in the window again.

FIGURE I-7: Security panel in Options dialog box

Select this check box to turn on Malware Protection

Select this check box to turn on Phishing Protection

Click to display Security panel

FIGURE I-8: Mozilla's sample phishing site with Phishing Protection turned on

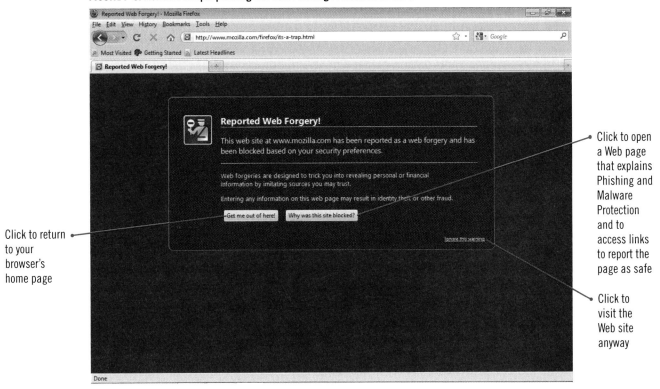

Click to open a Web page that explains Phishing and Malware Protection and to access links to report the page as safe

Click to return to your browser's home page

Click to visit the Web site anyway

Commonsense precautions

If you receive an email purporting to be from your bank, credit card company, or any company with which you do business, and the email asks you to click a link to verify your personal identification information, don't click the link. Instead, open a new browser window, type the URL of the company directly into the Address bar, and check your account information in the usual way. If you receive an email from a company with whom you do not do business telling you that your account has been compromised or asking you to check your account status, again, do not click the link in the email. If you want to follow up with the company, open a new browser window and contact them using a Contact link on the company's Web site, or contact them by phone.

Strengthening Security in Internet Explorer

Programs that travel with applications to a browser and execute on the user's computer are security risks. A **Java applet** is a program written in the Java programming language that can execute and consume a computer's resources. A **JavaScript program**, instructions (**scripts**) written in the JavaScript programming language, can send information to another computer over the Internet. For example, a cleverly written JavaScript program could examine your computer's programs and email a file from your computer back to a Web server. **ActiveX controls** are Microsoft's technology for writing small applications that perform some action in Web pages, but these components have full access to a computer's file system. For example, a hidden ActiveX control in a Web page could scan a hard drive for PCX and JPEG files and print them on any network printer. Most Java applets, JavaScript programs, and ActiveX controls are beneficial, but you should take steps to protect your computer from potential attacks that use them. Perhaps the simplest strategy is to prevent these programs from running. You want to be sure that the club's Web site will be compatible with users' security settings. You decide to investigate how to disable your Web browser from running Java and JavaScript programs and ActiveX controls.

STEPS

🛑 *If you are using Firefox, skip to the next lesson.*

1. **Click the** Tools button **on the Command bar, click** Internet Options, **then click the** Security tab

    The Security tab of the Internet Options dialog box opens with Internet selected as the Web content zone. See Figure I-9. The Local intranet zone contains any computers on your LAN. The security settings for this zone are minimal. Unless you add sites to the Trusted sites and Restricted sites zones, all Web sites are in the Internet zone.

TROUBLE

If the Default level command is grayed out and not available, your security level is already set to the default level of Medium-high. Skip Step 2.

2. **Click** Default level

    The default security level is Medium-high, and a description of the security level appears next to the slider. As noted in the dialog box, the default setting of Medium-high will cause the browser to prompt you before it downloads potentially unsafe content and prevents the browser from downloading unsigned ActiveX controls.

QUICK TIP

Protected Mode means that the only place files are downloaded without the express consent of the user is to the Temporary Internet Files folder.

3. **Drag the slider up to the top of the slider bar**

    The security level is changed to High. This provides the highest level of security as you are using the Internet; Java applets, JavaScript programs, and ActiveX controls are not allowed to run. However, this means that some safe Web sites that use these Web programs will no longer work properly.

4. **Click** Custom level

    The Security Settings - Internet Zone dialog box opens, similar to the one shown in Figure I-10.

QUICK TIP

Signed ActiveX controls are ActiveX controls that Internet Explorer has identified as controls created by software developers with a digital certificate.

5. **Scroll down the Settings list box to view the available options**

    The list box allows you to specify how to deal with many different types of Web page content and programs, including ActiveX controls, Java applets, and scripts.

6. **Click** Cancel

    The Security Settings dialog box closes.

7. **Click** Cancel

    The Internet Options dialog box closes without changing your security settings.

FIGURE I-9: Security tab in the Internet Options dialog box

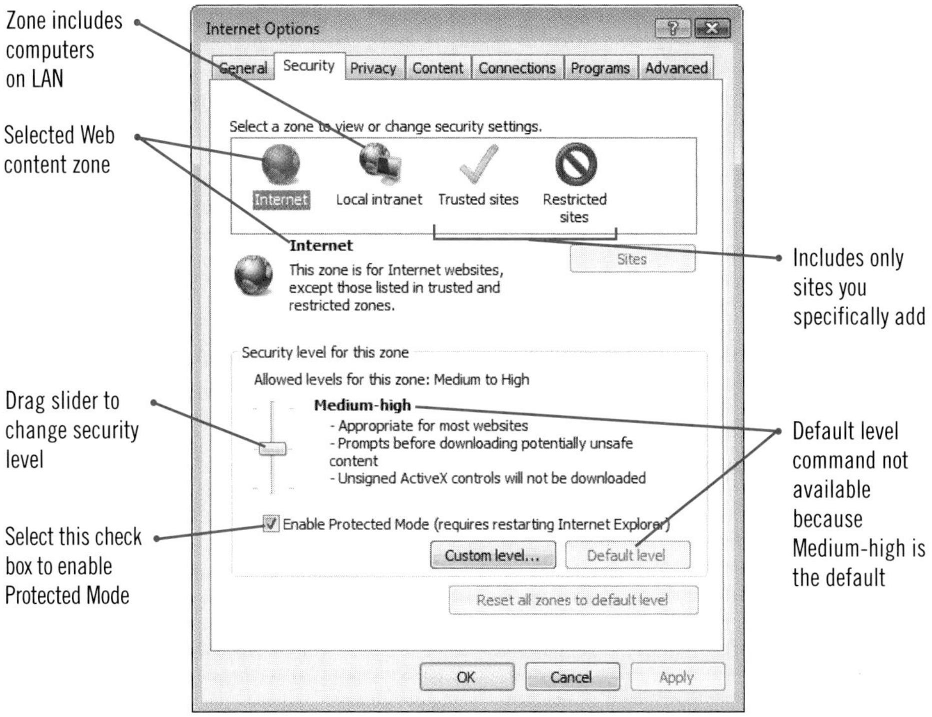

Zone includes computers on LAN

Selected Web content zone

Drag slider to change security level

Select this check box to enable Protected Mode

Includes only sites you specifically add

Default level command not available because Medium-high is the default

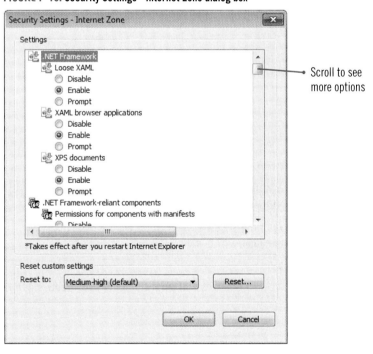

FIGURE I-10: Security Settings - Internet Zone dialog box

Scroll to see more options

Internet

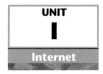

UNIT
I
Internet

Strengthening Security in Firefox

Programs that travel with applications to a browser and execute on the user's computer are security risks. A **Java applet**, a program written in the Java programming language, can execute and consume a computer's resources. A **JavaScript program**, instructions (**scripts**) written in the JavaScript programming language, can send information to another computer over the Internet. For example, a cleverly written JavaScript program could examine your computer's programs and email a file from your computer back to a Web server. Most Java applets and JavaScript programs are beneficial, but you should take steps to protect your computer from potential attacks that use them. Perhaps the simplest strategy is to prevent these programs from running. ▓▓▓ You want to be sure that the club's Web site will be compatible with users' security settings. You decide to investigate how to disable your Web browser from running Java and JavaScript programs.

STEPS

 If you are using Internet Explorer, skip to the next lesson.

1. **Click** Tools **on the menu bar, click** Options, **then click the** Content icon **at the top of the Options dialog box**

   The Content panel of the Options dialog box opens. See Figure I-11.

2. **Note whether the Enable JavaScript and Enable Java check boxes are selected, then click the** Enable JavaScript check box **to select it, if necessary**

   When this check box is selected, JavaScript programs are allowed to run.

3. **Click** Advanced **next to Enable JavaScript**

   The Advanced JavaScript Settings dialog box opens, as shown in Figure I-12. These options allow you to decide what scripts are allowed to do when you view Web pages.

4. **Click** Cancel

   The Advanced JavaScript Settings dialog box closes.

QUICK TIP

Firefox does not support **ActiveX controls**, which are Microsoft's technology for writing small applications that perform some action in Web pages.

5. **Click the** Enable Java **and** Enable JavaScript check boxes **to clear them, if necessary**

   Now as you are using the Internet, Java applets and JavaScript programs are not allowed to run. However, this means that some Web sites that use these Web programs will no longer work properly. You need to enable Java to view some Web sites.

6. **Click the** Security icon **in the bar at the top of the dialog box, then, if necessary, click the** Warn me when sites try to install add-ons check box **to select it**

   When this option is selected, as shown in Figure I-13, Firefox warns you when a Web site is about to install active content (such as programs, plug-ins, and applets).

7. **Click** Cancel

   The Options dialog box closes without changing your security settings.

FIGURE I-11: Content panel in Options dialog box

Click to display Content panel

JavaScript and Java options

Click to see advanced JavaScript options

FIGURE I-12: Advanced JavaScript Settings dialog box

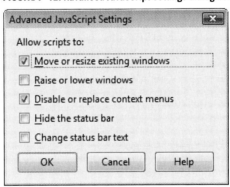

FIGURE I-13: Security panel in Options dialog box

Select this check box to display a warning dialog box when a site tries to install an add-on

Click to display Security panel

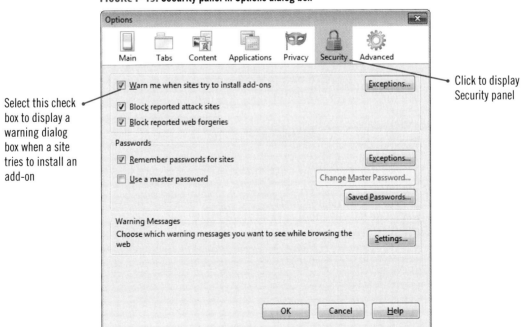

Checking Security Features on a Web Site

The **Secure Sockets Layer** (**SSL**) was the first widely used protocol for establishing secure, encrypted connections between Web browsers and Web servers on the Internet. SSL was revised several times and is still used. In 1999, SSL version 3 was improved and reissued by the Internet Engineering Task Force as **Transport Layer Security** (**TLS**). Web pages that use a secure protocol are encrypted, and the site has a server certificate that users can access to authenticate its validity. Web pages secured by the secure protocol also have URLs that begin with https://, in which the "s" indicates a secure connection, and when the page is displayed in a Web browser, the browser displays an icon, usually a closed padlock. You know that you will have to use encryption and set up a secure page so that people feel safe providing their credit card numbers on the club's Web site. You want to learn more about how other sites do this. You recently purchased a book about advanced Web site design from Charles River Publishers. You remember that their Web site was secure, so you decide to investigate it.

STEPS

1. **Go to the Online Companion page for** Unit I, **then click the** Charles River Media link **under Lesson 7**

2. **Click the link for any title that appears on that page**
   A page describing the book you selected opens in the current tab.

3. **Click** Add to Cart
   The shopping cart page appears with the book you chose listed.

> **TROUBLE**
>
> If you are using Firefox and a new tab opens telling you the connection to delmarlearning.com is untrusted, click I Understand the Risks, click Add Exception, then click Confirm Security Exception. This sometimes occurs with Firefox and with Web sites having legitimate security certificates. If you are certain the Web site to which you are connecting is secure, you can continue accessing the site.

4. **Click** Continue Checkout **(or something similar)**
   The page changes to collect billing and shipping information from you. This page is secure, as indicated by the padlock on the right side of the Address or Location bar. In Internet Explorer, when a Web site has met more rigorous demands for proof of security from a certificate provider, it is granted an Extended Validation certificate and the Address bar is colored green. You can check the Web page's security features.

5. **If you are using Internet Explorer, click the** padlock **in the Address bar; if you are using Firefox, double-click the** padlock **at the right end of the status bar**
   If you are using Internet Explorer, the Website Identification dialog box opens. See Figure I-14. If you are using Firefox, the Page Info dialog box opens with the Security tab selected. See Figure I-15. (In Firefox, you can also click the highlighted domain name in the Location bar to open a box that identifies the certificate authority, and then you can click More Information to open the Page Info dialog box.) These dialog boxes indicate that the Web site is verified, which means that a digital certificate is on file and valid. The Firefox Page Info dialog box also specifically mentions that the page is encrypted.

6. **If you are using Internet Explorer, click the** View certificates link **in the Website Identification dialog box, then click the** Details tab; **if you are using Firefox, click** View Certificate
   If you are using Internet Explorer, you can scroll down the list on the Details tab to see information about the Web site's digital certificate. See Figure I-16. If you are using Firefox, the Certificate Viewer dialog box opens with information about the Web site's digital certificate. See Figure I-17.

7. **If you are using Internet Explorer, click** OK; **if you are using Firefox, click** Close, **then click the** Close button **in the Page Info dialog box title bar**

FIGURE I-14: Website Identification report in Internet Explorer

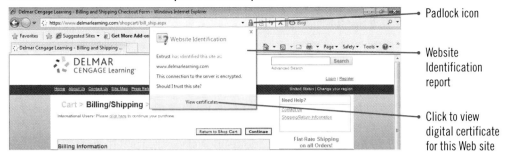

Padlock icon

Website Identification report

Click to view digital certificate for this Web site

FIGURE I-15: Security panel in the Page Info dialog box in Firefox

Highlighted domain name in Location bar

Security icon selected

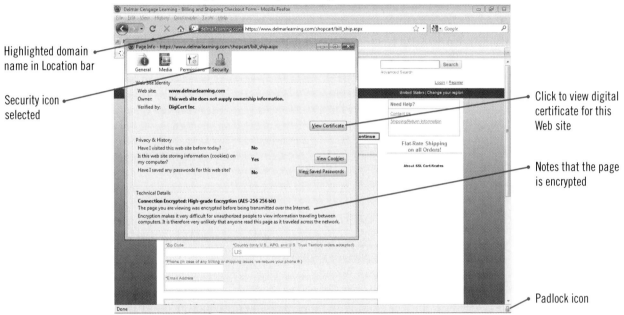

Click to view digital certificate for this Web site

Notes that the page is encrypted

Padlock icon

FIGURE I-16: Details tab in the Certificate dialog box in Internet Explorer

FIGURE I-17: General tab in the Certificate Viewer dialog box in Firefox

General tab selected

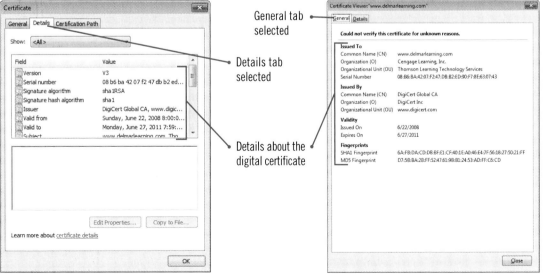

Details tab selected

Details about the digital certificate

UNIT
I
Internet

Understanding How Web Sites Track Users

Some companies attempt to collect marketing data by tracking users' movements on the Web. They do this by using cookies. A **cookie** is a small text file that a Web site stores on your computer and that contains information about your clickstream. A **clickstream** is sequence of links you click while visiting a Web site. Only the Web site that stored the cookie on your hard drive can read it, and it cannot read other cookies on your hard drive or any other file on your computer. You are considering using cookies on the Riverview Rowing Club's site. Before you make this decision, you decide to learn more about cookies that are helpful and cookies that could be considered intrusive, as well as other methods of tracking users' browsing.

DETAILS

Some methods used for tracking your browsing are described below:

- **Cookies That Enhance Browsing**

  Some cookies are helpful and record information that enhances your browsing. For example, on some Web sites, you provide the data stored in a cookie openly, such as when you enter a value in a field on a form. Other times, the cookie might silently record your behavior at a Web site. For example, an online bookstore might store your book preferences in a cookie. When you revisit the bookstore, the Web site might welcome you with your user name that you recorded in the form, and inform you of new books available by the same author as the one whose book you purchased previously.

- **Intrusive Cookies**

  - Some cookies are intrusive and are created without your consent. For example, some Web sites use cookies to collect information about your interests and then use this information to try to market products or services to you. Some Web sites have agreements with marketing companies that allow the marketing company to place images on a Web site; these images are linked to the marketing company's site. This means the marketing company can also place a cookie on your computer. These are known as **third-party cookies**. Any time you visit any site on which the marketing company has an image, the marketing company's cookie sends data back to the marketing company.

  - A **Web bug**, sometimes called a **clear GIF** or a **transparent GIF**, is a small, hidden graphic on a Web page or in an email message that is designed to work in conjunction with a cookie to obtain information about the person viewing the page or email message and then send that information to a third party. The hidden graphic is usually a GIF file with a size of one pixel, which is approximately the same size as the period at the end of this sentence. Figure I-18 shows the part of a Web page that contains a Web bug. To find a Web bug, you need to examine the HTML document that created the Web page. Figure I-19 shows a section of an HTML document that creates a Web bug in a Web page.

QUICK TIP

Often, if you do not want to see the ads in adware, you can pay a fee to the software publisher, which will provide you with a code to unlock the software and disable the ads.

- **Adware**

  Adware is software that includes advertisements to help pay for the product in which they appear. Many freeware and shareware programs are sold as adware, a practice that provides opportunities for developers to offer software at little or no cost to the user. Adware usually does not cause any security threats because the user is aware of the ads and the parties responsible for including them are clearly identified in the programs. Often, the advertisements are targeted to the user based on their browsing history.

- **Spyware**

  Spyware is a category of adware in which the user has little control over or knowledge of the ads and other monitoring features it contains. Spyware is generally considered to be malware. Some programs you install, especially freeware and shareware programs, might include spyware to track your use of the program and the Internet or to collect data about you. Some companies provide information to users about spyware, but many do not. **Ad blockers** and **antispyware programs** are programs that search for files written by known spyware. The results of a scan by one of these programs, Ad-Aware from Lavasoft, appears in Figure I-20.

FIGURE I-18: Web page containing a Web bug

Clear GIF file location

FIGURE I-19: HTML document containing a Web bug

```
<FRAMESET ROWS="*,20" BORDER=0 FRAMEBORDER=0 FRAMESPACING=0>
<!-- Start of           Tracking Code: Please do not remove -->
<SCRIPT language="JavaScript">
var axel = Math.random()+"";
var a = axel * 10000000000000;
document.write('<IMG
SRC="http://ad.           .net/activity;src=585966;type=counter;cat=oran;ord=1;num=' + a + '?"
WIDTH=1 HEIGHT=1 BORDER=0>');
</SCRIPT>
<NOSCRIPT>
<img src='http://127.0.0.1:3388/bug.cgi'>

</NOSCRIPT>
<!-- End of           Tracking Code: Please do not remove -->
```

Clear Gif file location

Cookie identification number generated for the current user

FIGURE I-20: Results of a scan in Ad-Aware

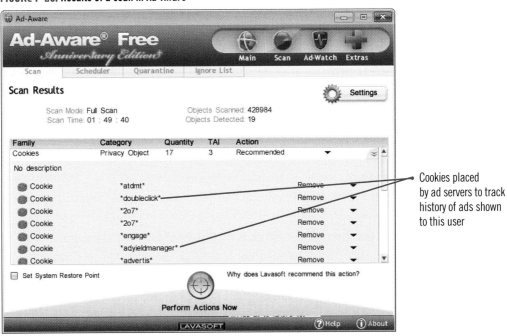

Cookies placed by ad servers to track history of ads shown to this user

Understanding pop-ups

Pop-ups are usually advertisements that appear in small windows in front of the current window. (Pop-ups that appear behind the current window are sometimes called **pop-unders**.) By default, both Internet Explorer and Firefox block pop-ups. To customize the Pop-up Blocker in Internet Explorer, click the Tools button on the Command bar, and then point to Pop-up Blocker. To turn the Pop-up Blocker on or off, click Turn On Pop-up Blocker or Turn Off Pop-up Blocker in the submenu. To specify on which sites pop-ups are allowed to appear, click Pop-up Blocker Settings to open the Pop-up Blocker Settings dialog box, type the URL in the Address of website to allow text box, and then click Add. To customize how Firefox blocks pop-ups, click Tools on the menu bar, click Options, and then click the Content icon at the top of the Options dialog box. To turn the pop-up blocker option on or off, select or deselect the Block pop-up windows check box. To specify on which sites pop-ups are allowed to appear, click Exceptions next to the Block pop-up windows check box to open the Allowed Sites – Pop-ups dialog box, type the URL in the Address of web site text box, and then click Allow.

Internet

Managing Browsing Tracks in Internet Explorer

One way to keep Web sites from tracking your browsing is to prevent cookies from being saved on your computer. However, if you visit a Web site that requires a membership, without a cookie, you might need to sign in every time you open a new Web page on the Web site. Fortunately, Internet Explorer can distinguish between different types of cookies, and you can block more intrusive cookies while allowing harmless ones, or you can block your computer from storing cookie files altogether. In addition, **InPrivate Filtering** is a feature in Internet Explorer that analyzes the content on Web pages you visit, and if the same content is used on several Web sites that you visit (in other words, third-party content), you can choose to block that content. You can also use the **InPrivate Browsing** feature, which opens a new browser window, and while you are browsing the Internet in that window, no cookies are stored, and the browsing history and temporary Internet files are deleted automatically when you close the InPrivate Browsing window. If you do not use InPrivate Browsing, you can manually delete all traces of your browsing history. As you continue your investigation, you decide to investigate how to change your Web browser preferences relating to cookies and how to delete your browsing history.

STEPS

(STOP) *If you are using Firefox, skip to the next lesson.*

1. **Click the Tools button on the Command bar, click Internet Options, then click the Privacy tab in the Internet Options dialog box**

   The Privacy tab in the Internet Options dialog box opens. The Privacy tab contains a slider bar, which allows you to adjust your Web browser's privacy level to one of six preset specifications. The description of the cookies allowed for each setting appears next to the slider. In the InPrivate section of the Privacy tab, you can click the first check box to disable InPrivate Filtering. Figure I-21 shows the slider set to Medium and InPrivate Filtering turned on.

2. **Click Sites**

   The Per Site Privacy Actions dialog box opens. You can set rules for cookies from specific Web sites by typing the URL of a Web site in the Address of website text box, and then clicking Allow or Block.

3. **Click OK, then click Cancel in the Internet Options dialog box**

   The Per Site Privacy Actions dialog box and the Internet Options dialog box close. You can delete all the stored cookies and the browsing history on your computer.

4. **Click the Safety button on the Command bar, then click Delete Browsing History**

   The Delete Browsing History dialog box opens, as shown in Figure I-22. To delete your browsing tracks, you would select the check box next to each type of browsing history that you want to delete, and then click Delete. If you select the InPrivate Filtering data check box, then all of the saved data used by the InPrivate Filtering feature will be deleted and Web sites that were previously blocked from storing cookies will be able to store cookies again. Note that selecting the first check box in the list preserves cookies stored from any Web sites stored in your Favorites list.

5. **Click Cancel**

   The Delete Browsing History dialog box closes.

6. **Click Safety on the Command bar, then click InPrivate Browsing**

   A new browser window opens with *InPrivate* in the Address bar and in parentheses after the page title in the title bar. See Figure I-23.

7. **Click the Close button in the title bar of the InPrivate Browsing window**

FIGURE I-21: Privacy tab in the Internet Options dialog box

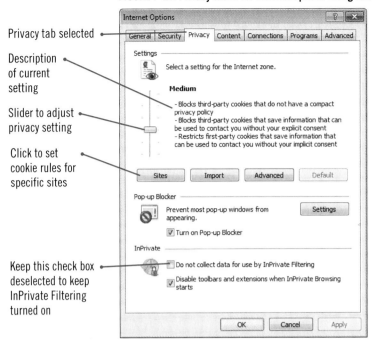

Privacy tab selected

Description of current setting

Slider to adjust privacy setting

Click to set cookie rules for specific sites

Keep this check box deselected to keep InPrivate Filtering turned on

FIGURE I-22: Delete Browsing History dialog box

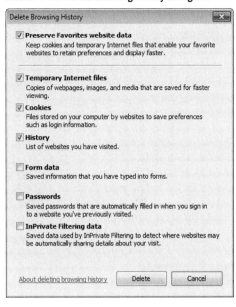

FIGURE I-23: InPrivate browser window

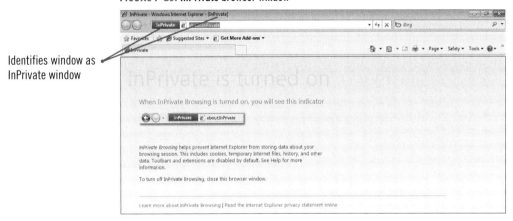

Identifies window as InPrivate window

Customizing the Internet Explorer Pop-up Blocker

Pop-ups are usually advertisements that appear in small windows that appear in front of the current window. (Pop-ups that appear behind the current window are sometimes called **pop-unders**.) By default, Internet Explorer blocks pop-ups. You can customize the Pop-up Blocker in Internet Explorer. Click the Tools button on the Command bar, and then point to Pop-up Blocker. To turn the Pop-up Blocker on or off, click Turn On Pop-up Blocker or Turn Off Pop-up Blocker in the submenu. To specify on which sites pop-ups are allowed to appear, click Pop-up Blocker Settings to open the Pop-up Blocker Settings dialog box, type the URL in the Address of website to allow text box, and then click Add.

UNIT
I

Internet

Managing Browsing Tracks in Firefox

One way to keep Web sites from tracking your browsing is to manage the cookies that are stored on your computer. Firefox can distinguish between types of cookies, and you can block more intrusive cookies while allowing harmless ones or you can block your computer from storing cookie files altogether. In addition, you can choose to block all third-party cookies. You can also use the **Private Browsing** feature, which opens a new browser window, and while you are browsing the Internet in that window, no cookies are stored, and the browsing history and temporary Internet files are deleted automatically when you close the Private Browsing window. If you do not use Private Browsing, you can manually delete all traces of your browsing history. As you continue your investigation, you decide to investigate how to change your Web browser preferences relating to cookies and how to delete your browsing history.

STEPS

 If you are using Internet Explorer, skip to the next lesson.

1. **Click** Tools **on the menu bar, click** Options, **then click the** Privacy icon **at the top of the Options dialog box**

   The Privacy panel in the Options dialog box allows you to manage your browsing tracks.

2. **Click the** Firefox will list arrow, **then click** Use custom settings for history

   The dialog box changes to display options for managing browsing tracks. See Figure I-24. You can adjust how long your browsing history is stored, choose to not store your download history or your search and form history, choose how long to store cookies, and choose to accept third-party cookies.

3. **Click** Exceptions

   The Exceptions - Cookies dialog box opens. You can set rules for cookies from specific Web sites by typing the URL of a Web site in the Address of web site text box, and then clicking Allow or Block. This is especially useful if you choose to block third-party cookies and you want to use the features on a Web site that require a third-party cookie to be stored on your computer.

> **QUICK TIP**
>
> To clear your browsing tracks every time you exit Firefox, click Tools on the menu bar, click Options, click the Privacy icon, click the Firefox will list arrow, click Use custom settings for history, then click the Clear history when Firefox closes check box to select it.

4. **Click** Close, **then click** Cancel **in the Options dialog box**

   The Exceptions - Cookies dialog box and the Options dialog box close. You can delete all the stored cookies and the browsing history on your computer.

5. **Click** Tools **on the menu bar, click** Clear Recent History, **then, in the Clear Recent History dialog box, click the** Details list arrow

   The Clear Recent History dialog box opens. See Figure I-25. To delete browsing tracks, click the Time range to clear arrow, select the time range, select the check box next to each type of browsing history that you want to delete, and then click Clear Now.

6. **Click** Cancel

   The Clear Recent History dialog box closes.

> **QUICK TIP**
>
> To start Firefox in a Private Browsing session, click Tools on the menu bar, click Options, click Privacy, select Use custom settings for history, then select the Automatically start Firefox in a private browsing session check box.

7. **Click** Tools **on the menu bar, then click** Start Private Browsing

   A dialog box opens asking if you would like to start Private Browsing.

8. **Click** Start Private Browsing

   A new browser window replaces the currently open browser window. *Private Browsing* appears in parentheses after the page title in the title bar, and a message reminding you that Firefox will not remember any history for this session appears in the window. See Figure I-26.

9. **Click** Tools **on the menu bar, then click** Stop Private Browsing

   The Private Browsing window closes and the previous browser session is restored.

Increasing Web Security

FIGURE I-24: Privacy panel in Options dialog box with custom settings for history displayed

Options for storing history

Select to accept cookies

Deselect to reject third-party cookies

Click to choose length of time to keep cookies

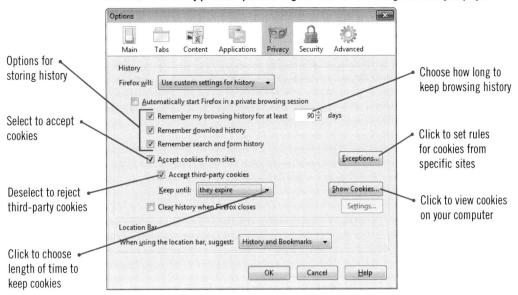

Choose how long to keep browsing history

Click to set rules for cookies from specific sites

Click to view cookies on your computer

FIGURE I-25: Clear Recent History dialog box

Details list arrow

Deselect to save login information for the current session

Keep deselected to retain site preferences

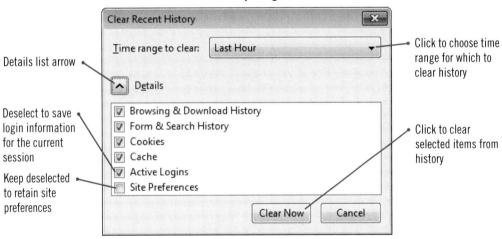

Click to choose time range for which to clear history

Click to clear selected items from history

FIGURE I-26: Private Browsing window

Identifies window as Private window

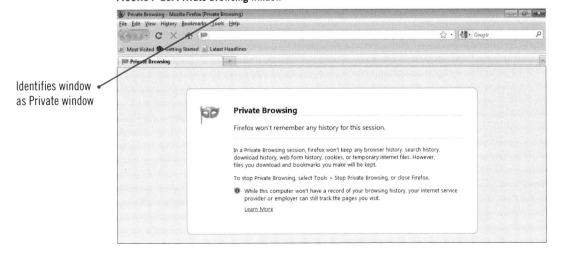

Protecting Email from Viruses and Interception

Although the Web is an important area to focus on for understanding Internet security, it's not the only area of concern. Protecting your computer when using email must go hand in hand with Web protection to eliminate the most common Internet-based threats to your computer. Fortunately, you can greatly limit your exposure to destructive programs carried by email by taking a few simple precautions, such as installing programs that protect your computer or verifying that your attachments are safe before you open them. ▰▰▰▰ As you conclude your preparatory research for the Riverview Rowing Club's Web site, you want to understand how email risks might affect the company's online strategy. You know that you will have a Contact link on the site, and you want to review the steps you and others at the club will need to take to limit their exposure to problems via email.

Some tools for protecting your computer from email threats are:

Some Webmail providers, such as Windows Live Hotmail, automatically check their users' email messages for viruses.

- **Antivirus Software**

  As explained earlier in this unit, viruses, worms, and Trojan horses are destructive programs that can wreak havoc on your computer, and antivirus software can block damage from any viruses, worms, or Trojan horses that you might receive by email and keep such programs from using your email program to reproduce. Figure I-27 shows a comparison chart on the TopTenReviews Web site of some popular antivirus programs. Because antivirus software is often available for free at colleges and universities, you should check with your instructor or system administrator to see if this software is available to protect your computer. If you plan to purchase antivirus software or download and use a free package, make sure you read current reviews to see which program will do the best job at protecting your computer. After you install antivirus software, you must run regular updates to keep the antivirus protection up-to-date since new viruses are constantly being written.

- **Handling Email Attachments**

  You can increase your email security by modifying your email practices. Don't save or open attachments from anyone—even people you know well—without scrutinizing the email message first. An attachment ending with .exe is a program file; opening it runs the program on your computer with unknown consequences. Always be sure you know what a program will do and that you're certain of the sender's identity before opening it. In addition, because worms replicate by sending nonsense messages to people listed in the victim's address book, make sure the accompanying email message makes sense and is specific to you. If the message is short and general, even if it's from a friend, it might simply be a worm's trick to get you to open the attachment. If you get a lot of email every day, using antivirus software can be a worthwhile investment because it can find and delete any viruses, worms, or Trojan horses attached to email messages before they are visible in your email program.

- **Encryption Software**

  If you use email to send sensitive information, such as business information or financial data, it's good practice to use encryption software for email. Like Web browser encryption, email encryption scrambles a message's contents in a way that can only be decoded by the intended recipient; therefore, a packet sniffer cannot be used to illegally intercept the contents of email messages.

FIGURE I-27: Comparison of antivirus programs on TopTenReviews

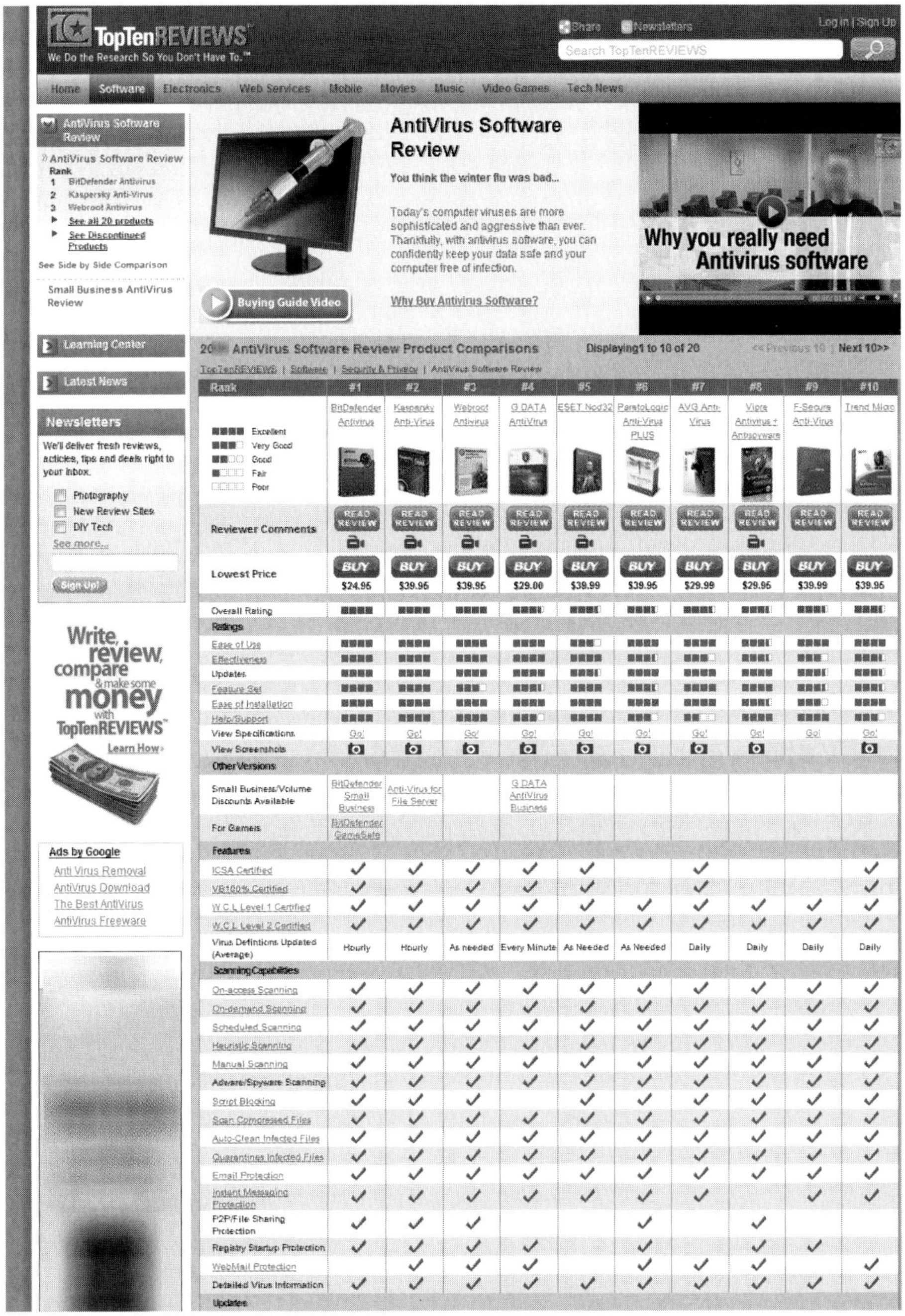

Dealing with spam

As spam has grown to become a serious problem for all email users and providers, new approaches have been devised or proposed to combat it. Some of these approaches require new laws to be passed, and some require technical changes in the mail-handling systems of the Internet. In January, 2004, the U.S. CAN-SPAM (Controlling the Assault of Non-Solicited Pornography and Marketing) law went into effect. Researchers who track the amount of spam noted a drop in the percentage of spam messages in February and March, 2004. However, by April the rate was back up. It appeared that spammers slowed down their activities after the CAN-SPAM law was passed to see if they would actually be prosecuted. For the most part, they were not, and the spammers went right back to work. Unfortunately, CAN-SPAM and similar laws are ineffective at preventing spam because many spammers use email servers located in countries that do not have (and that are unlikely to adopt) antispam laws, and spammers can move their operations from one server to another in minutes. For now, the best way to make spammers easier to find and ban or prosecute is to make changes in the way email is sent over the Internet.

Practice

For current SAM information including versions and content details, visit SAM Central (http://samcentral.course.com). If you have a SAM user profile, you may have access to hands-on instruction, practice, and assessment of the skills covered in this unit. Since we support various versions of SAM throughout the life of this text, you will want to check with your instructor for instructions and the correct URL/Web site to access those assignments.

▼ CONCEPTS REVIEW

Identify the purpose of the dialog boxes shown in Figures I-28 and 1-29 if you are using Internet Explorer and in Figures I-30 and I-31 if you are using Firefox.

FIGURE I-28

1.
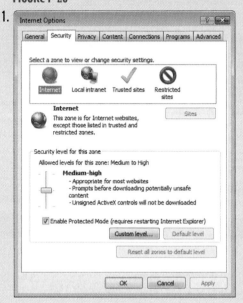

FIGURE I-29

2.
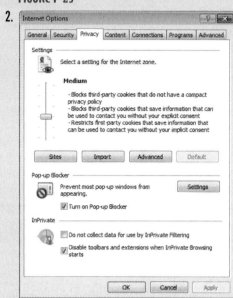

FIGURE I-30

3.

FIGURE I-31

4.

Match each term with the statement that best describes it.

5. **ActiveX control**
6. **Phishing**
7. **Security**
8. **Clickstream**
9. **Digital certificate**
10. **Sniffer program**
11. **Cookie**
12. **Encryption**

a. An encrypted and password-protected file that contains information to authenticate and prove a person's or organization's identity

b. Trying to obtain confidential information from people via email

c. The protection of assets from unauthorized access, use, alteration, or destruction

d. The sequence of links you click while visiting a Web site

e. Scrambling and encoding data transmissions

f. A program that monitors and analyzes data packets as they travel over the Internet

g. Microsoft's technology for writing small applications that perform some action in Web pages

h. A text file that Web sites can use to track your browsing habits

Select the best answer from the list of choices.

13. **Web sites that look like they belong to one business but actually belong to someone else are:**
    a. authenticated.
    b. phooled.
    c. encrypted.
    d. spoofed.

14. **The best way to protect your computer against worms is to:**
    a. prevent Web sites from storing cookies on your computer.
    b. disable Web page programs in your Web browser.
    c. install antivirus software.
    d. use encryption software, such as PGP.

15. **A small, hidden graphic on a Web page or in an email message that is designed to work in conjunction with a cookie to obtain information about the person viewing the page or email message and to send that information to a third party is:**
    a. adware.
    b. a Web bug.
    c. a virus
    d. spyware.

16. **A _____ is when one computer tests all or some of the ports of another computer to determine whether its ports are open, closed, or stealth.**
    a. sniffer program
    b. phishing program
    c. virus
    d. port scan

17. **The process of identifying a user to a computer is called:**
    a. digital certification.
    b. user identification.
    c. user authentication.
    d. SSL protocol.

18. **A software program or hardware device that controls access between two networks is a(n):**
   a. ActiveX control.
   b. cookie.
   c. firewall.
   d. Java applet.

19. **Which of the following stores information about your clickstream?**
   a. ActiveX control
   b. Cookie
   c. Spyware
   d. Web bug

20. **The mathematical code used to decrypt data is a(n):**
   a. antivirus
   b. countermeasure
   c. key
   d. sniffer code

21. _____ **was the first widely used protocol for establishing secure, encrypted connections between Web browsers and Web servers.**
   a. SSL
   b. SST
   c. TLS
   d. TSL

▼ SKILLS REVIEW

1. **Use the SmartScreen Filter in Internet Explorer.**
   a. If you are using Internet Explorer, open the Microsoft SmartScreen Filter dialog box; if you are using Firefox, skip to Skills Review 2.
   b. Click the "What is SmartScreen Filter?" link at the top of the dialog box to open a Help window. Click some of the arrows or plus signs next to topics to read about the SmartScreen Filter. Close the Help window when you are finished.
   c. Close the Microsoft SmartScreen Filter dialog box without changing the setting.
   d. Click the Safety button on the Command bar, point to SmartScreen Filter, then click Check This Website. If a dialog box opens asking you to confirm that you know that information will be sent to Microsoft, click the Don't show this again check box to deselect it, then click OK. Wait for the process to complete.
   e. In the dialog box that appears telling you that the current Web page is not a reported phishing Web site, click OK.

2. **Use Phishing and Malware Protection in Firefox.**
   a. If you are using Firefox, open the Security panel in the Options dialog box; if you are using Internet Explorer, skip to Skills Review 3.
   b. If necessary, deselect the Block reported attack sites and Block reported web forgeries check boxes, then click OK.
   c. Go to the Online Companion page for Unit I, then click the Firefox Phishing Test site link under Skills Review 2. Read the information on Mozilla's It's a Trap! Web page.
   d. Return to the Online Companion page for Unit I, then click the Firefox Malware Test site link under Skills Review 2. Read the information on Mozilla's It's an Attack! Web page.
   e. Return to your browser's home page.
   f. Open the Security panel in the Options dialog box, then, if the Block reported attack sites and the Block reported web forgeries check boxes were selected prior to this exercise, click them to select them, then click OK.

3. **Strengthen security in Internet Explorer.**
   a. If you are using Internet Explorer, open the Internet Options dialog box; if you are using Firefox, skip to Skills Review 4.
   b. Switch to the Security tab, if necessary.
   c. Click Default level if it is not grayed out, then drag the slider to High and read the description of the settings.
   d. Drag the slider down as far as it can go.
   e. Open the Security Settings – Internet Zone dialog box.
   f. Scroll down and examine the settings for ActiveX controls, then click Cancel.
   g. Click Cancel in the Internet Options dialog box.

4. **Strengthen security in Firefox.**
   a. If you are using Firefox, open the Options dialog box; if you are using Internet Explorer, skip to Skills Review 5.
   b. Switch to the Content panel in the Options dialog box, if necessary.
   c. Select the Enable JavaScript check box, if necessary, then open the Advanced JavaScript Settings dialog box.
   d. Examine the options in the dialog box, then click Cancel.
   e. Clear the Enable Java and Enable JavaScript check boxes, if necessary.
   f. Click Cancel in the Options dialog box.

5. **Check security features on a Web Site.**
   a. Go to the Online Companion for page Unit I, then click the Amazon.com link under Skills Review 5.
   b. Perform a search or follow links to find a book that you want to purchase.
   c. After you have selected a book that you like, click Add to Shopping Cart.
   d. Click Proceed to Checkout. (If the Internet Explorer Security dialog box appears warning you that a Web site wants to open Web content using a program on your computer, and if the name of the program in bold in the dialog box is Adobe Shockwave Player, click Allow.)
   e. Enter your email address in the top text box, then click Sign in using our secure server.
   f. Click the padlock icon in the Address bar in Internet Explorer or double-click the padlock icon in the status bar in Firefox.
   g. Open the Certificate dialog box and examine the certificate for this Web site. Close all open dialog boxes when you are finished.

6. **Manage browsing tracks in Internet Explorer.**
   a. If you are using Internet Explorer, open the Internet Options dialog box; if you are using Firefox, skip to Skills Review 7.
   b. Switch to the Privacy tab, if necessary.
   c. Drag the slider down to Low, if necessary, and read the description of the types of cookies that would be blocked with this setting.
   d. Drag the slider up to High and read the description of the types of cookies that would be blocked with this setting.
   e. Open the Per Site Privacy Actions dialog box.
   f. Add www.microsoft.com as a site that is always allowed to leave cookies on your computer.
   g. Remove www.microsoft.com from the list of Managed websites, then close the open dialog boxes.
   h. Open the Delete Browsing History dialog box.
   i. Close the dialog box without making any changes.
   j. Open an InPrivate Browsing window.
   k. Go to any of your favorite Web sites that you have not visited today.
   l. Return to your browser's start page, click the Favorites button, then click the History tab in the Favorites Center. Sort the list by order visited today, then by Web site. Verify that the Web site you just visited in the InPrivate Browsing window is not in the History list.
   m. Exit your browser.

7. Manage browsing tracks in Firefox.

 a. If you are using Firefox, open the Options dialog box; if you are using Internet Explorer, skip this Skills Review exercise.

 b. Switch to the Privacy panel in the Options dialog box, then display the custom settings for history.

 c. Open the Exceptions – Cookies dialog box.

 d. Add www.microsoft.com as a site that is always allowed to leave cookies on your computer.

 e. Remove www.microsoft.com as a site that is always allowed to leave cookies on your computer.

 f. Close the Exceptions - Cookies dialog box, then click Cancel in the Options dialog box.

 g. Open the Clear Recent History dialog box, expand the Details list, if necessary, then close the dialog box without deleting any stored information.

 h. Open a Private Browsing window.

 i. Go to any of your favorite Web sites that you have not visited today.

 j. Return to your browser's start page, click History on the menu bar, then click Show All History. Double-click Today in the pane on the right, then verify that the Web site you just visited in the Private Browsing window is not in the History list.

 k. Click the Close button in the Library window title bar.

 l. Exit your browser.

▼ INDEPENDENT CHALLENGE 1

You're interning in a lawyer's office for a summer. Because you understand some of the technical aspects of Internet security, your manager has asked you to evaluate security programs that allow you to encrypt email messages. She is considering using one for sensitive communications.

 a. Go to the Online Companion for page Unit I, click one of the links to a download site under Independent Challenge 1, then search for a program that will let you encrypt email messages.

 b. Find at least two programs that you think will work.

 c. Click the links to the publishers' Web sites and read more detailed information on the sites explaining how the programs work.

 d. Write at least three paragraphs summarizing your findings. Include a description of the basic features of each program, minimum computer system requirements, and the differences between them.

 e. Close your Web browser.

▼ INDEPENDENT CHALLENGE 2

In class, you're discussing how browsers can track your browsing history. You decide to investigate how this is done.

a. Clear your browser history, start a new browser session, then visit five different Web sites. At least one of them should be a retail site.

b. Open the browser History list and examine how the sites you visited are listed.

c. If you are using Internet Explorer, examine the Web page privacy policy on the current page to see the list of Web sites with content on that page. If you are using Firefox, open the Privacy panel in the Options dialog box, then click **Show Cookies** to see the cookies that have been stored on your computer during this session.

d. If you are using Internet Explorer, start an InPrivate Browsing session. If you are using Firefox, open the Privacy panel in the Options dialog box, click **Show Cookies**, then click **Remove All Cookies**; close the open dialog boxes, then start a Private Browsing session.

e. Visit three additional Web sites, then check the History list again. Are the three additional Web sites listed?

f. If you are using Firefox, view the cookies. Are there any listed?

g. Close the InPrivate Browsing window in Internet Explorer or use the Stop Private Browsing command in Firefox.

h. If you are using Firefox, open the Cookies dialog box again. Are any cookies listed?

i. Write two paragraphs that explain how cookies and the History list track your browsing, and describe what happens when you use the InPrivate or Private Browsing feature.

j. Close your Web browser.

▼ INDEPENDENT CHALLENGE 3

Three times in the last six months, someone has successfully penetrated the computer system at Bolton Brokerage Services and defaced the home page in the same way that a person might use spray paint to add graffiti to a highway underpass or public restroom. The owner has hired you to look into the security measures he should take to prevent the break-ins his business is experiencing.

a. Go to the Online Companion page for Unit I, then click the **SecurityMetrics Free Port Scan link** under Independent Challenge 3.

b. Click the option to run a free port scan on your computer. It might take several minutes for the port scan results to appear. (**STOP:** Do not run a port scan on a public computer unless you have permission to do so from your lab's administrator.)

c. Use your browser's Print button to print the results page. In a report addressed to the owner, answer the following questions.
   • How secure is your computer?
   • What actions can you take to protect any open ports?
   • If you do not have any open ports, what actions have you already taken to protect your computer? (If you are in a public computer lab and do not have access to security information, explain the countermeasures that you believe are in place to secure open ports.)

d. Return to the Online Companion page for Unit I, then click the **VeriSign link** under Independent Challenge 3.

e. Use the VeriSign Web site to determine the cost of Secure Sockets Layer certificates. When you find this information, use your browser to print it.

Advanced Challenge Exercise

■ Return to the Online Companion page for Unit I, click one of the links to a download site under Independent Challenge 3, then search for ZoneAlarm.

■ Download the free version of ZoneAlarm and install it on your computer. (**STOP:** If you are working on a public computer or in a lab, make sure you have permission to install software before installing ZoneAlarm.)

■ Run ZoneAlarm, then try to return to the Online Companion. Describe what happens, then give permission for your browser to access the Internet.

■ If you don't want to run ZoneAlarm every time you start your computer, click the Preferences tab in the ZoneAlarm program window, click the Load ZoneAlarm at startup check box to remove the check mark, then click Yes in the warning box that appears.

f. Close your Web browser.

▼ REAL LIFE INDEPENDENT CHALLENGE

Now that you understand more about Internet security and potential risks associated with using the Internet, you want to take steps to secure your Internet use. Start by finding out about your school's or employer's antivirus and antispyware resources.

a. Ask your instructor or system administrator if your school makes antivirus and antispyware software available to students and staff.

b. If your school does not make antivirus and antispyware software available, ask your instructor or system administrator about the school's plan for safe computing. Find out if other safeguards are in place to limit exposure to viruses for users of the school's computers. Summarize your research in a paragraph, then write another paragraph analyzing what you've found. State whether you think students and staff at your school are adequately protected against viruses, and why.

c. If your school does make antivirus and antispyware software available, download it to your computer and install it. Use information on your school's Web site along with the software's help section to understand and enable its main features. Also download the most recent virus definitions from the software company's Web site. Then write a paragraph describing the steps you took to download and install the software, and another paragraph summarizing the software's features.

d. Find out how your school protects computers from spyware.

Advanced Challenge Exercise

- Go to the Online Companion page for Unit I, click one of the links to a download site under Real Life Independent Challenge, then search for Ad-aware, a software program that detects and removes adware.
- Read the description of Ad-aware, then download and install the free version of the program. (STOP: If you are working on a public computer or in a lab, make sure you have permission to install software before installing Ad-aware.)
- Click the Scan button, then click Scan Now.
- Once the scan is complete, examine the list of results. Click the Action list arrow next to the objects you want to delete, select an action to perform or leave Recommended as the selection, then click Perform Actions Now.
- Click the Close button in the Ad-aware title bar to exit the program.

e. Close your Web browser, if necessary.

▼ VISUAL WORKSHOP

Open the dialog box shown in Figure I-32 if you are using Internet Explorer or open the dialog box shown in Figure I-33 if you are using Firefox and add the Web site shown in the figure to the list of sites from which cookies are blocked. Close the dialog box, go to the Online Companion page for Unit I, then click the link to The New York Times under Visual Workshop. Click the Register Now link, fill in your information, then click the link to complete the registration. What happens? Return to your browser's home page, then remove www.nytimes.com from the list of sites from which cookies are blocked.

FIGURE I-32

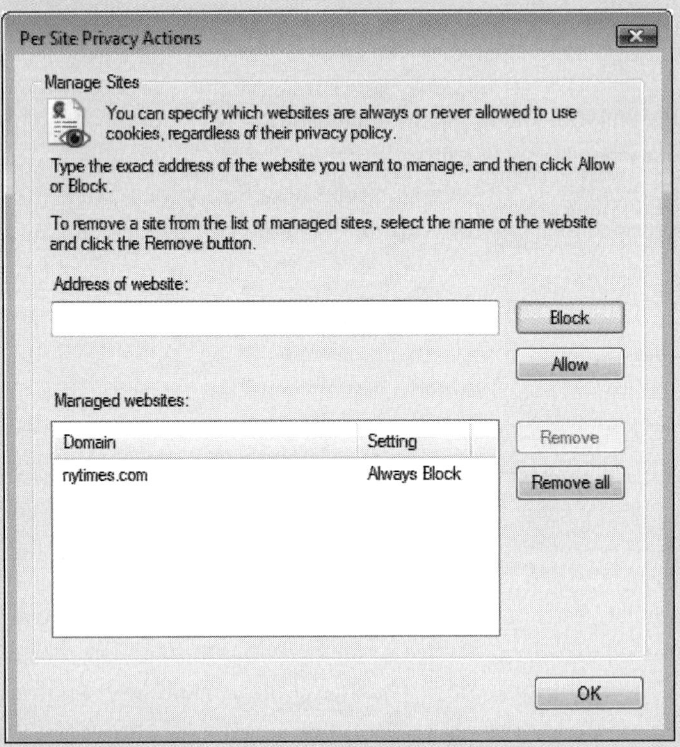

FIGURE I-33

Increasing Web Security

Using Other Email Programs

The steps in Unit C, *Using Email,* cover Windows Live Mail version 2009, which is freely available from Microsoft's Web site, and Microsoft Live Hotmail, Microsoft's Webmail service. There are many other email client programs available, including Windows Mail version 6, which is included with Windows Vista, Outlook Express, which is included with Windows XP, Mozilla's Thunderbird 2, and Gmail, another Webmail service. This appendix covers some of the significant differences between each of these four email programs and the ones discussed in Unit C.

OBJECTIVES

Using Windows Mail version 6

Using Outlook Express

Using Thunderbird 2

Using Gmail

Using Windows Mail Version 6

Windows Mail version 6 is the mail client software that comes with Windows Vista. There are a few differences between Windows Mail version 6 and Windows Live Mail Version 2009. Start by reading the Windows Live Mail lessons and steps in Unit C, and then refer to this lesson when you need additional information.

DETAILS

- **Starting Windows Mail**

  To start Windows Mail, click **Start** on the taskbar, point to **All Programs**, then click **Windows Mail**.

- **Examining the Windows Mail program window**

  Figure 1 shows the Windows Mail program window. The elements in the Windows Mail program window are similar to those in the Windows Live Mail program window, as discussed in Lesson 2, "Starting Windows Live Mail and Exploring the Mail Window" in Unit C, *Using Email*. Note that the Outbox is listed as a folder in the folders list in Windows Mail. Also note that the default setup in Windows Mail is for the reading pane, which is called the Preview Pane in Windows Mail, to display at the bottom of the window, although you can change this. Note also that Windows Mail includes a menu bar.

- **Sending an Email Message**

  To open a New Message window in Windows Mail, click the **Create Mail button**.

- **Checking Incoming Mail**

  To check to see if there are any new messages on the server using Windows Mail, click the **Send/Receive button**. To open a message in the Message list in its own window, double-click it.

- **Attaching a File to an Email Message**

  In Windows Mail, the Attach button has an icon of a paper clip on it.

- **Saving an Email Attachment in Windows Mail**

  To save an attachment in Windows Mail, click the message to select it in the Message list, click the **paper clip icon** that appears in the message header in the Preview Pane, then click **Save Attachments**.

QUICK TIP
You can copy messages from one folder to another in Windows Mail.

- **Organizing Email Messages**

  To create a new folder in Windows Mail, click **File** on the menu bar, point to **New**, then click **Folder**.

- **Deleting Email Messages**

  To permanently delete messages from the Deleted Items folder in Windows Mail, right-click **Deleted Items** in the folders list, then click **Empty 'Deleted Items' Folder** on the shortcut menu.

- **Maintaining a Contacts List in Windows Mail**

  To open the Contacts window in Windows Mail, click the **Contacts button** on the toolbar. See Figure 2. To open a new contact card, click the **New Contact button** on the toolbar. This opens the Properties dialog box. Adding the contact information in Windows Mail is very similar to Windows Live Mail, although you will notice slight differences in the dialog box names and text box labels. Also, in Windows Mail, you can add a **nickname**, which is a shortened name for the contact, to the contact card. Then you can type the nickname in the To or Cc box in a message window and Windows Mail will find the email address associated with that nickname.

- **Creating a Contact Group in Windows Mail**

  To create a contact group in Windows Mail, open the Contacts window, then click the **New Contact Group button** on the toolbar.

FIGURE 1: Windows Mail program window

Menu bar

Toolbar

Folders list

Inbox folder

Message header (this message might not appear in your list)

Message list (you might have additional messages listed)

Preview pane

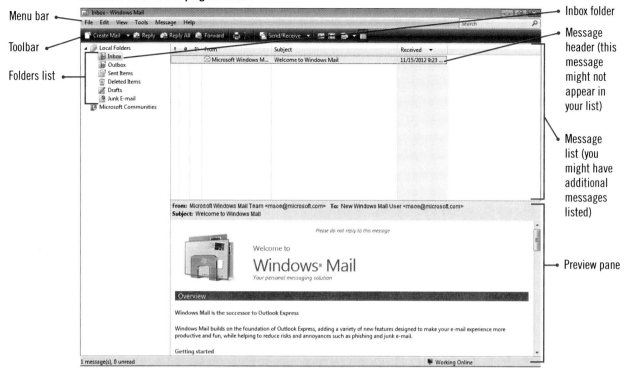

FIGURE 2: Windows Mail Contacts window

Log-in name on computer; yours might differ

Click to add new contact

Contacts list

Click to delete selected contact

Preview of selected contact

Click to create new contact group

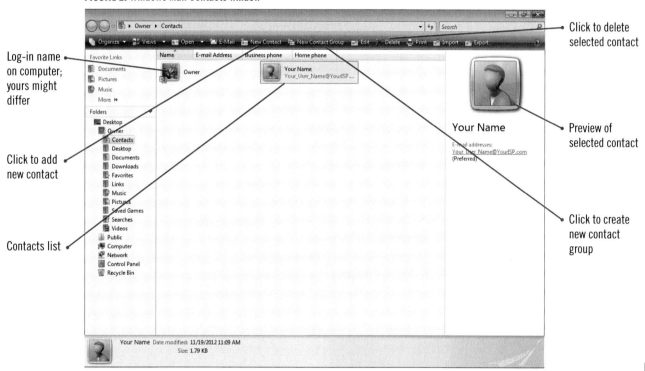

Setting up a Windows Mail account

The first time you start Windows Mail, the Your Name dialog box opens with the Display name text box ready for you to type your display name, which is the name you want to appear in the From text box when you send an email message to someone else. To set up your Windows Mail account, type your display name, click Next, and then continue following the directions in the dialog boxes to finish setting up your Windows Mail account. If the Your Name dialog box does not appear automatically, click Tools on the menu bar, and then click Accounts to open the Internet Accounts dialog box. Click Add to open the Select Account Type dialog box, click E-mail Account in the list, click Next, and then continue to follow the directions in the dialog boxes to finish setting up your Windows Mail account.

Using Outlook Express

Outlook Express is the mail client software that comes with Windows XP. There are very few differences between Windows Live Mail and Outlook Express. Start by reading the Windows Live Mail lessons and steps in Unit C, and then refer to this lesson when you need additional information.

DETAILS

- ## Starting Outlook Express
  To start Outlook Express, click **Start** on the taskbar, point to **All Programs**, then click **Outlook Express**.

- ## Examining the Outlook Express program window
  Figure 3 shows the Outlook Express program window. The elements in the Outlook Express window are similar to those in the Windows Live Mail program window, as discussed in Lesson 2, "Starting Windows Live Mail and Exploring the Mail Window" in Unit C, *Using Email*. Note that Outlook Express does not have a Junk e-mail folder. Because you can customize the program window by resizing, hiding, and displaying different panes and their individual elements, your screen might look different from Figure 3.

- ## Checking Incoming Email
  To check to see if there are any new messages on the server, click the **Send/Recv button** on the toolbar.

- ## Attaching a File to an Email Message
  The Attach button has a paper clip on it.

- ## Saving an Attachment in Outlook Express
  To save an attachment in Outlook Express, click the **paper clip icon** on the right edge of the message header in the Preview pane, click **Save Attachments**, then click **Browse** in the dialog box that opens to navigate to the folder in which you want to save the file.

- ## Deleting Email Messages
  To permanently delete messages from the Deleted Items folder in Outlook Express, right-click the **Deleted Items folder**, then click **Empty 'Deleted Items' Folder** on the shortcut menu.

- ## Maintaining a Contacts List in Outlook Express
  The Contacts list in Outlook Express is called the **Address Book**. To open the list of contacts in Outlook Express, click the **Addresses button** on the toolbar. Figure 4 shows the Address Book window. To add a new name to the Address Book, click the **New button** on the toolbar, then click **New Contact**.

QUICK TIP
If you want to add additional group members, add them before you click OK to close the Select Group Members dialog box.

- ## Creating a Contact Group in Outlook Express
  To create a new group in Outlook Express, click the **New button** on the toolbar in the Address Book window, then click **New Group** to open the Properties dialog box. On the Group tab, type a name for the group in the Group Name text box, click **Select Members** to open the Select Group Members dialog box, click the contact you want to add, click **Select**, then click **OK**. The Select Group Members dialog box closes and the contacts you added appear in the Group Members list in the Properties dialog box. The Group Name Properties dialog box is shown in Figure 5.

Setting up an Outlook Express account

The first time you start Outlook Express, the Your Name dialog box opens with the Display name text box ready for you to type your display name, which is the name you want to appear in the From text box when you send an email message. To set up your Outlook Express account, type your display name, click Next, and then continue following the directions in the dialog boxes to finish setting up your Outlook Express account. If the Your Name dialog box does not appear automatically, click Tools on the menu bar, and then click Accounts to open the Internet Accounts dialog box. On the Mail tab, click Add, and then click Mail.

FIGURE 3: Outlook Express program window

Menu bar

Toolbar

Folders list

Unread message

Read message

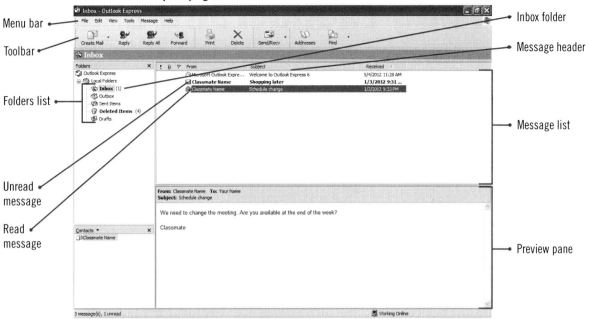

Inbox folder

Message header

Message list

Preview pane

FIGURE 4: Address Book window in Outlook Express

Click to add new contact

Click to delete selected contact

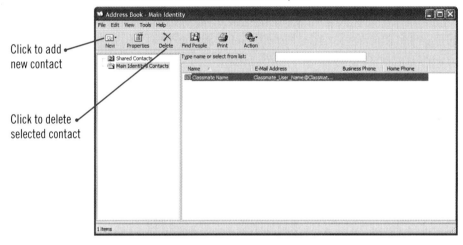

FIGURE 5: Group Name Properties dialog box in Outlook Express

Group contains one member

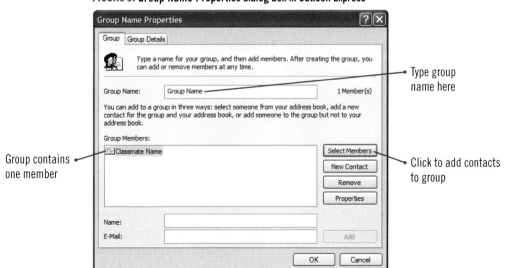

Type group name here

Click to add contacts to group

Using Thunderbird 2

Thunderbird 2 is free mail client software that you can download from Mozilla, the same company that created Firefox. There are a few differences between Windows Live Mail and Thunderbird. Start by reading the Windows Live Mail lessons and steps in Unit C, and then refer to this lesson when you need additional information.

DETAILS

- **Starting Thunderbird**

  To start Thunderbird, click the **Start button** on the taskbar, point to **All Programs**, click **Mozilla Thunderbird**, then click **Mozilla Thunderbird**.

QUICK TIP

The first time you start Thunderbird, you might not see all of the folders in the All Folders list. Some folders, such as the Drafts and Sent folders, do not appear until you have a need for them.

- **Examining the Thunderbird program window**

  Figure 6 shows the Thunderbird program window. The elements in the Thunderbird program window are similar to those in the Windows Live Mail program window, as discussed in Lesson 2, "Starting Windows Live Mail and Exploring the Mail Window" in Unit C, *Using Email*. Note that the folder that contains deleted messages is called the Trash folder, and Thunderbird does not have a Junk e-mail folder. Thunderbird does include a filter that evaluates mail as it comes in and marks suspected junk email as Junk. Then you can delete all email marked as Junk. Because you can customize the program window by resizing, hiding, and displaying different panes and their individual elements, your screen might look different from Figure 6.

- **Sending an Email Message in Thunderbird**

  To create a new message, click the **Write button** on the toolbar. To add a Cc email address, click the empty box below the To name you added, click the **To list arrow** in this box, then click **Cc**.

- **Checking Incoming Mail in Thunderbird**

  To check to see if you have any new messages, click the **Get Mail button** on the toolbar.

- **Saving an Email Attachment in Thunderbird**

  To save an attachment, click the message to select it in the Message list, right-click the attached file in the Preview pane, then click **Save As** on the shortcut menu.

- **Organizing Email Messages in Thunderbird**

  To create a new folder, click **File** on the menu bar, point to **New**, then click **Folder**.

- **Deleting Email Messages in Thunderbird**

  To delete a message, drag it to the Trash folder; to permanently delete the messages you place in the Trash folder, right-click the **Trash folder**, then click **Empty Trash**.

- **Maintaining a Contact List in Thunderbird**

  The Contacts list in Thunderbird is called the **Address Book**. To open the list of contacts in Thunderbird, click the **Address Book button** on the toolbar. The Address Book window is shown in Figure 7. To add a new contact, click the **New Card button** on the Address Book window toolbar.

- **Creating a Contact Mailing List in Thunderbird**

  To create a new mailing list, click the **New List button** on the Address Book window toolbar to open the Mailing List dialog box. (See Figure 8.) Type a list name in the List Name text box, type email addresses in the list at the bottom of the dialog box, then click **OK**.

Setting up a Thunderbird account

The first time you start Thunderbird, the Account Wizard opens displaying the New Account Setup dialog box. Click the Email account option button, if necessary, and then click Next. Type your name in the Your Name text box; this is the name you want to appear in the From text box when you send an email message. Click in the Email Address text box, type your email address, and then click Next.

Continue following the directions in the dialog boxes to finish setting up your Thunderbird account. If the New Account Setup dialog box does not appear automatically, click Tools on the menu bar, and then click Account Settings to open the Account Settings dialog box. Click Add Account to open the New Account Setup dialog box.

FIGURE 6: Thunderbird program window

Menu bar

Toolbar

All Folders list

Message header

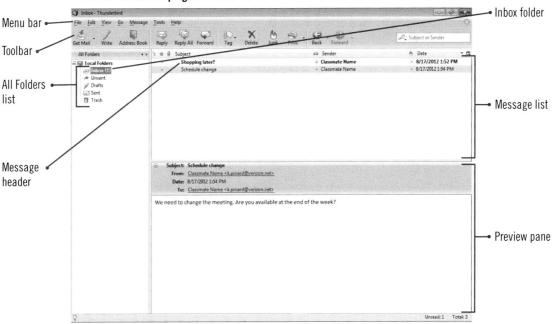

Inbox folder

Message list

Preview pane

FIGURE 7: Address Book window in Thunderbird

Click to add new contact

Your name might not appear in the list; your list might contain additional items

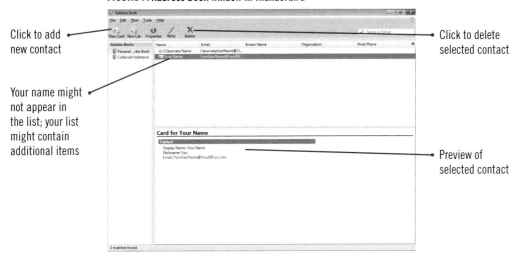

Click to delete selected contact

Preview of selected contact

FIGURE 8: Mailing List dialog box in Thunderbird

Type email addresses of group members here

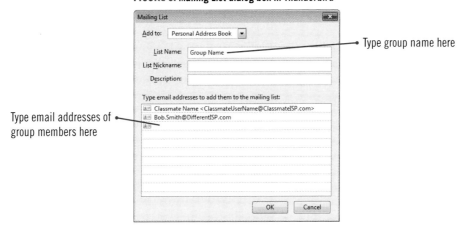

Type group name here

Internet

Using Gmail

Gmail is Google's Webmail service. As with Hotmail, you need to sign in with a user name and password to use the service. Start by reading the Hotmail lessons and steps in Unit C, and refer to this lesson when you need additional information.

DETAILS

ADDITIONAL INFORMATION

- **Connecting to Gmail**

  Start your browser, go to the Online Companion page for the **Appendix**, then click the **Gmail link**. Type the username you received when you registered with Gmail in the Username text box, type your password in the Password text box, then click **Sign in**.

QUICK TIP

Click a label to show only those messages with that label.

- **Examining the Gmail Mail Window**

  Figure 9 shows the Gmail Mail window. The elements in the Gmail Mail window are similar to those in the Windows Live Hotmail window, as discussed in Lesson 3, "Connecting to Your Hotmail Account and Exploring the Mail Window" in Unit C, *Using Email*. However, Gmail organizes mail by using labels instead of folders. The system labels cannot be changed or deleted, although they can be hidden (or shown). The system labels are the **Inbox**, **Sent Mail**, **Drafts**, **Spam** (similar to the Junk folder in Hotmail), and **Trash** labels, as well as the **Starred** label, which is applied to messages you have flagged by clicking the star in the Message list; the **Chats** label, which is automatically applied to instant message conversations you save; and the **All Mail** label, which, as the name suggests, is applied to all mail. In addition, note the following differences:

  - **Search Mail text box:** Allows you to search your email messages or the Web.
  - **Archive button:** Allows you to archive your messages, which removes them from the Inbox, but keeps them available when you click the All Mail label.
  - **Report spam button:** Allows you to report a selected message to Gmail as spam.
  - **More actions button:** Allows you to perform specific actions on selected messages.
  - **Refresh link:** Checks the Gmail server to see if you have any new messages.

- **Sending a Message and Checking Incoming Mail in Gmail**

  To create a new message, click the **Compose Mail link** above the Labels list; to add a Cc email address, click the **Add Cc link** below the To text box.

- **Saving an Attachment in Gmail**

  To save an attachment, open the message, then click one of the links below the attachment filename.

- **Viewing Replies and Forwarded Messages in Gmail**

  A **conversation** is a message and all of the replies to that message. To read messages in a conversation, click a message that has a number in parentheses after the message header summary. The conversation opens, as shown in Figure 10. To read a message in the middle of the conversation thread, click the visible portion of the message to expand it.

QUICK TIP

Messages can have more than one label.

- **Organizing Messages in Gmail**

  You use labels instead of folders to organize messages. To organize a message, click its **check box** in the Message list, click the **Labels list arrow**, then click a label or click **Create new** to create a new label.

- **Deleting Email Messages in Gmail**

  To delete a message, click its **check box** in the Message list, then click the **Delete button**. To permanently delete messages, click the **Trash link** in the Labels list, then click the **Delete forever button**.

- **Maintaining a Contacts List and Creating a Contact Group in Gmail**

  Click the **Contacts link** below the Labels list. To add a contact, click the **New Contact button**, type the contact information, then click the **Save button**. To create a group, click the **New Group button**, type a group name, click **OK**, click **All Contacts**, click the check box next to contacts you want to add, click the **Groups button**, then click the group name.

FIGURE 9: Gmail Mail window

Search Mail text box

Archive button

Click to open a new message window

Labels list

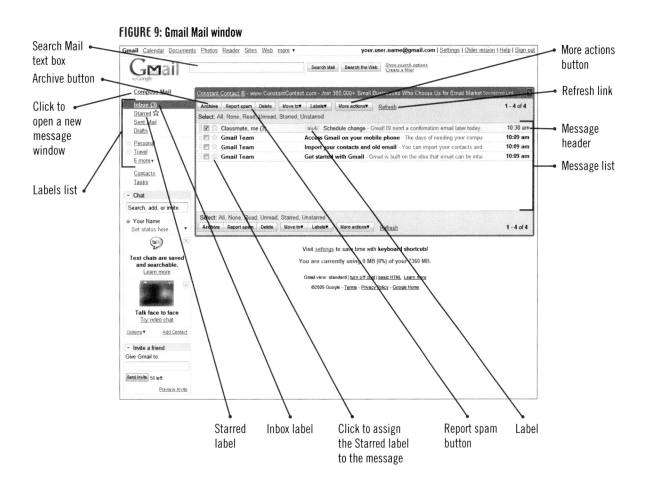

More actions button

Refresh link

Message header

Message list

Starred label

Inbox label

Click to assign the Starred label to the message

Report spam button

Label

FIGURE 10: A conversation in Gmail

Additional messages in the conversation

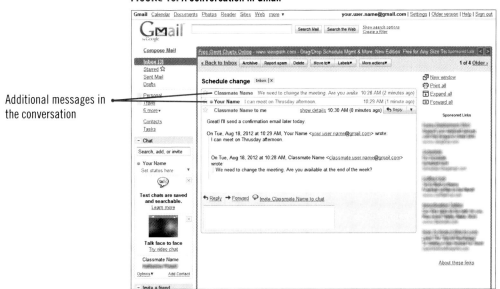

Signing up for a Gmail account

Gmail, like most Webmail services, provides free email service to anyone with an Internet connection. Before you can use it, you need to establish a user account. To do this, go to the Online Companion page for the Appendix, and then click the Gmail link.

Click the Create an account button to go to the Create an Account page, and then enter the required information (your name, country, security question, and so on).

Internet

Glossary

Accelerator In Internet Explorer, a type of add-on program that is actually a shortcut to another Web site.

Acceptable use policy (AUP) A written policy at most schools and companies that specifies the conditions under which you can use their Internet connection.

Active tab The tab on top in a browser window.

ActiveX control Microsoft's technology for writing small applications that can download to your computer and run; used by Web page designers to enrich and personalize a user's interaction with a Web page; can also be written with malicious intent, however, destabilizing programs and even risking data loss on a user's computer.

Ad blocker A program that searches for files written by known spyware and blocks them from your computer.

Add-on A browser extension that enhances your browsing experience, such as a toolbar that lets you access a search engine without opening its Web site.

Address bar In Internet Explorer, a text box at the top of the browser window that indicates the URL of the current Web page and into which you can type a new URL then press [Enter], or click the Go button to go to another Web page; in Firefox, *called* Location Bar.

Address book *See* contact list.

Administrative address The email address to which you send mailing list commands.

Administrator A person assigned to oversee a mailing list.

Advanced Research Projects Agency Network (ARPANET) An experimental WAN that consisted of four computers networked together by DARPA researchers in 1969.

Advanced Systems format (asf) A proprietary Windows Media Player file format that will play only in Windows Media Player.

Adware A general category of software that includes advertisements to help pay for the product in which they appear.

Aggregator Software that lets you receive newsfeed content.

AIM *See* AOL Instant Messenger.

Animated GIF A file that combines several images into a single GIF file so that the images can be displayed one after the other to simulate movement.

Annotations Summaries or reviews of Web pages in some subject guides.

Announcement list A mailing list that sends messages to subscribers, but does not allow subscribers to post to the list; similar to a newsletter.

Anonymous FTP The method of logging in to a publicly accessible FTP server without having a personal account.

Antispyware program A program that searches your computer for files written by known spyware.

Antivirus software Software that protects your computer from viruses, worms, and Trojan horses.

AOL Instant Messenger (AIM) AOL's instant messaging software available to anyone (even those people without AOL accounts) for use on the Web.

API *See* Application Programming Interface.

Application Programming Interface (API) A means of communication with an operating system or some other program to handle specific tasks such as displaying content on the screen or printing.

Archive A compressed file in WinZip.

Archived file *See* compressed file.

ARPANET *See* Advanced Research Projects Agency Network.

Asf *See* Advanced Systems format.

Attachment A separate file sent with an email message.

AU format The audio file format used by the UNIX operating system.

AUP *See* acceptable use policy.

Avatar An online character that a game player uses to represent him or herself.

AVI format An uncompressed file format used for video on the Web that can be played using the same software that plays many other multimedia file types, including the player that comes with Windows.

Back button A button on a Web browser toolbar that allows you to go back to a previously viewed Web page.

Bandwidth A measure of the amount of data that can be transmitted simultaneously through a communications circuit.

Banner ad An advertisement that appears in a box on a Web page (usually at the top, but sometimes along the side or bottom of the page).

Bcc Short for blind carbon or courtesy copy; in an email program, the text box in which you type the email address(es) of recipient(s) to whom you want to send a copy of an email message without the knowledge of the other addressee(s).

Because It's There network The original name for BITNET.

Because It's Time network (BITNET) A network of computers organized by the City University of New York.

bit A single unit of data stored in a computer.

BITNET *See* Because It's Time network.

Blog (Web log) An online journal in which the blogger posts entries for public viewing; some blogs contain commentary on current events.

Blogger A blog owner.

Bluebugging When a hacker gains access to a device that uses Bluetooth and all of its functions without the owner's consent.

Bluejacking When a hacker sends an anonymous message in the form of a phone contact that is displayed on a device that uses Bluetooth in an attempt to surprise the owner, express a comment or opinion, or to make a social connection.

Bluesnarfing When a hacker is able to detect the signal from a Bluetooth device and gain access to its data, listen in on phone calls, and send email messages from the victim's device.

Bluetooth A technology that provides short-wave radio links between electronic devices.

Bookmark In Firefox, a shortcut on a menu to a Web site; in Internet Explorer, *called* favorite.

Boolean operator Words that specify the logical relationship between the elements they join; the most common are AND, OR, and NOT; *also called* logical operator.

Bot Short for *robot*, a computer that sends malware to or communicates with other computers without the owner's knowledge to harm those computers or act with other bots to harm Web servers; *also called* zombie; *see also* Web robot.

Browse To use your computer and Internet connection to view Web pages.

Browser *See* Web browser.

Browser extension A program that enhances the capabilities of Web browsers by allowing a Web browser to perform a task that it was not originally designed to do.

Brute force attack The act of using a program to enter character combinations until the attacked computer system accepts a user name and password, which allows the attacker access to the system.

Bug An error in software that could cause the program to halt, malfunction, or damage the user's computer.

Bulletin board An information posting area on a network.

CA *See* certificate authority.

Cable A method of connecting to the Internet used by individuals and businesses that uses the customer's television cable; connection speeds range from 300 Kbps to 10.0 Mbps.

Cable modem A special type of modem required to create a cable connection to the Internet through a cable television company.

Café latte attack *See* evil twin attack.

Calendar window In Windows Live Hotmail, the page that provides the user with an electronic calendar.

Category A group or list of two or more email addresses stored as one contact; *also called* group *or* mailing list.

Category 1 cable A type of twisted-pair cable that transmits information more slowly than other cable types; used by telephone companies for years to wire residences and businesses.

Category 5 cable, **Category 5e cable**, and **Category 6 cable** Newer types of twisted-pair cable that transmit data faster than coaxial cable.

Cc Short for carbon or courtesy copy; in an email program, the text box in which you type the email address(es) of recipient(s) to whom you are sending a copy of an email message.

Certificate authority (CA) A trusted third party that verifies a digital certificate holder's identity and issues the digital certificate.

Chat Real-time communication on the Internet or on the Web.

Chat room A public area in which anyone who is registered with the chat service can come and go.

Circuit switching A method for data transmission once commonly used by telephone companies in which all data transmitted from a sender to a receiver travels along a single path.

Clear GIF *See* Web bug.

Clearinghouse *See* subject guide.

Clickstream The sequence of links you click while visiting a Web site.

Client A computer connected to a server.

Client/server network A network consisting of one server that shares its resources with multiple clients.

Clip art A collection of individual icons, shapes, and other graphics.

Closed discussion forum, **mailing list**, or **newsgroup** A discussion forum, mailing list, or newsgroup in which the list administrator must either reject or accept a request to become a list member.

Coaxial cable An insulated copper wire encased in a metal shield that is enclosed with plastic insulation.

Command A request to a list server to take a prescribed action.

Command bar Contains the buttons and menus that allow you to access and use all the features of the Internet Explorer browser.

Commerce service provider (CSP) A common name for large ISPs that sell Internet access along with other services to businesses.

Communications circuits The circuits through which data travels in network connections.

Complete Web page A Web page and all of its individual associated files saved to a disk; the Web page is saved as an htm file and the associated files are stored in a folder with the same name as the file you saved followed by an underscore and the word "files."

Compressed file A file created after using a file compression program to reduce a file to a fraction of its original size; *also called* an archived file.

Computer Science Network (CSNET) A network founded by the National Science Foundation (NSF) for educational and research institutions that did not have access to the ARPANET.

Contact Each person that you add to a Contact list.

Contact card The information about a contact stored in a Contact list.

Contact list Stores people's names and email addresses, as well as other information, such as the person's postal address and telephone number; *also called* address book.

Contacts window In Windows Live Hotmail, the page on which the Contact list is stored.

Cookie A small text file that a Web site stores on your computer and that contains information that makes your Web-browsing experience simpler and more personalized by storing information about your clickstream.

Copyright A right granted by a government to the author or creator of a literary or artistic work.

Countermeasure A procedure, program, or hardware that detects and prevents a computer security threat.

CSNET *See* Computer Science Network.

CSP *See* commerce service provider.

Cyberbully To use Internet communication such as email, instant messages, or online social networks to harass, threaten, or intimidate someone.

DARPA *See* Defense Advanced Research Projects Agency.

Data packet A small chunk of data.

DDoS attack *See* Distributed denial of service attack.

Decrypt To reverse the encryption of data.

Deep Web Dynamic Web pages and other Web pages that can be accessed only with a user name and a password; *also called* hidden Web *or* invisible Web.

Defense Advanced Research Projects Agency (DARPA) An agency created by the U.S. Department of Defense in the early 1960s to examine ways to connect its computers to one another and to weapons installations distributed all over the world.

Deleted folder In Windows Live Hotmail, the folder in which you store messages you delete until you permanently delete them; in Windows Live Mail, *called* Deleted items folder.

Deleted items folder In Windows Live Mail, the folder that stores messages you delete until you permanently delete them; in Windows Live Hotmail, *called* Deleted folder.

Demodulation The process of converting an analog signal back into digital form.

Digital certificate An encrypted and password-protected file that contains information to authenticate and prove a person's or organization's identity.

Digital object identifier (DOI) Assigned by CrossRef, an independent registration agency, to provide a uniform way to identify scholarly academic journals and similar documents and provide a persistent link to their locations on the Internet.

Digital Subscriber Line (DSL) A method of connecting to the Internet used by individuals and businesses that creates a high-speed connection using the customer's telephone wiring; connection speeds range from 100 Kbps to 9.0 Mbps.

Discussion forum *See* Web-based discussion forum.

Discussion group *See* mailing list.

Distributed database A database stored in multiple physical locations with portions of the database replicated in the different locations.

Distributed denial of service attack (DDoS attack) An attack on a Web server in which an attacker uses his or her own computer as well as zombie computers to bombard a server or other computer with so many messages that the network's bandwidth resources are consumed and the organization's computer communications are disabled.

DOI *See* digital object identifier.

Domain name The equivalent of an IP address that uses words and abbreviations; in an email address, the name of the computer that stores the email for a user.

Download To receive a file on your computer from another computer over a network.

Download Manager In Firefox, the window that opens when you download a file, and which lists files and programs you have downloaded.

Download site A Web site that contains freeware and shareware programs organized in categories.

Drafts folder In an email program, the folder in which messages that you are not yet ready to send are saved.

DSL *See* Digital Subscriber Line.

DSL modem A special type of modem required to create a DSL connection to the Internet.

Dynamic Web page A Web page generated when a user submits a query; the Web server searches the database and generates a Web page on the fly that includes information from the database.

Electronic mail *See* email.

Email (electronic mail) An electronic message transferred between two or more devices connected to a network.

Email address A unique identifier for an individual or organization that is connected to the Internet, consisting of a user name, the at sign (@), and the domain name.

Email list *See* mailing list.

Emoticon A form of electronic body language represented by a group of keyboard characters that represent a human expression when viewed together by tilting your head to the left.

Encryption The process of scrambling and encoding data transmissions using a mathematically based program.

Evaluation software A free, but restricted, version of software; *sometimes called* limited edition (LE) software.

Evil twin attack An attack on a computer using a hotspot in which the hacker gathers information about an access point, and then uses that information to set up his own computer to use the real access point's signal to impersonate the real access point; *also called* café latte attack.

Exploratory question A type of question for searching the Internet that starts with a general, open-ended question that leads to other, less general questions, which result in multiple answers.

Extensible Markup Language *See* XML.

Fair use The use of a copyrighted work that includes copying it for use in criticism, comment, news reporting, teaching, scholarship, or research.

FAQ *See* frequently asked questions.

Favorite In Internet Explorer, a shortcut on a menu to a Web site; in Firefox, *called* bookmark.

Favorites Center In Internet Explorer, a pane that opens to the left of the browser window and that contains a list of favorites on your computer as well as the history list and feeds to which you have subscribed.

Feed A file that contains summaries of stories and news from a Web site.

Fiber-optic cable A cable through which information is transmitted by pulsing beams of light through very thin strands of glass.

File compression program A program that reduces the size of a file, creating a compressed file.

File decompression The process of restoring a compressed file to its original form; *also called* file extraction *or* file expansion.

File expansion *See* file decompression.

File extraction *See* file decompression.

File Transfer Protocol (FTP) A set of rules established to enable users to transfer files between computers.

Firewall A software program or hardware device that controls access between two networks and controls port scans and other incoming traffic by rejecting it unless you have configured the firewall to accept the traffic.

Flame To use automated programs to send messages to multiple chat rooms simultaneously; also, to send profane and vulgar messages and threats to individuals.

Flash Player A popular animation browser extension from Adobe that lets your Web browser display simple animations, user interfaces, static graphics, movies, sound, and text that were created using Adobe Flash software.

Folder list In an email program, a list of folders in which email messages are stored.

Forum *See* Web-based discussion forum.

Forward To send an email message that you receive to someone else.

Forward button A button in a browser that, when clicked, brings you forward one page in the history list.

Freeware Software that is fully functional and available to users at no cost and with no restrictions.

Frequently Asked Questions (FAQ) A document that contains the answers to common questions that users ask about a mailing list and its subject.

From In an email program, the text box that contains the sender's name, email address, or both.

FTP *See* File Transfer Protocol.

FTP client program A program that resides on your computer and allows you to transfer files between your computer and another computer connected to it using the rules for FTP.

FTP server A server that uses FTP to transfer files rather than HTTP; *also called* FTP site, remote server, *or* remote site.

FTP server program A program that runs on an FTP server allowing file transfer to and from the server by FTP and managing FTP access to the server's files.

FTP session The interaction between your computer and the remote computer after you connect to the FTP server.

FTP session profile A collection of information about an FTP server.

FTP site *See* FTP server.

Full privilege FTP *See* named FTP.

GIF (Graphics Interchange Format) A compressed file format that uses lossless compression technology and can contain up to 256 colors.

Graphic An image or art incorporated into a document.

Graphic Interchange Format *See* GIF.

Graphical user interface (GUI) A method of interacting with a computer that uses text, pictures, icons, and other graphical elements to present information and allow users to perform a variety of tasks.

Group A group or list of two or more email addresses stored as one contact; *also called* category *or* mailing list.

Grouping operator *See* precedence operator.

GUI *See* graphical user interface.

Helper app *See* helper application.

Helper application A browser extension that calls a separate program that is launched to display or play some files; *also called* helper app.

Hidden Web *See* deep Web.

History feature A list of Web sites you've visited over the past days or weeks.

Hit A Web page indexed in a search engine's database that contains text that matches a search expression.

Home button A button on a Web browser toolbar that allows you to return to the home page (or start page) for your Web browser.

Home page The main Web page that all the Web pages in a Web site are organized around and link back to; also the first Web page that opens when you start your Web browser; also a Web page that a Web browser displays the first time you use it. *See also* start page.

Hot spot A wireless access point to a LAN that offers Internet access to the public.

HTML *See* Hypertext Markup Language.

HTML anchor tag An HTML tag that links multiple HTML documents together.

HTML document A text file that contains the Web page content and instructions in HTML tags for formatting that content.

Hybrid search engine An Internet tool that combines a search engine and a Web directory.

Hyperlink *See* link.

Hypermedia link Hyperlinks that connect to computer files that contain pictures, graphics, and media objects such as sound and video clips.

Hypertext link *See* link.

Hypertext Markup Language (HTML) A text markup language that marks text with a set of tags that defines the structure and behavior of a Web page.

Hypertext server A computer that stores files written in the hypertext markup language and lets other computers connect to it and read those files; *also called* Web server.

IANA *See* Internet Assigned Numbers Authority.

IAP *See* Internet access provider.

ICANN *See* Internet Corporation for Assigned Names and Numbers.

ICQ Pronounced "I seek you," one of the most popular instant messaging software programs available, with over 220 million worldwide users.

IETF *See* Internet Engineering Task Force.

IM *See* instant message.

Inbox folder In an email program or in Webmail, the folder in which messages that the user receives are stored.

Inclusion operator *See* precedence operator.

InPrivate Browsing A feature of Internet Explorer 8 that allows you to open a new browser window and surf the Web without recording anything in the History list, storing files in the Temporary Internet Files folder, or recording cookies.

InPrivate Filtering A feature of Internet Explorer 8 that analyzes the content on Web pages you visit, and if the same content is used on several Web sites that you visit, allows you to block that content.

Installation wizard A series of dialog boxes that help you complete the installation process of a program step-by-step.

Instant message (IM) A message sent over the Internet that is received almost as soon as it is sent.

Intellectual property A general term that includes all products of the human mind.

Interconnected network *See* Internet.

Internet "Internet" with an uppercase "I" is a collection of computers all over the world that are connected to one another; "internet" with a lowercase "I" is a system of networks connected to each other, short for *interconnected network*.

Internet Assigned Numbers Authority (IANA) An organization operated by ICANN that manages IP addresses as well as a few other duties crucial to keeping the Internet running.

Internet access provider (IAP) *See* Internet Service Provider.

Internet Corporation for Assigned Names and Numbers (ICANN) A nonprofit organization chartered by the U.S. government that is responsible for managing domain names; in order to establish a Web site, a Web site owner *must* register its domain name with an ICANN-approved registrar.

Internet Engineering Task Force (IETF) A volunteer group that is the main body that develops new Internet standards and makes technical contributions to the engineering of the Internet and its technologies.

Internet host Computers that connect a LAN or a WAN to the Internet.

Internet Protocol (IP) A set of rules for routing individual data packets over the Internet.

Internet Protocol address (IP address) A unique number by which each computer connected to the Internet is identified.

Internet Relay Chat (IRC) A communications program that requires IRC client software to connect to an IRC server.

Internet service provider (ISP) A company that provides access to the Internet for individuals and businesses.

Internet Society (ISOC) An international organization whose goal is to promote Internet standards so that people all over the world have access to the Internet; its members work with the IETF to develop and promote Internet standards.

Intranets LANs or WANs that use the TCP/IP protocol but do not connect to sites outside the firm.

Invisible Web *See* deep Web.

IP *See* Internet Protocol.

IP address *See* Internet Protocol address.

IRC *See* Internet Relay Chat.

ISOC *See* Internet Society.

ISP *See* Internet service provider.

Janet *See* Joint Academic Network.

Java applet A program written in the Java programming language that Web pages can download to your computer and run; used by Web page designers to enrich and personalize a user's interaction with a Web page; however, can also be written with malicious intent, destabilizing programs and even risking data loss on a user's computer.

JavaScript program Instructions written in the JavaScript programming language that can send information to another computer over the Internet.

Join *See* subscribe.

Joint Academic Network (JANET) A network established in the United Kingdom to link universities in that country.

Joint Photographic Experts Group *See* JPEG.

JPEG (Joint Photographic Experts Group) A compressed file format that uses lossy compression technology and can store over 16 million colors.

Jump To open a new Web page in a browser by clicking a link.

Junk email Unsolicited email usually selling an item or service; *also called* spam.

Junk email folder In Windows Live Mail, the folder to which possible junk emails are automatically sent when they arrive in the Inbox.

Junk folder In Windows Live Hotmail, the folder to which possible junk emails are automatically sent when they arrive in the Inbox; also, in some email programs or Webmail, the folder to where possible junk email messages are automatically filed when they are copied from the server; *also called* spam folder.

Key The mathematical code used to decrypt encrypted data.

Key logger A program that runs in the background and sends your keystrokes to someone else so they can discover your user names and passwords.

Keyword A word in a search expression.

LAN *See* local area network.

License To pay a fee for the full, unrestricted use of a program.

License agreement A contract between the publisher of the software and the person who is installing the software that usually states that the software cannot be copied and resold and details restrictions for the software's use.

Limited edition (LE) software *See* evaluation software.

Link Text, a graphic, or another Web page element that connects to additional data on the Web when the user clicks it; *also called* hypertext link *or* hyperlink.

List address The email address mailing list members use to send a message to all members of the list; *also called* list name.

list administrator The person assigned to oversee an open discussion forum, mailing list, or newsgroup; can reject or accept membership requests.

List moderator The person responsible for discarding any messages that are inappropriate for or irrelevant to the list's members and for accepting or rejecting membership requests to a closed discussion forum, mailing list, or newsgroup.

List name *See* list address.

LISTSERV A mailing list established by BITNET.

Load The process of a Web page appearing in a Web browser window.

Local area network (LAN) A group of computers no more than a few thousand feet apart connected through NICs.

Local computer Your computer when you use FTP to download programs; *also called* local site.

Local site *See* local computer.

Location bar In Firefox, a text box at the top of the browser window that indicates the URL of the current Web page and into which you can type a new URL and press [Enter] or click the Go button to go to another Web page; in Internet Explorer, *called* Address bar.

Location operator A word (the most common is NEAR) that lets a user search for keywords that appear close to each other in the text of a Web page; *also called* proximity operator.

Logical operator *See* Boolean operator.

Login The combination of a user name and password that identifies a user to a computer.

Lossless compression Technology that reduces the file size without any loss of data.

Lossy compression Technology that eliminates redundant and unnecessary data in an image to reduce the file size.

Lurk To observe messages on a mailing list or a newsgroup without posting any new messages.

Mail client software A program that lets a user send and receive email and store email on the user's computer.

Mail server A server that runs special software for handling email tasks.

Mail window The interface in an email program that allows a user to compose, send, receive, and manage emails.

Mailing list A list of names and email addresses for a group of people who subscribe to the list; *also called* email list *or* discussion group. *See also* category *and* group.

Malware Short for *malicious software*, a broad term that means any program that runs on your computer without your permission and usually performs undesired tasks.

Mashup A Web site created by the services from two different sites using the APIs from one or both sites to create a completely new site that uses features from one or both.

Meetup In-person meeting arranged over the Internet, often via a political Web site.

Menu bar In a Windows program, contains the File, Edit, View, and Help menus and other specialized menus that allow you to use the features of the program.

Message body The part of the email that contains the actual message.

Message body pane The part of the message window that displays the actual email message.

Message header All the information about an email message, including the recipients' and sender's email addresses, a subject line and, sometimes, the filename of an attachment.

Message list In an email program, the list containing the message headers of the messages in the selected folder.

Meta-search engine A search tool that searches multiple search engines simultaneously.

Microblog To send short messages, usually 140 characters or fewer, on a very frequent schedule.

MIDI (Musical Instrument Digital Interface) format A file format used for creating small sound files that digitally records information about each element of the sound, including its pitch, length, and volume.

MILNET (Military Network) One of the two networks that ARPANET split into that is reserved for military uses that required greater security.

Military Network *See* MILNET.

MMOG, MOO, and **MUD** Short for massively multiuser online game, MUD object-oriented, and multiuser dungeon; three types of online adventure games that allow hundreds, and even thousands, of users to assume character roles and to play at the same time, interacting with each other.

Modem Short for modulator-demodulator; a device that converts signals from digital to analog and back again between a computer and a transmission line.

Moderated discussion group, **mailing list**, or **newsgroup** Group communication in which all messages are read and evaluated for appropriate and relevant content by a list moderator before they are sent to members in the discussion group, mailing list, or newsgroup.

Modulation The process of converting a digital signal to an analog signal.

Modulator-demodulator *See* modem.

Moving Picture Experts Group format *See* MPEG format.

MP3 format *See* MPEG Audio Layer 3 format.

MPEG Audio Layer 3 (MP3) format The audio portion of a compressed video format that yields files slightly lower in quality than WAV files, but 90 percent smaller.

MPEG (Moving Picture Experts Group) format A common file format for video on the Web that uses lossy compression technology and can be played using the same software that plays many other multimedia file types, including the player that comes with Windows.

Multimedia The collective term for sound, animation, and video.

Musical Instrument Digital Interface format *See* MIDI format.

Named FTP The method of logging in to a computer on which you have an account (with a user name and password) and using that account to send and receive files; *also called* full-privilege FTP.

NAP *See* network access point.

Natural language query A type of search expression that allows users to enter a question exactly as they would ask a person that question.

Netiquette A term coined from the phrase "Internet etiquette" that refers to the set of commonly accepted rules that represent proper behavior on the Internet.

Network Two or more computers connected to each other that share resources, such as printers or programs.

Network access point (NAP) The physical locations where networks connect to the Internet.

Network backbone The long-distance lines and supporting technology that transport large amounts of data between the network access points.

Network card *See* network interface card.

Network interface card (NIC) A removable circuit board used to connect a computer to a network by running a cable from the NIC to a server or to another client.

Network operating system Software that runs on a server and coordinates how information flows among its various clients.

Newsgroup An online discussion group that is part of the Usenet database and requires a newsreader to be able to read the messages, which are stored and sorted by topic on a server connected to the Internet; messages are sorted by topic.

Newsreader Software required by some newsgroups to access messages in the newsgroup.

News search engine A search engine that searches only online news sites.

News server A server that stores a Usenet newsgroup.

NIC *See* network interface card.

Nickname A shortened name for a contact.

NSFnet A network run by the National Science Foundation that merged with CSNET and BITNET to form one network that could carry much of the network traffic that had been carried by the ARPANET.

Online social group *See* virtual community.

Open architecture philosophy The philosophy that ensures that each network connected to the ARPANET could continue using its own protocols and data-transmission methods internally.

Open discussion forum, **mailing list**, or **newsgroup** A discussion forum, mailing list, or newsgroup that automatically accepts all subscribers.

Optical carrier (OC) Fiber-optic cables used to connect to the Internet in a variety of bandwidths ranging from OC3, approximately 15 times faster than a fast connection provided by a cable television company, to OC192, approximately 1,000 times faster than a fast connection provided by a cable television company.

Outbox or **Outbox folder** In an email program or Webmail, the folder in which messages waiting to be sent are stored.

Packet sniffer Software that can monitor and analyze the data packets and capture user names, passwords, and other personal information from unencrypted files as they travel on the Web; *also called* sniffer program.

Packet switching A method of sending information over a network in which files and messages are broken down into electronically labeled data packets.

Page title The name of the Web page that appears in the browser title bar and in the tab.

PDF format A file format that allows documents to maintain a consistent layout and format on different computers when viewed using Adobe Reader.

Peer-to-peer (PTP) The process of transferring files directly from one computer to another without using a server.

Petabyte Approximately 10^{15} (1,000,000,000,000,000) bytes.

Pharm To redirect users of a specific Web site to a spoofed site without their knowledge or consent and without clicking a link in an email message.

Phish To try to obtain confidential information from people via email by pretending to be a familiar organization or institution, such as a bank.

Phishing site *See* spoofed site.

Plagiarism The failure to cite the source of material that you use in a published medium.

Plain old telephone service *See* POTS.

Plug-in A browser extension that a Web browser starts to display or play a specific file type.

Podcast A subscription audio or video broadcast that is created and stored in a digital format on the Internet.

Podcasting The practice of posting an audio or video feed for subscribers to play or watch at their convenience on their computers or MP3 players.

Podcatching software Software you use to subscribe to a podcast and check for and download new podcasts.

Pop-under A pop-up that appears behind the current window.

Pop-up A small window that appears in front of the current window and that usually contains an advertisement.

Port Permits traffic to enter and leave a computer.

Port scan Using a computer to test all or some of the ports of another computer to determine whether its ports are open, closed, or stealth.

Post (n.) A message sent to a mailing list or newsgroup or placed on the Web site of a Web-based discussion forum.

Post (v.) To send a message to a mailing list or newsgroup or place a message on the Web site of a Web-based discussion forum.

Postcardware Software that you can use freely for no charge, but the programmer requests you mail a postcard from your hometown in return for your use of it.

POTS (plain old telephone service) A method of connecting to the Internet used by individuals and small businesses using regular phone lines; connection speeds range from 28.8 Kbps to 56 Kbps.

Precedence operator A way of clarifying the grouping within a complex Boolean expression usually indicated by parentheses; *also called* grouping operator *or* inclusion operator.

Printer friendly link A link that, when clicked, opens a Web page containing the same information as on the original Web page, but formatted like a printed page rather than a Web browser window.

Private Browsing A feature of Firefox that allows you to open a new browser window and surf the Web without recording anything in the History list, storing files in the Temporary Internet Files folder, or recording cookies.

Private chat A chat that occurs between individuals who know each other and are invited to participate in the chat.

Profile A brief description of the user's personality, likes and dislikes, and a picture, among other information that is posted on the user's page in an online social group.

Protected mode In Windows Vista, the default secure mode in which files are downloaded only to the Temporary Internet Files folder unless express consent of the user is given.

Proximity operator *See* location operator.

PTP *See* peer-to-peer.

Public chat A chat that occurs in a chat room in which anyone who is registered with the chat service can come and go.

Public domain Information that you can freely copy without requesting permission from the source.

Pull technology A method of obtaining information from the Web by allowing subscribers to "pull" content to their computers when they want it.

Push technology A method of obtaining information from the Web by sending content to users who request it.

Query *See* search expression.

QuickTime A proprietary video format developed by Apple Computer that works equally well on Windows and Macintosh computers and which requires the QuickTime player to play.

Reading pane In Windows Live Mail and in Windows Live Hotmail, the pane that displays the contents of the selected message in the message list.

RealAudio format A proprietary compressed audio format developed by RealNetworks, Inc.

Real-time Occurring in the current instant.

Really Simple Syndication (RSS) A file format that makes it possible to share updates such as headlines, weather updates, and other Web site content via a newsfeed.

RealVideo format A proprietary compressed video format developed by RealNetworks, Inc.

Refresh button In Internet Explorer, a button that allows you to load again a Web page that currently appears in your Web browser so that you can view the latest information (such as news headlines); in Firefox, *called* Reload button.

Reload button In Firefox, a button that allows you to load again a Web page that currently appears in your Web browser so that you can view the latest information (such as news headlines); in Internet Explorer, *called* Refresh button.

Remote server *See* FTP server.

Remote site *See* FTP server.

Results page A page provided by a search engine that includes links to Web pages that match the search expression.

Router A computer on a network that determines the best way to move the data packet forward to its destination while traveling through the network.

Routing algorithm A program that determines the best path for data packets being routed on a network.

RSS *See* Really Simple Syndication.

Satellite A method of connecting to the Internet that uses a satellite dish receiver; connection speeds range from 125 Kbps to 500 Kbps.

Script A program written in JavaScript that Web pages can download to your computer and run; used by Web page designers to enrich and personalize a user's interaction with a Web page; can also be written with malicious intent, however, destabilizing programs and even risking data loss on a user's computer.

Search box A text box in a Web browser in which you can type keywords, and then press [Enter] or click the Search button to search for Web pages that contain the keywords using your default provider.

Search engine A Web site or part of a Web site that finds Web pages containing a search expression and displays a list of search results.

Search expression The words or phrases you enter when you conduct a search; *also called* query.

Search filter A search expression that eliminates Web pages from a search by specifying a language, date, domain, host, or page component (such as a URL, link, image tag, or title tag) or by specifying that the results pages will contain all or any of the keywords.

Secure File Transfer Protocol (SFTP) A network protocol used to transfer files over a secure connection.

Secure Socket Layer (SSL) A protocol for information traveling over the Internet that encrypts information in a secure channel on top of the TCP/IP Internet protocol; Web pages that use SSL are encrypted, the site has a server certificate that users can access to authenticate its validity, and the pages have URLs that begin with *https://*.

Security The protection of assets from unauthorized access, use, alteration, or destruction.

Self-replicate To create, and in some cases distribute, a copy.

Sent folder In Windows Live Hotmail, the folder that contains copies of messages you sent; in Windows Live Mail, *called* Sent items folder.

Sent items folder In Windows Live Mail, the folder that contains copies of messages you sent; in Windows Live Hotmail, *called* Sent folder.

Server A computer that accepts requests from other computers that are connected to it and shares some or all of its resources, such as printers, files, or programs, with those connected computers.

Server certificate A file that authenticates a Web site for its users so the user can be confident that the Web site is genuine and not an imposter and to ensure that the transfer of data between a user's computer and the server with the certificate is encrypted.

SFTP *See* Secure File Transfer Protocol.

Shareware Software that is usually available for free during a short evaluation period, after which you must license it.

Shockwave Player A browser extension from Adobe that lets you view animated, three-dimensional interfaces, interactive advertisements and product demonstrations, multiuser games, streaming CD-quality audio, and video that was created using Adobe Director software.

Signed ActiveX control An ActiveX control that Internet Explorer has identified as controls created by software developers with a digital certificate.

Single-file Web page A Web page and all of its supporting elements, including text, graphics, and links, stored in a single file when the Web page is saved to a disk.

Smiley An emoticon consisting of a colon, a hyphen, and a close parenthesis :-) so that it looks like a smile.

Sniffer program *See* packet sniffer.

Social bookmark A favorite or a bookmark saved to a public Web site that you can access or share from any computer connected to the Internet.

Spam (n.) *See* junk email.

Spam (v.) To send unsolicited and irrelevant messages to a chat room.

Spam folder *See* junk folder.

Specifications Sets of standards for the Web.

Specific question A type of question for searching the Internet that you can phrase easily and has only one answer.

Spider *See* Web robot.

Sponsored link A link connected to the search expression that a company pays to place near the top of the results page.

Spoofed site A Web site that looks like it belongs to one organization but actually belong to someone else; *also called* phishing site.

Spyware A category of adware that tracks your use of the program and the Internet or collects data about you without the user having control over or knowledge of the ads and other monitoring features it contains.

SSL *See* Secure Socket Layer.

Start page The first Web page that opens when you start your Web browser or the Web page that a Web browser displays the first time you use it. *See also* home page.

Static Web page An HTML file that exists on a Web server computer.

Status bar The bar at the bottom of a program window that indicates the status of the document or provides important information for the user; in a browser, when you point to a link, its URL appears in the status bar.

Stop button A button on a Web browser toolbar that allows you to stop loading the contents of a Web page.

Streaming transmission When a Web server sends the first part of a file to a Web browser, and then, while the browser begins playing the file, sends the next segment of the file.

Strong key An encryption key that is 128 bits or longer.

Strong password A password that consists of random strings of letters not found in a dictionary, including numbers and special characters, and combinations of uppercase and lowercase letters.

Subject In an email program, the text box in which you summarize the main topic of an email message.

Subject guide A Web site that organizes links in categories and subcategories; *also called* clearinghouse, virtual library, *or* Web bibliography.

Subscribe To send an email message to the administrative address of a mailing list or submit information on a Web page form so that you can start receiving the mailing list; *also called* join.

T1 and **T3 connections** Methods of connecting to the Internet used by large companies and organizations that offer a higher grade of service for connecting to the Internet than telephone service does; connection speed is 1.544 Mbps for T1 connections and 44.7 Mbps for T3 connections.

Tab Allows you to display a Web page in a browser window; when multiple tabs are open, you can easily navigate from page to page by clicking the tab for the page you want to view.

Tabbed browsing Switching between multiple Web pages in the same Web browser window.

Tag One of a set of codes used in HTML codes, that define the structure and behavior of text, graphics, and other content on a Web page; or one-word descriptions of the blog content or pages on social networking sites that bloggers and page owners use to categorize their content.

Tag cloud A list of tags in which the most popular tags used by people using the service appear in a larger font size, making it possible to see which keywords are being used as tags the most.

TCP *See* Transmission Control Protocol.

TCP/IP (Transmission Control Protocol and Internet Protocol) A suite of rules that includes a tool to facilitate file transfer and another to access computers that aren't part of a user's immediate network over the Internet.

Telnet A protocol that allows users to log on to a remote server.

Terabyte Approximately 10^{12} (1,000,000,000,000) bytes.

Text To send and read instant messages using a cell phone.

Third-party cookie A cookie placed on your computer by a Web site that stores content, usually an image, on the Web site you are visting.

Thread Messages in a mailing list, Web-based discussion group, or newsgroup arranged by discussion or topic.

Title bar In a program window, the top bar that shows the name of the open document and the name of the program; also contains the Minimize, Restore Down/Maximize, and Close buttons.

TLD *See* top-level domain.

TLS *See* Transport Layer Security.

To In an email program or in Webmail, the text box in which you enter the email address(es) of the recipient(s).

Today window In Windows Live Hotmail, the page that appears when you first log into your Hotmail account and displays the total number of messages in your mailbox and the percentage of your storage space on the Hotmail server that you have used.

Toolbar In a Windows program, a bar that contains buttons to execute commands that allow you to use the program.

Top-level domain (TLD) The last part of a domain name.

Transfer protocol The set of rules that computers use to move files from one networked computer to another.

Transmission Control Protocol (TCP) The set of rules that computers on a network use to establish and break connections.

Transmission Control Protocol and Internet Protocol *See* TCP/IP.

Transparent GIF *See* Web bug.

Transport Layer Security (TLS) An improved version of SSL.

Trojan horse A program that hides inside other programs, and then causes problems when the other program is downloaded and run (similar to a virus).

Tweet (n.) A microblog post.

Tweet (v.) To post a message to a microblog.

Twisted-pair cable A type of cable that consists of two or more insulated copper wires twisted around each other and enclosed in a layer of plastic insulation.

Undiscoverable mode The state of a device that uses Bluetooth when it is disabled from broadcasting its signal.

Uniform Resource Locator (URL) The address that tells the Web browser the transfer protocol to use when transporting the file, the domain name of the computer on which the file resides, the path name of the folder or directory on the computer on which the file resides, and the filename.

Unmoderated discussion group, mailing list, or **newsgroup** Group communication in which messages are not read or evaluated for appropriate and relevant content by a list moderator before they are sent to members in the discussion group, mailing list, or newsgroup.

Upload To send a file from your computer to another computer over a network.

URL *See* Uniform Resource Locator.

Usenet An acronym for User's News Network, the first newsgroups started in 1979 by a group of students and programmers at Duke University and the University of North Carolina.

User authentication The process of associating a person and his identification on a Web page with a very high level of assurance.

User-generated content Content on Web sites created by the user.

User identification The process of identifying a user to a computer, usually with a login.

User name The part of an email address that the ISP uses to identify you.

User's News Network *See* Usenet.

V

Virtual community A place on the Internet where a user can post a profile of him or herself and then post a blog or share information; *also called* online social group.

Virtual library *See* subject guide.

Virus A program that runs without your permission on your computer and performs undesired tasks, such as deleting the contents of your hard disk.

W

3C *See* World Wide Web Consortium.

WAN *See* wide area network.

Wave (WAV) format An uncompressed file format that digitizes audio waveform information at a user-specified sampling rate and can be played on any Windows computer that supports sound.

WAV format *See* Wave format.

Web *See* World Wide Web.

Web 2.0 A term that indicates a change in the way people use the Web, just like a version change in a software program indicates that a new release of the software that is better than the old version.

Web-based discussion forum Similar to a mailing list, but members put their messages on a Web site instead of sending them via email.

Web-based email service *See* Webmail.

Web bibliography *See* subject guide.

Web browser Software that lets users browse HTML documents and move from one HTML document to another; *also called* browser.

Web bug A small, hidden graphic—usually a GIF file with a size of one pixel—on a Web page or in an email message designed to work in conjunction with a cookie to obtain information about the person viewing the page or email message and to send that information to a third party; *also called* clear GIF *or* transparent GIF.

Web directory A list of links to Web pages compiled by human editors or computers organized into hierarchical categories.

Web log *See* blog.

Webmail (Web-based email service) A service that allows you to send and receive email by using a Web browser and the service's Web site.

Web page A document that is formatted in HTML to be viewed using a Web browser.

Web robot A program that automatically searches the Web to find new Web sites, updates information about old Web sites that are already in the database, and deletes information in the database when a Web site no longer exists; *also called* bot *or* spider.

Web server *See* hypertext server.

Web services Data shared via APIs.

Web site A collection of related Web pages.

Web slice A type of RSS update that is available to Internet Explorer users.

WEP *See* Wired Equivalent Privacy.

White page directory A search engine based on the printed telephone directory that enables a user to search for addresses and telephone numbers for individuals as you would in a white pages phone book.

Wide area network (WAN) Several LANs connected together.

Wi-Fi *See* wireless fidelity.

Wi-Fi Protected Access (WPA) A new security protocol that provides better encryption than WEP by encrypting individual data packets with different keys.

Wiki A Web site that is designed to allow multiple users to contribute content and edit existing content quickly.

WiMAX Short for Worldwide Interoperability for Microwave Access, a wireless fidelity technology being developed for use in metropolitan areas that will have a range of up to 31 miles.

Windows Live Messenger Microsoft instant messaging program.

Windows Media Audio (wma) format A proprietary Windows Media Player file format that will play only in Windows Media Player.

Windows Media Video (wmv) format A proprietary Windows Media Player file format that will play only in Windows Media Player.

WIPO *See* World Intellectual Property Organization.

Wired Equivalent Privacy (WEP) A security protocol for Wi-Fi networks that works by encrypting data sent over the network.

Wireless A method for connecting to the Internet that uses high-frequency radio waves; connection speeds range from 722 Kbps to 54 Mbps.

Wireless fidelity (Wi-Fi) A short-range wireless network that connects a wireless access point to wireless devices located within a distance of approximately 200 feet.

Wireless LAN (WLAN) A LAN in which the computers are connected wirelessly, without using cables.

Wireless LAN PC card *See* WLAN card.

Wireless network A network that uses technologies such as radio frequency (RF) and infrared (IR) to link computers.

Wireless wide area network (WWAN) WANs connected using newer technologies that allow faster data transfer over longer distances.

Wire service An organization that gathers and distributes news to newspapers, magazines, broadcasters, and other organizations that pay a fee to the wire service; *also called* press agency *or* news service.

WLAN *See* wireless LAN.

WLAN card A circuit board in a computer that allows a user to connect to the Internet without cables as long as the user's computer is within range of a wireless access point that is connected to the Internet; *also called* wireless LAN PC card.

WMA format *See* Windows Media Audio format.

WMV format *See* Windows Media Video format.

WPA *See* Wi-Fi Protected Access.

World Intellectual Property Organization (WIPO) An agency of the United Nations whose purpose is to develop international standards to protect the rights of intellectual property holders.

World Wide Web (Web) A subset of the computers on the Internet in which resources on the Internet are organized in a way to make them easily accessible to all users.

World Wide Web Consortium (W3C) An international organization that establishes specifications, or sets of standards, for the Web.

Worm A self-replicating program that causes problems by reproducing so many times that it uses all available computer resources or it sends itself as an attachment to email messages to everyone in the contact list on the infected computer.

WWAN *See* wireless wide area network.

XML (Extensible Markup Language) A markup language that uses customized tags to describe data and its structure.

Yellow page directory A search engine that specializes in finding businesses, which are grouped by type and location as in the yellow pages phone book.

Zip file Another name for a compressed file because .zip is the most common file extension for compressed files; *also called* zipped file.

Zipped file *See* zip file.

zombie *See* bot.

Index